Deaths of (

The Hidden S

CW01401842

Alison Liebling is a Senior Research Associate at the Cambridge Institute of Criminology and a Staff Fellow and Tutor at Trinity Hall, Cambridge. Her publicatons include *From Custody to Community: Throughcare for Young Offenders* (1992); *Suicides in Prison* (1992); *Deaths in Custody: International Perspectives* (1994); *Deaths in Custody II: Caring for Prisoners at Risk* (1996) and *Privatising Prisons: Rhetoric and Reality* (1997). In 1997 she was awarded a Leverhulme Special Research Fellowship to carry out a project entitled *Shaping Prison Life*.

Deaths
of
Offenders

The Hidden Side of Justice

PROCEEDINGS OF A CONFERENCE HELD
AT BRUNEL UNIVERSITY, UXBRIDGE, ENGLAND
JULY, 1997

Edited by **Alison Liebling**

WATERSIDE PRESS

on behalf of

Deaths of Offenders
The Hidden Side of Justice

Published 1998 by
WATERSIDE PRESS
Domum Road
Winchester SO23 9NN
Telephone or Fax 01962 855567
INTERNET:106025.1020@compuserve.com

On behalf of
The Institute for the Study and Treatment of Delinquency
(ISTD)
King's College London,
Strand,
London WC2R 2LS
Telephone 0171 873 2822   Fax 0171 873 2823

ISBN Paperback ISTD 0 901 541 48 6. Waterside Press 1 872 870 61 9

Cataloguing-in-Publication Data A catalogue record for this book can be obtained from the British Library

Cover John Good Holbrook Ltd, Coventry

Printing and binding Antony Rowe Ltd, Chippenham.

Contents

Introduction   *vii*

PART ONE POLITICS, THEORY AND INQUIRY

1 Deaths in Custody: The Politics and Language of Culpability in Post-modern Britain *Mick Ryan*   *21*

2 Changing Perspectives on Deaths of Prisoners *Richard Tilt*   *33*

3 'Man Passeth Away Like a Shadow': Deaths Associated with the Australian Criminal Justice System, Six Years After the Royal Commission into Aboriginal Deaths in Custody
   David MacDonald   *44*

4 Prison Suicide and the Nature of Imprisonment
   Alison Liebling   *64*

5 Untoward Deaths in Special Hospital Care: Implications of These and Other Inquiries *Herschel Prins*   *75*

6 Deaths of Offenders: The Coroner's Inquiry
   Richard Whittington   *85*

PART TWO DEATHS OF OFFENDERS IN POLICE CUSTODY: SPECIAL ISSUES

7 Investigating Deaths in Police Custody
   John Cartwright   *95*

8 Investigating Suspicious Deaths in Police Custody
   Tony Ward and Deborah Coles   *105*

9 What Are the Lessons From Tragedies?
   Nicholas Long   *120*

10 Self Harm and Suicide by Detained Persons: A Study
   Alan Ingram, Graham Johnson and Ian Heyes   *145*

PART THREE VOICES OF PRISONERS, FAMILIES AND SUPPORT GROUPS

11 The Right to Life and the European Convention On Human Rights *John Wadham (with the assistance of Richard Wald)* *151*

12 Recognising Responsibilities to Familes
Paul Edwards and Audrey Edwards *158*

13 Black Deaths in Custody: A Human Rights Perspective (Transcript) *Lee Jasper* *174*

14 Deaths In Custody; What Lessons?: An Overview of the Nigerian Situation *Uju Agomoh* *182*

PART FOUR PREVENTION OF DEATHS IN CUSTODY

15 Prevention of Suicides in the Dutch Criminal Justice System
Eric Blaauw, Frans Schilder and Stef van de Lande *201*

16 Jail Suicide: Preventing Future Casualties
Lindsay M. Hayes *224*

17 Impact of the Custodial, Controlled Environment and Inmate/Patient Behaviour on Practices of Some Health Care Providers: Recommendations for Resolution of this International Problem *Joseph R. Rowan* *234*

18 Deaths in the Care of the State: Issues and Lessons
Vivien Stern *238*

References *246*

Cases Cited *254*

Speakers' Biographical Details *255*

Delegates *258*

Expanded List of Contents *262*

ISTD are most grateful to all who contributed so much to the conference which was the origin of this collection of papers. Particular thanks should go to the Home Office and the Prison Service of England and Wales and HM Prison Service of Northern Ireland for financial support for core costs. The Home Office Programme Development Unit kindly supported the costs of bringing a group of delegates from Eastern Europe, and the generosity of the British Council allowed our Nigerian speaker to attend.

I would like to record our thanks to all our speakers and contributors, and to everyone who worked so hard on the event itself. Appreciation is also due to Bryan Gibson and his staff at Waterside Press, for their dedication and professionalism. Finally I would particularly like to thank Dr Alison Liebling, who has contributed so significantly to the three conferences ISTD has organized on this painful theme, and has edited all three sets of conference papers. I know that this is a subject dear to her heart. We are indeed lucky to have someone with Alison's gifts, sensitivity and humanity working in this field.

Julia Braggins
November 1997

Introduction

This is probably the most difficult thing I will be asked to write. It is for me a very emotional subject. I work in a jail. My time spent here consists of 48 or more hours a week. I treat this place as a second home. I live and eat with the people I work with and the people that are housed in this jail for four days in a row. During my four days away from here my life is my family. So I guess in a way I have two separate lives . . . I get a great feeling of satisfaction when I can talk to my 15-year-old and she says 'Thanks'. I also get a great feeling of satisfaction when I am at work and inmates personally ask for me because they want to talk or want information on different ways to possibly make their lives better 'when they get out'. Most times, I need only listen, allowing them to figure out what they want to do. I was fairly new at this job when I met an inmate who I will call 'Tee'. I had been working nights for about a month when Tee came up to the bars in his cell and asked if he could talk to me in private. He was quiet that night and, because of the way he hugged the bars and spoke so desperately, I tried to quickly finish what I was doing and went back to his cell. I took him to the library where it would give us the privacy he seemed to need. He sat down in one of the chairs and I turned down the television to lessen the distraction. I sat in the chair next to him and said 'What's up?' He immediately started crying, hard. He wanted to talk and began to choke out that a visit that morning with his wife had hurt him. She told him that his best friend had moved into the house and she wanted a divorce. He cried and cried. I eventually got him to talk about something more positive. He talked about what his plans were when he got out of jail. He even laughed at times and remembered the good times he had had with his little boys. Then he would cry again wishing he could see them. Before he went back to his cell he had some fruit and made a phone call. The call made him upset and he cried again. I wished I could do more but what could I do? Give him encouragement? Tell him everything would be OK? I did. When he stopped crying and seemed to have settled down I put him back in his cell.

I found Tee dead in his cell at 5.00 a.m. He was hanging from the bars with a sheet tied tightly around his neck. He was wearing only his underpants. He was white and blue and purple and red. His eyes were open. His mouth was closed. His feet were touching the ground. He was holding onto the bars. *Why didn't he just stand up?* . . . When I looked at my partner I felt like I would explode. I felt like it was me that killed this man. My partner's eyes were so big, it seemed everything went in slow motion. 'What, please tell me. Tell me what? Tell me, tell me'. My mind was racing, my heart was beating hard. We touched him. He was looking at us. Oh, God.

After that first shock had passed things started happening. Notifications, documentation. It seemed like people were coming from everywhere. I probably held together for about 30 minutes. Then I lost it. I cried and cried. All I could think about was what exactly I had done that night. Why did I miss it? I killed this man. It was all my fault. I ruined not only my life and career but also the lives of my co-workers. I was taken home and left in the care of a friend. My head was pounding. I had to tell my story over and over. Every time I got to the part of seeing Tee hanging there, I cried. Every dream I had was of finding him and trying to save him, but he always died . . . I cried for days. I had nightmares for weeks. And forever I will have the memories . . . I have learned a lot. The hard way. I am back to work, still learning, and on the way I am trying to pass on what I have learned. If there was a way to sensitise people to the importance of 'knowing' when somebody needs help. But just try to imagine as you walk through your jail how and where a suicide could take place. Take the time to picture in your mind every possible area where you might find somebody. How would you get to them? What would you do first? What are the dangers? Where is your back-up? Run through every scenario you can possibly imagine. This is not just a tedious task. It is your job. It is your life. Think about it.

So now that I have written my thoughts down, how do I really feel? The anger, the hurt, the guilt, the shame. Every emotion all piled on top of one another. The feeling of not being able to face anybody. Reliving it every once in a while because it just does not go away. The look on everybody's face when it first happened. The dreams of trying over and over to save him and he always dies. The alienation when the shift was broken apart. Trying to say I'm sorry. Looking at that cell. The depression, not sleeping, my friends and family not knowing what to say or how to act. Knowing that this will never go away. Having to answer so many questions, wishing they could understand. I felt like I killed him, that it was all my fault. Everybody said don't blame yourself. Even though you know that is true you can't help but feel responsible. I didn't want anybody to feel sorry for me . . . I talked with our jail psychologist briefly twice. Nobody else would talk about it around me. Or talk to me, almost as if it were taboo. We never talked as a shift ever again'.

(Prison officer, cited in Hayes: this volume, *Chapter 16*)

This book arises from the third in a series of international conferences on the theme of deaths in custody organized by the Institute for the Study and Treatment of Delinquency (ISTD). From the first moment of the conference, it was clear that this type of event remains a challenging and delicate task. The conference sought to bring together all those people touched by deaths in custody: practitioners in the police, prison and probation services, voluntary organizations, officials from relevant Home Office departments, academics, campaigning organizations, prisoners and ex-prisoners and the families of those who have died in custody. Participants came from many countries; and it was especially noteworthy that very many of the participants, including some of our Eastern European delegates, were 'returnees' from previous meetings. The conference was opened and chaired by Sir Louis Blom-Cooper, chair of National Victim Support, and Dr Andrew Coyle, Director of the International Centre for Prison Studies.

This collection contains all of the plenary papers and most of those workshop papers which were submitted for publication. The content of the papers will inevitably reflect the differences of position and perspective held by participants. There was a stronger emphasis on deaths in police custody at this conference than in previous years, an inevitable result of the high profile deaths of Shiji Lapite, Richard O'Brien and Wayne Douglas and the controversial investigations which followed in the United Kingdom (see *Chapters 7* and *8*, this volume). At the time of going to press, the Crown Prosecution Service was facing two major inquiries, including an inquiry into its handling of deaths in custody cases (see *Chapter 8*, this volume). The European Committee for the Prevention of Torture and Inhuman or Degrading Treatment or Punishment (CPT) was beginning an unprecedented special visit to Britain, prompted by these cases. This was an interesting development to set against an international context in which, for example, the advent of the Australian Royal Commission into 'Aboriginal Deaths in Custody' and its aftermath seems to have shifted the highest proportion of deaths in custody from police cells to prison custody (see *Chapter 3*). The 'role of the inquiry'—at whatever level—can be a significant and complex one (see *Chapter 5*).

The papers are organized around four broad themes: *Part One: Politics, Theory and Inquiry* begins with Professor Mick Ryan of the University of Greenwich, on 'Deaths in Custody: the Politics and Language of Culpability' (*Chapter 1*). His opening plenary set the scene, tracing the history of interest in deaths in police and prison custody in the United Kingdom through the 1970s and 1980s, and outlining the role of ordinary people in bringing them to the forefront of media and political attention. The role of the organization INQUEST has been a highly significant part of this history. Professor Ryan illustrated how significant and unresolved these political issues of accountability and principle remain in 1997.

Richard Tilt, Director General of the Prison Service in England and Wales, gave a very honest and well received account of 'Changing Perspectives on Deaths of Prisoners' (*Chapter 2*). He congratulated ISTD for organizing this third conference on such an important theme, confirming his commitment on behalf of the prison service to reducing the number of such deaths wherever possible, and to engaging seriously and openly with families and other interested parties when such tragedies did occur. He welcomed the parents of Christopher Edwards, who died by homicide in Chelmsford prison in 1994, and who were able to join us for the duration of the conference. Their important contribution is included in this collection. 'We are not complacent', he told a highly involved and largely critical audience. 'There will always be more work to be done'. He congratulated those prison staff through whose sterling efforts lives had been saved.

The third paper in this volume is by David McDonald, of the Australian National University (*Chapter 3*). Six years ago, the Australian Royal Commission into 'Aboriginal Deaths in Custody' presented its report into the epidemic of Aboriginal deaths in custody which occurred in the mid-1980s. Despite massive attention being given to the problem nationally since then, the incidence of custodial deaths in Australia has not fallen, although the patterns have changed dramatically, with a higher proportion of the deaths now occurring in prison rather than police custody. David McDonald referred to the extent and patterns of death among people serving non-custodial correctional orders, observing that their death rates were probably much higher than those of prison inmates. The paper concluded on a pessimistic note, suggesting that trends in contemporary Australian society were such that it was unlikely that the incidence of Australian deaths in custody and deaths in other sectors of the criminal justice system would fall, at least over the short term. The lives of people in the hands of the state continued 'to pass away like shadows'.

Chapter 4 contains my own contribution and is entitled 'Prison Suicide and the Nature of Imprisonment'. The paper argues that suicide and self-injury in prisons have been the subjects of considerable international research in recent years. There has not been a link drawn between the results of these studies and our understanding of the prison experience. Prison suicide rates are high and are increasing. Large groups amongst prisoner populations share those characteristics associated with increased suicide risk in the community: adverse life events, negative interpersonal relationships, social and economic disadvantage, alcohol and drug addiction, early contact with criminal justice agencies, poor educational and employment history, low self-esteem, poor problem-solving ability and low motivational drive. Arguably, the prison population is almost selected to be at risk of suicide. The psychological resources of prisoners (and their variability over time) have been insufficiently examined. This neglect has resulted in a failure to understand the nature of the prison experience, particularly for vulnerable groups. What *does* prison demand of the imprisoned? How *do* we understand the nature of the prison experience? We need to know more about what being in prison *feels like*. In the debate over the existence of the lasting harms of imprisonment, those prisoners who have died by suicide have never had a voice. The chapter shows, using research on suicide, and autobiographical accounts of confinement in extreme situations, how readily understandable—and yet how remote from most research accounts—such suffering can be.

Chapter 5, by Professor Herschel Prins of Loughborough University on 'Untoward Deaths in Special Hospital Care: Implications of These and Other Inquiries' develops the theme of the role of inquiries into deaths in custody based on his experience as chairman of the 'Blackwood Inquiry' into the death of Orville Blackwood in Broadmoor Hospital in 1991. He outlines the managerial and political pressure such inquiries face, and produce, and the high expectations held by interested parties. In their report (Prins *et al*, 1993), the authors raised the question of the fear of violence amongst staff: are their fears in particular situations exacerbated by institutionalised racist stereotypes? If so, how can such fears, which have major consequences for the sorts of decisions made about individual patients, be understood and overcome? Should such inquiries take place in public or private? Should the reports be made public? What is the most effective way of ensuring that the truth is 'achieved', without bias or injustice? Families need to know what happened, even where such a process is an ordeal for all concerned. What is the best way of ensuring that 'what happened to them should not happen to others in the future' (Grounds, 1997)?

There were many workshops presented at the conference, many of which developed these themes further. The topics covered included the prevention of deaths in USA and Dutch police stations and jails, the treatment of self-harm in special hospitals for women, the impact of deaths on police and probation staff, the role of the European Convention On Human Rights, deaths in Nigerian prisons, suicide in Hungarian prisons, asylum seekers, the role of the coroner, motivating health care and custodial staff, youth suicide in prison, a presentation from the Suicide Awareness Support Unit, several police contributions (see further below), two presentations by INQUEST, a workshop by Trevor Walt, the chaplain of Broadmoor Hospital, and the presentation by Audrey and Paul Edwards on the death of their son, which is included below. We were all torn between competing sessions. The first of the workshop papers included in this volume is by Richard Whittington, the Birmingham coroner, who talked about the role of the coroner's inquiry (*Chapter 6*). Its purpose, he told us, reflected in its inquisitorial nature, is to establish the truth. The coroner has considerable discretion—to call witnesses, to disclose documents, to direct the jury, and to make recommendations afterwards. The reaching (or sociologically, the 'making') of a verdict can be a complex and lengthy process. Again, as in the inquiry process discussed above, competing agendas can inform this process, to different degrees.

Part Two: Deaths of Offenders in Police Custody: Special Issues contains those papers which dealt most directly with deaths in police custody. The particular deaths of three individuals (Shiji Lapite, Richard O'Brien and Wayne Douglas) linked many of these presentations, and we felt it was a significant aim of the conference to encourage various perspectives to be heard. First, a plenary presentation by John Cartwright, deputy chairman of the Police Complaints Authority, on 'Investigating Deaths in Police Custody' (*Chapter 7*). He outlined the role of the Police Complaints Authority (PCA) in investigating such deaths under Section 88 Police and Criminal Evidence Act 1984 and in recommending disciplinary action. There are around 47 deaths per year. The majority are 'natural causes', or they are alcohol or drug-related; a proportion are suicides; and a small number are traffic-related incidents. The use of force, particularly on arrest, raises major concerns. There have been verdicts of unlawful killing brought in cases where the restraint techniques used were regarded as unreasonable. Such issues have formed the basis of several of the inquiries carried out by the PCA. The role of the PCA in collecting and disseminating information about deaths in custody, in pressing for changes to training and procedure, and for further research, has increased, with most police forces now making voluntary referrals to the PCA in all cases of deaths in custody.

The paper by Tony Ward and Deborah Coles (*Chapter 8*) on 'Investigating Suspicious Deaths in Police Custody' continues this theme of the effectiveness of the investigative process, concentrating on the deaths of Richard O'Brien, Shiji Lapite, and Wayne Douglas in 1994 and 1995. The decisions taken by the Director of Public Prosecutions not to prosecute following two verdicts of unlawful killing were recently quashed by the High Court. How are such investigations shaped, and whose interests do they serve? The disproportionate number of deaths of black people following violent incidents involving the police has been raised by the Police Complaints Authority and by the United Nations Committee on the Elimination of Racial Discrimination. The authors argue that public trust depends on a credible, thorough and fair investigative process. Eliminating conscious or unconscious speculation and theory from this process is a difficult and uncertain business, the need for which is barely acknowledged in practice, and yet this complexity is clearly understood in several well-known accounts of the inquest process: see for example, Douglas (1967), Taylor (1982), Atkinson (1982), and Scraton and Chadwick (1987). The fairness of proceedings can depend more on the personal qualities of the investigator (or in the case of inquests, the coroner) than on procedures, where there is considerable scope for discretion. Ward and Coles identify a need for reform, widely shared by many of those affected, including some sections of the police service and the PCA. This 'readiness' for change was reflected during discussions at the conference.

Chapter 9, 'What Are the Lessons From Tragedies?', follows from the paper by Ward and Coles, again concentrating on the implications of the deaths of Brian Douglas and Wayne Douglas in the South London borough of Lambeth during 1995, where Nicholas Long is chair of the Community-Police Liaison Group. The paper summarises progress made following the recommendations of a report (*Lessons from Tragedies: Deaths in Custody in the Metropolitan Police District 1986-1995*, Community-Police Consultative Group for Lambeth (1996)) submitted to CPCG and published after the inquest of Brian Douglas. The report recognised that public confidence in police practice needs to be increased, and that procedures both throughout custody and following a death should be improved. The work of the Lambeth group was a first step in providing more information and working towards improved practice.

Finally, in this part, is a brief paper by inspectors Alan Ingram and Graham Johnson and principal officer Ian Heyes, based on their detailed research carried out in Lancashire on 'Self-harm and Suicide by Detained Persons' under the Police Research Award Scheme (see Ingram *et al*, 1997, *Chapter 10* of this work). The research aimed to improve on existing knowledge by collecting and analysing available information on 52 deaths in police custody over a five year period and carrying out a survey of 47 incidents of self-harm in Lancashire police custody over a six month period. The research led to 19 recommendations and the development of a suicide awareness booklet for police custody staff.

Part Three: The Voices of Prisoners, Families and Support Groups begins with a paper by John Wadham, the Director of Liberty, on 'The Right to Life and the European Convention On Human Rights'. In this paper, he anticipates the impact of the incorporation of the right to life contained in the European Convention On Human Rights into domestic law. The Labour government announced in the Queen's Speech in May 1997 that it intends to incorporate the provisions of the European Convention on Human Rights into United Kingdom Law. Article 2, The Right to Life, is 'the most basic human right of all'. It 'places the state both under a positive obligation to take adequate measures to protect the right to life as well as a negative obligation not to take life other than in certain defined circumstances' (see Wadham, 1998, *Chapter 11* of volume). This duty has implications for the proper investigation of deaths in custody, the training of police and prison officers, the implementation of procedures and the adequacy of such procedures and for remedy where there are arguable violations. John Wadham's paper is a helpful account of this intention and its implications.

Chapter 12, 'Recognising Responsibilities to Families', is by Paul and Audrey Edwards, the parents of Christopher Edwards. Their contribution to the conference throughout was brave, and valuable, and we are very pleased that their contribution is amongst the papers included in this publication. They tell the tragic story of their son's illness and his eventual remand into prison, where he was killed by his cell mate. Their angry and bewildered reaction to these events was deepened by the difficulties they experienced in receiving information and assistance about the death and events leading up to it. They attended the conference, and wrote the paper, in order to seek improvements. Their main concern is that inquiries should be held in public, that families should be advised and supported and that proceedings should be 'user-friendly' and not (as they experienced) hostile or distancing. As representatives of the wider community, families should be the first, and not the last, point of concern for the institutions involved. Too often, Paul and Audrey Edwards felt, institutions became energised by instant damage limitation, rather than taking a self-critical look at 'the truth' and at the lessons to be learned. They told how their pragmatic and trusting but distant view of the criminal justice system, as ordinary people, had been transformed as they became its victims. Why should this be so, they asked, and what could they do to avoid such experiences for families in the future?

This paper, and the recommendations made by Paul and Audrey Edwards, is followed by the transcript of a plenary presentation by Lee Jasper, director of the 1990 Trust, on 'Black Deaths in Custody: A Human Rights Perspective'. Lee Jasper continued with the theme of incorporating the European Convention On Human Rights into United Kingdom law. He spoke as a representative of black communities, arguing that it is young black men who are disproportionately the subject of police attention, and sometimes violence. The stop and search figures are, he argued, the tip of the iceberg. Deaths in custody, he went on to say, represent the culmination of a whole series of discriminations. Like Professor Herschel Prins, Lee Jasper identified stereotypes, and responses to stereotypes, as part of the black experience of life in the community and in custody, for those who come into contact with it. He referred to the Lambeth Police Consultative Group as one welcome opportunity for police and the community to work together, to combat racism and to develop constructive alternatives. He argued for a working dialogue—rather than confrontation and litigation.

Chapter 14, by Uju Agomoh, provides 'An Overview of the Nigerian Situation'. Uju Agomoh shows how the high number of deaths in Nigerian prisons are not due to suicide, but are more likely to be from natural causes (or execution). Little official data is recorded on the numbers or causes of such deaths. The vast majority of the deaths occur amongst remand prisoners. Overcrowding, lack of sanitation, lack of beds and clothing, poor medical facilities, lack of food and water, prolonged incarceration, harsh treatment and lack of contact with families all contribute to the high figures. This sober and detailed account constitutes a valuable and rare overview of the state of life and death in Nigerian prisons.

Part Four: The Prevention of Deaths in Custody contains three papers, by Dr Eric Blaauw *et al*, and by Lindsay Hayes and Joseph Rowan, who have attended all three conferences, and who have both been major players on an international level in the translation of information into practice. Eric Blaauw, a forensic psychologist from the university of Amsterdam, gave a presentation on the 'Prevention of Suicides in the Dutch Criminal Justice System' (*Chapter 15*). As elsewhere, the rate of suicides in custody is increasing in Dutch police and prison systems, particularly amongst unsentenced prisoners. Suicides and deaths due to intoxication are the main concerns, although both the causes and approaches to prevention vary according to the places of detention concerned. He distinguishes between police cells and houses of detention (remand centres). A sudden rise in the number of suicides in houses of detention during 1995 and 1996 led to a re-evaluation of prevention methods, a major conference and a programme of suicide prevention training. Dr Blaauw carefully reviews the literature, and considers possible preventive approaches based on a programme of research carried out by his team. Considerable attention is being paid to the suicide problem in The Netherlands, by practitioners and universities.

Lindsay Hayes talked about 'Jail Suicide: Preventing Future Casualties' (*Chapter 16*). He illustrated his case using four case studies, arguing that attitudes can influence suicides, that all such deaths have to be thoroughly examined for the lessons to be learned, and that staff involved in such incidents need support. Institutions can be judged by their responses to such tragedies. Joe Rowan talked about 'The Impact of the Custodial, Controlled Environment and Inmate/Patient Behaviour on Practices of some Health Care Providers' (*Chapter 17*), arguing that staff can be too ready to attribute manipulative motives to prisoners and patients in distress. He argued that practitioners need to be encouraged to be team workers. The higher their self-respect, the greater their capacity to operate co-operatively and positively with others.

Our final plenary was by Vivien Stern, Director of Penal Reform International (*Chapter 18*). The aims of PRI are to promote the development and implementation of the international human rights instruments relating to law enforcement; to end discrimination in penal measures, and to abolish the death penalty. Deaths in custody, she said, 'are at the heart of the human rights concern about custody'. The title of her paper was 'Deaths in the Care of the State: Issues and Lessons'. Her chilling account of the conditions she has witnessed in many prisons in the United Kingdom, in Eastern Europe and elsewhere, and of the questions asked of prisoners before execution in some of the States of America, brought home the scope and significance of the conference theme. The Universal Declaration On Human Rights, she reminded us, was signed on 10 December 1948. Never again, its signatories had hoped, would it be possible for people to treat other human beings in inhumane ways. The potential for such inhumanities is always present in prison.

The conference was closed with a few carefully chosen words by Dr Andrew Coyle, who summarised some of the main themes to have emerged, noted some of the more difficult issues to have been considered by participants, and managed to send us away feeling optimistic, despite the very real tensions and criticisms of practice expressed during several of the sessions.

Inevitably, there were contributions to the conference which we have not been able to include or represent fully here. Two governors from Cornton Vale, Scotland's only prison for women, gave one of the workshops for which we do not have a written paper. This was a powerful presentation, with Kate Doneghan and Moira McAlpine describing with a quiet dignity their struggle to come to terms with, and move beyond, a tragic series of suicides by young women prisoners which occurred at Cornton Vale between 1996 and 1997. Their descriptions of the impact of these suicides upon staff—those who discover the deaths, those who knew and cared for the women beforehand, and those who must deal with the families—was moving and informative. Their attempts to understand and ameliorate the problems faced by their population resonated with an audience well versed in such tragedies in their working environments, and in some cases, in their own lives. Such presentations made the regular, free-flowing, small discussion groups a necessary feature of each day, to enable delegates and presenters to share their own experiences, to respond to the content of presentations and the exchanges which followed them, and to attempt to deal with some of the emotions raised by the conference programme. The role of the Samaritans, who led several of the discussion groups, steered post-group feedback sessions for group leaders, and who contributed their own workshops on Listener schemes, is not reflected in the collection of papers here. They know what a major role they have played, and continue to play, for those who live and work in prison, and for many of those who deal with prison matters.

It was not a deliberate strategy of the conference organizers to strike a particular note or steer the proceedings in any particular direction, but it is interesting that these three conferences have each had a distinct tone and flavour. The first deaths in custody conference was, as we have recorded, chilling (Liebling and Ward, 1994). Few of the delegates at that first meeting will ever forget the powerful exchanges which took place between angry, bereaved families and individual 'defenders of the state'. This was necessary, and valuable. The topic needed to be aired, the agenda was emotive and individuals were defensive. Despite tense moments, the conference was well received, and individuals voiced a wish for the group to remain in touch, and to come together in the future, to review progress.

The second conference, in 1994, sought to provide opportunities for progress or good practice to be shared, and the prison services of England and Wales and Northern Ireland were pleased to be given the opportunity to share new, carefully planned strategies with delegates from many countries. The Samaritans were invited to outline the advantages of Listener schemes, then evolving rapidly in a new era of 'caring for the suicidal'. Joe Rowan and Lindsay Hayes from the USA presented similarly optimistic visions of best practice, and experiences of reducing suicide rates in prison service establishments. There were more sober presentations throughout—how could this be otherwise? But there were some who felt that this second conference was, in places, 'complacent'.

The third conference aimed to expand a little, to look beyond prisons, special hospitals and police cells and to draw in experiences from other areas of criminal justice. Inevitably, it was influenced by the widespread interest in several specific and highly controversial deaths in police custody. It was conceived in a less optimistic era, with suicide rates remaining very high, several years of austerity to contend with, and, in England and Wales, the prospect of a new administration with a highly cautious approach to criminal justice reform. The tone of the third conference was, in one sense, somewhere between the earlier two—realist, sober, honest and self-critical. In another sense, it moved significantly beyond the first two in its more ambitious attempt to bring together larger numbers of the most significant players—prisoners, their families, with those practitioners in whose hands they find themselves. The discussions were above all, honest. There were genuine and moving attempts by participants to share their perspectives, and to listen to those of others. However sober our feelings about current criminal justice policy, at the level of the individual—those representing prisoners and prisoners ' families, campaigning organizations, research and practice—a will to justice, truth and co-operation was powerfully expressed. This felt like an important step forward.

There was drinking, dancing and (sometimes heated) conversation in the two evenings of the conference, including a wine reception and a dinner, attended by prison governors and other practitioners from the local area. These social events were a welcome part of the conference event, and provided opportunities for further, less formal exchange, and for letting off steam (particularly for the conference organizers!) I left the conference with a renewed sense of the significance and potency of this topic. It goes to the heart of our deliberations about justice, the use of power, and the kind of society we want to live in. I also had a renewed sense of there being a great deal of 'kinship' feeling amongst the delegates. A spirit of community was present throughout, despite some very real differences of perspective and position. As several participants put it:

> How do we move institutions from looking after themselves, to looking after those in their care? . . . We want to have confidence in professionals; we want to understand and be understood; we want a credible community to live in, that we can trust.

I hope that in this collection of papers, readers will recognise and be moved by the commitment of those who continue to work in this field.

Acknowledgements
I would like to thank ISTD—especially Stephanie Hayman, the conference organizer, and other members of the conference steering group: Julia Braggins, Kathy Biggar, Martin McHugh and Graham Towl, for all their hard work at every stage of the conference and since, and for 'being there'; also Carol Martin and Nic Groombridge for their role as discussants and their involvement in the conference more generally. I would also like to thank Andrew Coyle, Bill Baker, Valodia Bernardo, and Meena Ahmed for playing such a valuable role both behind the scene and variously, at the scene. What a team! My thanks are also due to Nicola Padfield and Keith Bottomley for reading a draft of and sections of the manuscript respectively, and for their helpful comments.

Alison Liebling November 1997

PART ONE

Politics, Theory and Inquiry

CHAPTER 1

Deaths in Custody: The Politics and Language of Culpability in Post-modern Britain

Mick Ryan

The sudden or unexpected death of anyone in custody, whether it occurs in a prison, in a police station or in a secure psychiatric hospital, is above all else a great personal tragedy which can blight the lives of those families and friends who are left behind to grieve. Given that all of us here know and appreciate this pain, that is why we are here, it seems a little insensitive, perhaps, to introduce—as my title does—politics into the discussion.

Making general or abstract political points rather than focusing on specific and concrete measures; trying to apportion blame and responsibility on hard pressed staff, civil servants and politicians rather than securing some sort of consensus about the way forward; surely such an approach is wholly negative and one which will do little to ensure that these essentially personal tragedies are kept to a minimum? I have some sympathy with this view, but if we carry it to its logical extreme then we would inevitably fail to address a number of very important, wider questions.

We would remain ignorant, for example, about why such deaths suddenly became an issue in Britain during the 1980s. In other words, we will fail to contextualise the object of our concern. Relatedly, and arguably even more importantly, we would also fail to understand why such deaths are a matter of concern for those who worry about our civil rights, a question which, in its turn, will lead us on to the vexed question of culpability, or perhaps more accurately, the constant official denial of culpability in these cases.

I would argue that we need to address these wider questions first, because they have provided the inspiration, the direction even, for some of those very practical changes and reforms that most of us here today would support, and which this conference will no doubt go on to debate in some detail in its workshops. We have to dirty our hands, so to speak, with politics and culpability first, and so let me start by trying to contextualise the British debate about deaths in custody, to ask why the debate got going when it did.

Sudden and unexpected deaths in custody: growth of public concern
Perhaps the most important point to make about these deaths is that they had always been with us in Britain. Week in week out, month in month out, people had died suddenly and unexpectedly in police, prison and secure psychiatric custody, but few people paid them much attention.

Looking back at newspaper reports and lobby journals in the 1940s, 1950s and 1960s these deaths went mostly unreported. Indeed, widespread public concern over these only came towards the end of the 1970s when the long post-war consensus which had seen modest economic growth and full employment in Britain was well and truly over.

You will recall that the 1970s saw a series of industrial and social conflicts in Britain which threatened to destabilise what looked like an increasingly fragile political order reeling under the impact of a quadrupling of oil prices and resurgent nationalism in Northern Ireland. The struggle to secure this order took various forms, including draconian legislation to combat both internal and external terrorism; the tightening of immigration controls and the re-vamping of the race relations industry in an attempt to combat racism and the newly emerging National Front.

Police
One of the indelible features of this period was the growing distrust of police by large sections of the public, particularly in large metropolitan areas. The sources of this distrust were many. The Metropolitan Police, for example, was seriously damaged by allegations of widespread financial corruption and the planting of evidence on innocent suspects, while on Merseyside the heavy handed policing by some divisions led to serious concern. Allegations of racism, especially around the operation of the 'sus' laws, turned black youth in particular against the police. This led to the mobilisation of black communities around individual cases and their participation in the monitoring of local police practice and in the wider, national campaign in Britain to secure greater police accountability.[1]

As important as all these concerns were, it is arguable that it was the general direction of public order policing, and in particular, the role of special patrol groups (SPGs) which caused most concern, particularly to organizations like the National Council of Civil Liberties (NCCL). Answering directly to headquarters through their own command structure, these SPGs were distributed around London as mobile units to respond to defined high crime areas and to provide, if required, saturation policing.[2]

The violent potential of this policy was soon realised in Red Lion Square on the other side of London. This was the scene of an anti-fascist demonstration in opposition to the National Front which had secured permission to hold a meeting in Conway Hall. After some demonstrators broke through a cordon designed to isolate the hall, a decision was made to clear the square using two Special Patrol Group units and mounted police. It was in the course of this operation that a young student, Kevin Gately, was killed. This fatality, and the role of the SPG, caused public alarm and a full public enquiry was ordered by the home secretary Merlyn Rees and carried out by Lord Scarman.[3]

A second fatality in similar circumstances, that of Blair Peach, occurred at yet another anti-fascist rally in Southall in 1979. It was the deaths of Kevin Gately and Blair Peach and also those of Liddel Towers and Jimmy Kelly in Gateshead and Liverpool respectively that ignited a widespread public campaign around the issue of deaths in police custody and during arrest. The issue quickly reached Parliament's attention and became the subject of a Select Committee Inquiry.[4]

By this time, *Dixon of Dock Green* and the consensual society he had policed was long gone and police were on the brink of receiving huge extra resources from the new Conservative government to reinforce the law and order clampdown which was to intensify during the Thatcher years as the New Right consolidated its grip on the levers of power.[5]

Prisons
The question of prison deaths also became an issue around the same time. The 1970s saw increasingly repressive and troubled regimes in British prisons. With the decline in the rehabilitative ideal there was a greater emphasis on segregation, militarisation and medicalisation. The policy of segregation was driven by the belief that British prisons were being destabilised by a few 'bad apples'. If these troublesome prisoners could be isolated, then peace would return. But this was a sadly wrong diagnosis, initially encouraged, it has to be admitted, by academic research.

Indeed, it was trouble in the segregation unit that led to the virtual destruction of Hull prison in 1975, which was sparked off by the rumour that a young prisoner had been forcibly injected. The growing use of the 'liquid cosh' as it came to be known, led to real concern during this period as prison dosage rates, particularly of psychotropic drugs like Largactil, escalated and the Home Office was eventually forced to admit that such drugs were being used for control purposes.[6] Dosage rates were notably high in some women's prisons.

It has to be said that the authorities were as unforthcoming about this abuse as they were about the specially trained prison officer MUFTI squads which were introduced to counter the growing threat of prison riots, and which had been introduced without any sort of public debate.[7]

It was during this period, as many of you here may remember, that Barry Prosser was brutally beaten to death in Winson Green prison near Birmingham, and a few years later that a young black rastafarian Richard Campbell committed suicide at Feltham having arguably been placed in isolation for no good reason, and certainly without any serious consideration of his background.[8] These cases and many others at the time, some suicides, others not, made deaths in prison custody as sensitive a political issue as deaths in police custody and during arrest as their families mobilised to get some answers.

I have taken sometime today to explain why the issue of deaths in police and prison custody came into the public domain because I want to challenge the idea that some politicians, prison and police officials try to put about, namely, that concern over these matters is merely the result of the activities a few radical agitators with a hidden political agenda. The truth is regrettably very different and not so easy to dismiss. The mechanisms of formal social control during the last two decades of the authoritarian consensus have, at great expense to the public purse, been enlarged, and strengthened, and the pressure they exert on certain sections of our community have been deliberately intensified.

Families

This was the real context of the growing public concern with deaths in police, prison and psychiatric custody, and it is a testimony to the power and strength of individual prisoners and patients, of various local communities, often working class communities from inner city areas—many from the ethnic minorities—who bore the brunt of these policies and who mobilised radical campaign groups to defend themselves and secure justice; it was the result of their endeavours, their energies, rather than the agitation of political extremists that put deaths in custody onto the public agenda. We are talking here about a social movement, not 'agitprop'.

I would like to give the flavour of some of these campaigns by reading briefly from Tommy Banks' account of the Kelly campaign. He writes:

Two days after Jimmy Kelly was buried a mass meeting was called outside the 'Eagle and Child' pub in Huyton on a Sunday morning . . . I was elected as chairman of the Jimmy Kelly Committee . . . When we first started off, James Jardine, chairman of the Police Federation called us 'ragbags'. We were called left wingers, communists, criminal elements . . . police bashers,

24

you name it, we were called it. But we ignored all that and just went our own steady way having marches and protests about the case . . . We had support from the Liverpool Trades Council, the Sefton Trades Council. These bodies set up their own trade union inquiry into the question of police violence and then a conference was called at which we discussed how to take the campaign forward . . .

During the course of the campaign myself and Peter Cunningham, the secretary of the Action Committee went all over the country speaking . . . and raising funds. When we first formed the Jimmy Kelly Action Committee . . . we split into two sections, the Action Committee itself and a fund raising committee . . . because . . . when it came to the inquest there was no legal aid . . . The Kelly family, like most Merseyside people, live marginally above subsistence level and there was no way they could meet the considerable costs involved in the inquest. At the time of writing, we have still not raised the £14,000 which we need. But we have most of it . . . People were going from pub to pub, club to club, organizing dances, discos, fancy dress competitions—you name it, we did it. One night we raised a very large sum by holding a very successful cabaret evening, another time we had a river boat trip on the Mersey. The Liverpool dockers gave financial support as did members of the National Union of Seamen, which Kelly used to belong to. Even workers on one of the government's 12 month . . . Special Temporary Employment Programmes . . . donated money to our campaign. [9]

As you can see, those involved is this campaign were—as has so often been the case—decent, ordinary, confident and articulate working class people who simply cannot be crudely written off as being anti-establishment.

Defending civil rights

But why is so much fuss made about these deaths? Of course families want to know exactly what happened, to put right any procedural wrongs if they are discovered. This is something families often stress and take comfort from; it enables them to leave the inquest knowing (or believing) that at least something positive has come out of their personal tragedy. But why should the rest of us go to such trouble over the fate of those who have often deliberately chosen to break the law, about those who some might describe as the flotsam and jetsam of our society?

Why, as I put it earlier, appear to harass hard pressed politicians, police, prison officers and psychiatric nurses over these cases? Surely their jobs are difficult enough as it is? There are three separate but related answers to these several questions.

The first answer requires us to understand that while some, though by no means all, of those who die in custody have been guilty of anti-social behaviour, they are often far from being one dimensional characters. Indeed, I have been struck during my own research by how many of them were dutiful sons or daughters, loving partners or caring parents. It is the memory of these positive qualities which gives families and friends the energy to keep going and they deserve our attention and respect too.

The second answer is about the defence of our civil rights, the third and related one is about acknowledging culpability. Let us begin exploring these by starting with a truism.

In any society there are laws and there will be people who will disobey those laws who regrettably have to be arrested and eventually punished, sometimes with imprisonment. But when we take this very serious step of denying people their liberty in western societies we do so with certain safeguards. We do not strip these people of their legal right or their rights as human beings. We do not operate Gulags in the west where individuals are incarcerated and left to rot unheeded and unprotected, or driven to suicide by ill treatment, incompetence, neglect or despair.

Rather, we believe that those in custody retain many of the rights that they held in civil society, rights which can be, and often are, upheld and enforced by the courts, either in Britain or by the European Court of Human Rights in Strasbourg which was set up after the defeat of fascism in an attempt to secure civil rights and to place strict limits on the use of arbitrary state power.

In other words, in western liberal democratic societies we do not subscribe to the use of arbitrary power behind closed doors, say by police in the closed and largely secret world of the police van or the remand cell. Any hint of it quite properly excites our concern, our worst fears.[10] Of course, this is not just something that applies to police deaths. About prison deaths, for example, Judge Tumim suggested that these give rise to all manner of anxieties, even 'prejudices'.[11] Louis Blom-Cooper said much the same thing about deaths in secure psychiatric hospitals. In his comprehensive report on Ashworth he observed that they 'instinctively' incite curiosity, the suggestion that the death was 'unnatural'.[12]

It is, of course, to allay such fears and to raise, sometimes directly, though sometimes they are raised indirectly and almost by chance, critical questions about the possible use of arbitrary power, that investigations into sudden and unexplained deaths are carried out in free societies. Such investigations are inevitably highly political occasions.

Inquests

Take the British inquest, for example, which under the auspices of the coroner is charged with investigating sudden or unexplained deaths in this country. The state agency involved is in attendance and well represented, determined to demonstrate that the rule of law has been strictly adhered to, that those police, prison warders or psychiatric nurses involved in the death are beyond reproach. The press and television are also there to listen to the evidence, listen as the families or their legal representatives, question and cross question those involved in an attempt to discover the truth, to lay the facts before the jury, if there is one, and to secure what they take to be an appropriate verdict.

Of course, finding out just how the deceased spent his or her final hours is important in helping families and friends to cope with their grief, but beyond that, the quality of our liberal democratic society is at stake here. It is in such situations, in the interstices of the state, that power is routinely exercised, and where the massively uneven power ratio between the state and the individual is routinely demonstrated. If those who exercise that power in Britain feel hard done to and put under pressure on these occasions then I have some sympathy for their situation, but it is strictly limited because as things stand they easily have the best of it.

For example, there is no provision for families or friends to get legal aid enabling them to be adequately represented at inquests. This means that they will either have to cross question the legally represented police, prison or hospital authorities themselves, or face the daunting task of trying to raise the large sums of money to pay for a barrister to conduct their case for them. The iniquity of this, of course, is compounded by the knowledge that it is we as tax payers, including the bereaved, who will eventually pick up the bill for the legal fees incurred by the police, prison and hospital authorities through the public purse.

But even where families and friends do manage to raise money for legal representation, and some of them with the help of their local communities go to enormous lengths to do this, there is no guarantee that they will be able to prise open the files and discover exactly what happened since, among other things, advance disclosure of records and relevant files, of internal inquiries, of rule books, is still very much at the discretion of the authorities and the coroner, though it is true that following recent legislation formal efforts to disclose the medical records of deceased mental patients should have been made easier.

But overall, the situation is that the legal inquiry to discover the truth about a sudden or unexplained death in custody is often a tortuous, one sided affair. It is therefore difficult not to agree with the recommendation made by the former Chief Inspector of Prisons, Judge

Tumim that in general families and prison authorities should enter the inquest on a level playing field with the pooling of information.[13] And what applies to prison deaths should, in my view, obviously also apply to deaths in psychiatric and police custody.

The reluctance of the authorities to release all the relevant information in these cases inevitably, and often rightly in many cases, breeds suspicion. This is reinforced when those investigating these deaths find that the prison authorities, for example, go to great lengths to ensure that prison governors report to them any possible adverse public reaction to a sudden and unexpected death in their prison, that they should communicate to headquarters, immediately they are known, the names of those barristers who have agreed to represent the family or friends.

What then happens, in the words of Joe Whitty (who was the governor of Feltham when there were four tragic suicides in a very short space of time during the 1980s) is that Home Office officials and lawyers descend on the prison and begin a 'damage limitation exercise'.[14] Much the same process, or reaction, takes place when sudden or unexpected deaths take place in police cells and in psychiatric hospitals.

Denying culpability

No-one it seems is interested in admitting culpability. Indeed, quite the opposite, denial is the name of the game. I trust that up to a point I have explained why this is so. There is much at stake. The authorities and their political masters do not like to admit to the use of arbitrary power by their employees, or to admit that they themselves are guilty of neglect in its various forms, say for failing to put in place adequate procedures or safeguards. So the Prison Service Agency (as we must now learn to call it), the relevant Police Authority, the Special Hospitals Agency as was, they are always well represented by barristers at our expense, as are front line officers through their staff associations like the POA and the Police Federation.

Sometimes these various interests argue like ferrets in a sack. In the case of a suicide, for example, is it that the agencies' centrally devised procedures for suicide prevention are inadequate? Or is it that the local manager has not put them in place? Or is it the fault of the front line officer for not implementing the rule book? At inquests these various interests tussle with each other, each desperately trying to avoid being found culpable.

But even if the verdict goes against one of these interests, even where the inquest jury returns a verdict of unlawful killing, the Director of Public Prosecutions, the Crown Prosecution Service and the Police

Complaints Authority rarely bring criminal or disciplinary charges against the officers or nurses involved. The argument often is that the burden of proof in any subsequent criminal trial or disciplinary tribunal is more onerous than that required at an inquest; a conviction is unlikely and therefore proceedings unwarranted. Or in the case of the PCA, that its powers are limited. For whatever reasons those who are culpable go unpunished or uncensured, even in those cases where independent inquiry has more or less identified which agency or which individual is at fault.

You do not need me to tell you that this has a devastating effect on the families and friends of the deceased and the communities they represent, often, though by no means always, families who live in poorly resourced communities in material terms. They are often quite literally astonished at the outcome, their faith in British justice severely shaken.

If the inquest verdict on their relative or friend had been more ambiguous, say an 'open verdict' perhaps, or 'misadventure'—as it often is I must in fairness stress—then official inaction might make sense, be interpreted as reasonable by family and friends. But where the inquest verdict is quite unambiguous about where an unlawful act has been committed then reluctance of the authorities to act is interpreted as a denial of justice, as a cover up.

The fact that securing a conviction of serving police or prison officers is difficult as the cases of Barry Prosser and Joy Gardner have shown is surely to miss the point.[15]

Ways forward

I trust that I have said sufficient to suggest that something needs to be done to make the investigation of sudden or unexpected deaths in police, prison and psychiatric care more credible, to make those who are culpable answerable for their actions. There are a number of reforms on the table. For example, the pressure group INQUEST has a comprehensive range of reforms for the conduct of inquests. These include, most notably, the provision of legal aid to families in cases of deaths in custody, the far greater use of advance disclosure by police, prison and hospital authorities in such cases and so forth. The proposals here are on the whole quite modest, particularly if you are aware, as I am, of the sheer inadequacies of the inquest system in these cases which INQUEST's exemplary case work has consistently uncovered and exposed. This is what we might loosely call the reform agenda.

Another more root and branch proposal has come from the Institute of Race Relations (IRR) which, frustrated by the inquests into a number of controversial black deaths in custody, has called for an independent

Standing Commission on Deaths in Custody. The thinking behind this is that while the sort of reforms that I have just touched upon and which INQUEST advocates are necessary, they will not be sufficient to uncover the truth in cases where 'the motive for a cover up by those in authority is so strong.'[16]

What would happen under the IRR's proposal is that an interested party, a Board of Visitors perhaps, would approach the Commission over a suspicious death which would then be the subject of a full judicial, public enquiry, and where wrongdoing was uncovered, the Commission would have powers to recommend the taking of criminal or disciplinary proceedings against those concerned.

I should perhaps add here that since the IRR's original proposal the subject of black deaths in custody has attained an even greater public profile and INQUEST has forged a radical alliance on this controversial issue with a number of black campaign groups, for example, the 1990 Trust, the Newham Monitoring Project and the National Assembly Against Racism. In association with Liberty these groups gave evidence, which included proposals for reform, to the United Nations Committee on the Elimination of Racial Discrimination in Geneva during 1996.[17]

Conclusion

I hope the conference in its various sessions will take up the detail of these proposals, as singularly or in tandem they have both attractions and difficulties. However, in discussing the detail I trust that people will not forget that what is at stake here is public confidence in our political institutions, a confidence that can only be secured if lines of accountability are clearly understood, and perhaps above all, articulated in a way to secure and enhance political legitimacy.

I realise that modern government where the apparatus of the state is increasingly fragmented and dispersed through an archipelago of apparently unaccountable agencies, quangos and private operators may appear to make this difficult, at first sight at least. However, this very complexity, properly understood, could offer opportunities and lessons, and even more important, suggest that we need new ways of thinking about and articulating the important political principles which we apply in these matters.

For example, those of us here, and I would guess that we are probably in the majority, who fear that political accountability is likely to be lessened through the introduction of the private sector into the criminal justice system, must have been struck by the recent decision of Securicor to immediately re-deploy those of its employees who had failed to prevent the suicide of Peter Austin in a London magistrates' court. While the inquest showed that Securicor was far from blameless in responding to this tragedy in certain other respects, I cannot recall the Prison Service Agency ever acting quite so decisively in similar cases to reassure the public, though the Agency's director who is to follow me will no doubt argue that he and his managers are doing all they can.[18]

Of course, and in defence of the director and those other senior civil servants and politicians who are charged with running our prisons, police and psychiatric services generally, I do understand that there are limits to what they can do, what they can command. It is therefore important to remember, as Rose and Miller have so wisely reminded us, that the 'entities and agencies within governmental networks are not faithful relays, mere creatures of a controller situated in some central hub'.[19] But this realisation, the acknowledgement that the post- modern world we now all inhabit can no longer be seen as a set of simple one way relays, public or private, is no excuse for denying culpability, least of all by politicians who have legislated for these increasingly complex structures while at the same time maintaining the traditionalist, modernist language of ministerial responsibility and the supremacy of Parliament.

Such a discourse suggests, regrettably, that they have not yet woken up to the problems and subtleties of the post-modern order that they have themselves done so much to create, or yet found the political language with which to explain how their changing responsibilities should be discharged, spoken about feel so frustrated. This is a dangerous political vacuum which and understood. This goes some way at least to explaining why they feel so besieged, and why we and families and friends of the deceased will continue to have disruptive political consequences.

Mick Ryan is Professor of Penal Politics at the University of Greenwich, London. He has written extensively on British, European and American penal systems and has published a book on deaths in secure custody, *Lobbying from Below: INQUEST in Defence of Civil Liberties*.

ENDNOTES

1. M. Ryan, 1996, 'Lobbying from Below', INQUEST in *Defence of Civil Liberties*, UCL Press, London, *Chapter 2*
2. T. Jefferson, 1990, *The Case Against Paramilitary Policing*, Milton Keynes, Open University Press, *Chapter 2*
3. T. Ward, 1986, *Deaths and Disorder*, London, INQUEST, *Chapter 2*
4. P. Scraton and P. Gordon, 1984, *Causes for Concern*, London, Penguin,

Chapters 2 and 3

5. S. Hall *et al*, 1978, *Policing the Crisis*. London, MacMillan; and P. Scraton (ed.), 1976, *Law Order and the Authoritarian State*, Milton Keynes, Open University Press

6. J. Sim, 1990, *Medical Power in Prisons*, Open University Press, Milton Keynes; see also J. Sim, 1991, 'We are Not Animals, We are Human Beings', *Prisons, Protest and Politics in England and Wales 1969-970*, *Social Justice*, vol 18, no 3

7. M. Ryan, 1983, *The Politics of Penal Reform*, London, Longman, *Chapter 3*

8. G. Coggan and M. Walker, 1982, *Frightened for My Life*, London, Fontana, *Chapter 6*

9. T. Banks, 'The Death of Jimmy Kelly' (Unpublished and undated manuscript), *Chapter 4*

10. R. Burridge *et al*, 'The Inquest as a Theatre for Police Tragedy', *Journal for Law and Society*, 12: 25 -6, 1985

11. HM Chief Inspector of Prisons, 1990, *Suicide and Self- Harm in Prison Service Establishments in England and Wales*, London HMSO, cmd 1383, para 5; 9

12. *Report of the Committee of Inquiry into Complaints about Ashworth Hospital*, vol 1, London, HMSO,1992, 211

13. M. Ryan, *op cit.*, 77

14. TV documentary, 1996, 'First Sight; Who Dunnit?'

15. M. Ryan, ibid, 59

16. Institute of Race Relations, *Deadly Silence; Black Deaths in Custody*, London, IRR, 1991, 65/66

17. Update, *Agenda*, Liberty, 3, May 1996

18. I am grateful to Deborah Coles and Helen Shaw at INQUEST for details of this case which is scheduled for judicial review in July 1997

19. N. Rose and P. Miller, 'Political Power beyond the State; Problematics of Government', *British Journal of Sociology*, 1992, 43(2), 177- 205.

CHAPTER 2

Changing Perspectives on Deaths of Prisoners

Richard Tilt

Mr Chairman, I am very pleased to have been invited to address this conference. I am also pleased that ISTD has been able to organize and run the third conference on this vitally important subject. Let me start by emphasising that the preservation of human life is at the core of the Prison Service's duty of care to prisoners and our service to the public. It is something that I take very seriously: every death is one too many. It is implicit in our statement of purpose.

Prison Service Statement of Purpose

PRISON SERVICE STATEMENT OF PURPOSE

Her Majesty's Prison Service serves the public by keeping in custody those committed by the courts.

Our duty is to look after them with humanity and to help them lead law-abiding lives in custody and after release.

Deaths in prison custody are a profoundly serious matter for all those people whose lives are touched by them. For the family and friends of the deceased there are the pains of bereavement and the added pain that their loved one has died isolated from them and the community at large. For staff and prisoners there is the sense of loss and the impact of the death on the prison community. These two differing perspectives reveal tensions and potential conflicts but also some commonalities which are rarely recognised. I shall return to that later.

There are three main themes to this presentation. I want to describe the scale of the problem faced by the Prison Service in this most difficult area. I want to outline what we have achieved in addressing the issue. And finally I want to describe what I see as the key developments for the future. By way of preface let me clarify two necessary points: how we define and how we categorise deaths of prisoners.

33

Defining a death in prison custody is not always as straightforward as it might appear. Prisoners may be temporarily out of our custody, whether lawfully or unlawfully. Sometimes a prisoner might be unlawfully at large for a long time and we may never hear of the death. A pragmatic and sensible approach has to be adopted. As a general rule of thumb, we include *all* deaths where the prisoner is currently in the care and custody of prison staff or where the cause of death is directly related to an act occurring within our custody.

Categorising deaths in prison is not always straightforward. For apparent suicides, we use the term 'self-inflicted' death. We do not feel it would be fair to rely upon the exclusive verdict of 'suicide'—as strictly defined in the coroner's court—where verdicts of 'open', 'accidental', 'misadventure', or even 'natural causes', may be applied to self-inflicted deaths. Prison statistics on self-inflicted deaths are therefore likely to be over inclusive with slightly higher numbers than if we simply used suicide verdicts. I think this is the right approach—it is essential that we try and learn from all of these events. We do not wish to hide anything. This distinction is, however, important in any comparisons with rates of suicides in prison and the community.

Some difficulties arise when we try to understand deaths through drug overdose. It is not always clear whether an overdose was intentional. A judgment has to be made. Each death is considered carefully in the light of anything which may emerge at the coroner's inquest. The statistics, therefore, may have to be adjusted retrospectively in the light of any new evidence. I would emphasise that we are committed to being as accurate and as open as possible with our record keeping. I wish now to move on to the main substance of this paper.

Firstly, I would like to describe the scale of the problem. Deaths in prison custody fall into a number of broad categories: natural causes; self-inflicted; and homicide. In a typical recent year—1995—there were 117 deaths of which about half were self-inflicted.

Deaths during 1995

Deaths in Prisons in England and Wales 1995	
Self inflicted	59
Natural causes	56
Homicide	2
Total	117

- **Average Prison Population: 51,047**
- **Annual Throughput: 125,154**

The table also shows that deaths are, thankfully, rare. During this year the average daily population was over 51,000 and the overall throughput of prisoners was over 125,000.

Deaths by natural causes
Of all the kinds of death those by *natural causes* are perhaps the easiest to understand. Natural deaths refer to those which occur as a consequence of a known pathological process, such as coronary heart disease, or stroke. The majority of these deaths, although correctly identified as deaths in custody, actually occur within hospitals in the outside community.

Health care in prisons is based on the primary care model. The primary health care team comprises doctors and nurses who are available, as in the community, on a 24 hour, seven day a week basis. Such primary care is supplemented by visiting specialists and, where required, a prisoner may attend an outside hospital as an out-patient for assessment, diagnosis and treatment. In 1995/6 prisoners attended as National Health Service out-patients on almost 27,000 occasions.

As in the community, when a medical condition is more severe, complex or life threatening, the prisoner will be admitted to hospital for further treatment. In 1995/6 there were almost 2,500 in-patient admissions for physical conditions such as heart disease, stroke, lung disease and surgical conditions, such as appendicitis and hernia operations.

The major causes of natural death in the community amongst men are coronary artery disease, stroke and cancer. The pattern of mortality in prison mirrors that in the community. In the year ending 1995/6 there were 46 deaths of prisoners due to recognisable pathological processes; almost half were due to heart attacks or heart disease, eight per cent to a stroke and 15 per cent to cancer.

A number of prisoners with terminal illnesses, such as cancer related illnesses and AIDS, are released from prison on compassionate grounds to die in the community, either in a hospice, their own home, with friends, or in hospital. In 1996/7 eight prisoners were released early on grounds of cancer and three on account of AIDS related illness.

Those entering prison have often had less healthy lifestyles than the general population, having been more likely to abuse alcohol, tobacco and illegal drugs. They are more likely to suffer mental disorder and to be at increased risk of contracting communicable diseases.

The Prison Service is seeking to address all these factors through an increased focus on health promotion and healthy life styles. This should bring benefits to the general community, to which most prisoners return, as well as to the prison population. We will soon be making our first awards to a number of 'Health Promoting Prisons'—which have demonstrated a commitment to influencing up to ten aspects of healthy living, such as smoking reduction, healthy eating, and education about the risks of using drugs including those associated with blood borne viruses, such as Hepatitis B and C.

Self-inflicted deaths

Moving on to *self-inflicted deaths*. These types of deaths within prison have always given great cause for concern. Loss of life through a deliberate act of self-injury is a source of great sadness. Before examining the frequency with which they occur however, it is important to remember the *context* within which they occur. We know that the suicide rate among males under 35 in the United Kingdom has risen quite dramatically since the early 1980s. Although in more recent years the rise has tailed off.

Suicide rates in the community

Suicides and Undetermined Deaths in England and Wales Rate per 100,000 Population										
MALES										
Age	1985	1986	1987	1988	1989	1990	1991	1992	1993	1994	1995
15 - 24	12	13	15	17	16	18	17	17	16	16	15
25 - 34	20	20	21	23	22	24	25	23	21	23	23
35 - 44	22	21	21	25	22	24	26	26	22	22	23

There is no simple clear explanation for this rise. Various factors: economic, sociological and psychological may be involved. There will be some here at this conference who will be well versed in the complexities of the research in this area.

Whatever the causes, we do know that prisoners come from the community and in most cases return to the community. They include a significant proportion of those individuals from a background of heightened vulnerability: individuals with histories of drug/alcohol abuse, depression, and social deprivation. I think it is important to regard prison suicides not as an exclusively prison issue but also as a community problem. To clarify what I mean by that: it is not to deny the

36

importance that the additional pressure that imprisonment itself may place on those who are vulnerable, but to remember that some of that vulnerability relates to what is happening in prisoners' lives outside the prison walls. What is needed is a balanced perspective on the nature of the problem. Numbers of self-inflicted deaths in prisons in England and Wales have risen over the last 15 years.

Self-inficted deaths against average daily population

Self-inflicted Deaths in Prisons in England and Wales		
Year	Number of Deaths	Average Daily Population (thousands)
1983	27	43.5
1984	26	43.3
1985	27	46.2
1986	21	46.8
1987	46	48.4
1988	37	48.9
1989	48	48.5
1990	50	45.0
1991	42	44.8
1992	41	44.7
1993	47	44.6
1994	62	48.6
1995	59	51.0
1996	64	55.3

Displayed as a graph it shows a steady underlying annual increase of between 6 and 8 per cent with minor fluctuations year by year:

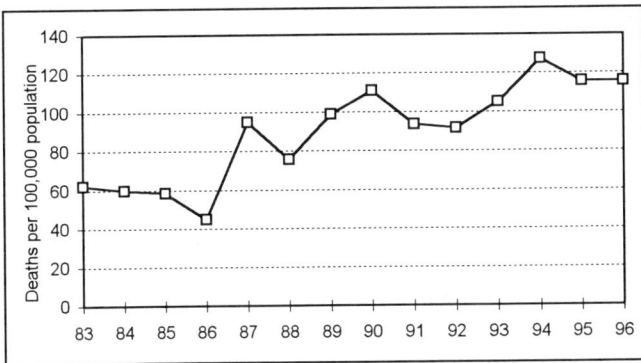

Self-inflicted deaths in prisons in England and Wales: rate per 100k population

37

Deaths in SPS and NIPS

It perhaps of note that both the Scottish and Northern Ireland Prison Services have experienced an increase in numbers of self-inflicted deaths in recent years.

Self-inflicted Deaths in Prisons, Northern Ireland and Scotland				
Year	Ireland	Ireland	Scotland	Scotland
	Number	Total Average Population	Number	Total Average Population
1985	2	2,107	6	5,273
1986	1	1,937	7	5,587
1987	1	1,981	7	5,446
1988	1	1,901	7	5,229
1989	1	1,815	6	4,986
1990	1	1,785	3	4,724
1991	1	1,796	4	4,839
1992	0	1,810	9	5,257
1993	0	1,934	5	5,637
1994	3	1,899	16	5,585
1995	2	1,762	10	5,626
1996	3	1,607	16	5,862

We take some encouragement that the rate of self-inflicted deaths in England and Wales has slowed a little during the last three years, at a time when the prison population has risen dramatically. In December 1992 the prison population stood at 40,600. It now stands at well over 61,000.

It is, of course, too early to say whether this slowing down of the rate marks a change in the underlying trend. It does highlight, however, the shortsightedness of judging the performance of the Prison Service by numbers of deaths, rather than the numbers of deaths in relation to the prison population at the time. Headlines such as 'record number of deaths' are singularly unhelpful when numbers actually indicate a reduction in the rate.

The question is often asked: 'how much more at risk are prisoners of suicide than the general community'? A number of attempts have been made to estimate the increased likelihood of risk. This is very difficult to do. Samples in community studies may be quite unrepresentative of those typically entering custody. We do not have sufficient information about levels of vulnerability of those at risk of imprisonment to be able to make valid comparisons. However, a word of caution is needed. If the information was available and if it demonstrated that risk of suicide was no greater within prison than in the community—it would not have any impact upon our primary goal, which is to do everything possible to reduce the risk of self-inflicted deaths occurring.

What has the prison service done about self-inflicted deaths?
We have a long tradition of developing, maintaining and reviewing strategies for reducing the risk of self-injury and suicide. The first instruction to Prison Service establishments on suicide prevention dates back to 1973. Following a review of suicides by the Chief Inspector in 1984 procedures were revised in the late 1980s. A further review was conducted by the Chief Inspector which reported in 1990. This led to an extensive review with revised instructions introduced during 1994, shortly before the last 'Deaths in Custody' Conference in Cambridge. There are workshops at this conference outlining its development, so I will not go in to it in detail. But it would be helpful for me to give an outline of its broad principles and how we are developing it.

Key features of strategy

- Multi-Disciplinary

- Local Suicide Awareness Teams

- Focus on Problems

- Multi-Agency

Further outlined, these key features are as follows:

- the foundation of the strategy is on a multi-disciplinary approach. We had been rightly criticised in 1990 for advocating, or at least implying, that the answers to suicide and self-injury rested entirely within the medical profession. Our current strategy rightly places the responsibility for identification of prisoners at risk and provision of help and support on *all* staff
- each establishment has a multi-disciplinary Suicide Awareness Team with responsibility for oversight of local practice within national policy
- the focus of our strategy is upon identifying the individual prisoner's problems rather than just dealing with the symptoms
- we have developed a strong multi-agency approach involving the

Samaritans. This partnership which has developed over the last ten years has been particularly encouraging. All establishments have links with the local Samaritans. In over 90 establishments the Samaritans involvement includes the training of prisoners as Listeners to provide peer group support to fellow prisoners in distress.

There are no simple, easy solutions for preventing suicide. Strategies are kept continually under review. The evidence so far is that our strategies are well-founded and sound in principle. There is of course always room for improvement; suicide prevention is a continuing developmental process. The following are some of the ways we are currently working to improve our strategies:

Work in progress

- Reception/Induction Screening
- Movement of Prisoners at Risk
- Improving Communications
- Understanding Self-Injury
- Improving Cell Design
- Research

Futher outlined, these items are as follows:

- re-examining how reception and induction of prisoners into establishments can be most effectively handled. We know this to be the period of highest risk of vulnerability. Time and resources are stretched, but we know the importance of creating a climate where prisoners will feel that they can express their concerns
- ensuring that procedures for the movement of prisoners at risk are consistent so that vital information is communicated between agencies within and without the prison
- making full use of IT in communicating information
- improving our understanding of what factors precipitate self-injury and how they can best be monitored
- improving the design of prison cells so that they can be made safer for both staff and prisoners
- continuing to conduct research into suicide and self-injury; the Prison Service hosts a research forum consisting of members both within and outside prisons.

This is not an exhaustive list—but just to give a flavour of the key areas of work.

This work needs to be seen against a context of what is realistically achievable. We could be forgiven for feeling that some of our critics create the impression that all suicides are preventable. We have to accept that in spite of the best efforts of staff some deaths may not be preventable. But at the same time we have to work *as if* they were. That is the real dilemma facing staff on a daily basis.

Homicides
Death by homicide in prison is extremely tragic but, thankfully in this country, rare.

1991	1992	1993	1994	1995	1996
2	2	3	3	2	2

Prisoner Homicides in England and Wales

Its rarity does not of course diminish the pain for those affected. Some of you may be aware of the independent inquiry into the tragic death of Christopher Edwards at Chelmsford prison in 1994. I am pleased that Christopher's parents have felt able to attend this conference so that they can share their perspective in such a painful experience. We have to learn from these dreadful tragedies. The independent inquiry will be reporting soon and along with the other agencies involved we will be considering its findings very carefully.

We are committed to doing everything possible to make prisons safer places. A framework for a strategic approach to reducing violence is presently being piloted in a number of prisons.

Deaths following restraint
Deaths of prisoners during or following restraint are a source of great concern. Control and restraint procedures are only used as a last resort when staff are faced with very difficult individuals who pose a severe threat to themselves and the safety of others. Control and restraint procedures are used hundreds of times each year with minimal harm. There have been seven deaths in the last nine years during or following restraint procedures. Of particular concern is death through *positional asphyxia*. The conditions which lead to it are poorly understood. It is the subject of continuing research. We have recently re-examined our instructions on control and restraint procedures. We have issued a reminder for staff to make them aware of the particular signs and symptoms of distress which may indicate a need for medical attention.

41

Aftermath of death

Finally in this paper I want to address some of the issues which follow in the aftermath of death. First and foremost, the death of a prisoner is a time of emotional shock. For staff there are important procedures to be followed. There are the tasks of identifying and notifying the next of kin, informing the police, notifying the coroner. I am conscious that some of these procedures have not always been handled well. However carefully and tactfully these procedures are carried out, there is an underlying sense of loss. Because, unlike other events in prison—an act has taken place which is irretrievable.

Self-inflicted or sudden deaths have a major impact upon prison staff and prisoners. We set great store on relationships between staff and prisoners. Where those relationships are at their strongest an unforeseen death can have the profoundest impact. The circumstances of the deaths themselves can be particularly unpleasant and traumatic for the staff and prisoners directly involved. There can be strong feelings of failure. It is a time for self-scrutiny and self-agonising. This is particularly so when there has been a sequence of deaths. With the benefit of hindsight it is, of course, always possible to identify things which might have been done differently.

We are only too well aware of the impact that a death has upon friends and family. We are committed to doing all that we can to help families in such a time of need. But as I say, I am not satisfied that we are always doing that as well as we could. It is a very emotional time. There will be questions which relatives and friends have which we can answer—and where we can our aim is to do so. But there will be some questions we cannot answer immediately simply because it takes time to piece together what has happened. There is a need for understanding on both sides of the prison walls.

I am pleased to say that since the first of these conferences was held in 1991, we have made significant improvements. It is now routine for families to be offered the opportunity to visit the prison if they wish. It is not uncommon for a memorial service to be held within the prison. That is not to say that we always get it right or that we have no more work to do. We are continually seeking to improve the relationship between the Prison Service and families and relatives after a death. We have been working with the organization INQUEST to see how we might improve our support to families in the light of their experience.

The coroner's inquest is, of course, held in public and is of great significance for the family in helping them find out and come to terms with what has happened. In recent years we have tried to increase the range of information to which families have access prior to the inquest. We acknowledge that there is more work to be done and we are currently examining how we can improve arrangements.

In a similar vein we have tried to improve the range of information which the coroner's office receives from us prior to the inquest. Of course, the coroner's inquiry is quite separate from our investigations into deaths and it is for a quite different purpose. We now routinely offer our reports to the coroner to assist in preparation for the inquest, although these reports currently remain outside of the public domain. However, we are currently reviewing our wider policy and practice on reporting to see how we can be more open.

Conclusion

This has been a wide-ranging overview of deaths of prisoners. I hope I have been able to give you a flavour of what we see as the key issues and how the Prison Service is addressing them. One issue which I have not mentioned is the fact that this is an area where we are judged almost exclusively on failure. A non-suicide or a life saved is not a statistic which reaches the attention of the public. We should not overlook the sterling effort of prison staff whose work on a daily basis results in lives saved. This is rarely recognised and I would like to take this opportunity to pay tribute to that.

In summary then, I wish to re-emphasise the commitment of the Prison Service to dealing with these very serious issues. As I have outlined, we have a programme of work which will help us improve the health of prisoners. We also have a programme of work to help assist us in our goal of providing help and support for those prisoners who are at risk of self-injury or suicide.

This is not easy work. It is a sensitive, but crucial area. We have made significant strides in recent years. But we are not complacent. There will always be more work to be done. We are deeply committed to doing all that we can to provide the best care for prisoners—and to reduce the likelihood of a death in prison custody.

Richard Tilt is Director General of the Prison Service which he joined in 1967. He served as governor of HMP Bedford and HMP Gartree, before becoming Deputy Regional Director for the Midlands. From 1992 to 1994 he was head of finance and resources in the Police Department. He became Director of Services for the Prison Service in 1994 and Director of Security and Programmes in 1995.

CHAPTER 3

'Man Passeth Away Like a Shadow': Deaths Associated with the Australian Criminal Justice System, Six Years After the Royal Commission into Aboriginal Deaths in Custody

David McDonald

Introduction[1]

In 1993 a 16-year-old Aboriginal lad was shot and killed by a police officer at Launceston in the Australian State of Tasmania. The circumstances were as follows; the quotations are from the coroner's findings.

The Tasmanian police had received information that an armed man was attempting to break into a shop. Two police constables were despatched to the scene, arriving there, in separate vehicles, at approximately the same time. One of the constables, walking around to the back of the shop, came upon an armed man. The officer attempted to unholster his service revolver but before he could do so the man came to within two or three metres of him and pointed his pistol at the constable's head. The constable told him to put the gun down but received no response. In the words of the officer (as recorded in the inquest findings) 'He kept walking towards me so I was backing away from him, and he still had the gun levelled at my head and I was thinking he was going to shoot me but I just, I raised both my hands'.

The constable backed up to his vehicle continuously pleading with or arguing with the young man to put down his gun. The other officer, seeing what had happened, had his service revolver drawn and pointing at the young man. He called out. The young man turned and pointed the revolver at the second constable. This gave time for the first constable to unholster his service revolver and point it at the young man. What we had then was a classic stand-off: the young man pointing his revolver at the head of one of the constables with both officers having their revolvers pointed at him. The officers pleaded with the young man telling him that unless he put down his gun they would have to shoot him but they did not want to do so. One of the constables described what happened next.

I said to this fellow, I said 'Look, put your gun down, we don't want to hurt you but there are two of us here, put the gun down and we'll just talk about it. We don't want to hurt you, we don't have to shoot you, put the gun down'. And he just, he said to me 'Go on, go on, shoot me then, I'll kill one of you'. And I said 'No, look, we don't want to hurt you, put the gun down and we can talk about this'. He said 'I'll kill one of you, then you can kill me, I don't care'.

The stand-off continued a little longer with both officers in fear of their lives. Finally, the young man stepped forward with his pistol still pointed at the officer's head. The officer stated 'Put the gun down now, I don't want to shoot you, but I will shoot you'. The lad took a further step forward, the officer was convinced that he was going to be shot and so pointed his revolver at the young man's stomach and fired. The young man died a little later from haemorrhage from the iliac vessels.

This death in custody, or a police operation, is a terrible tragedy, obviously for the young man, but also for his family and for the two police constables involved and, in turn, their families. It is easy to imagine how such an incident has a long term deleterious impact on all concerned. The incident captures, however, a number of the central themes of this paper, namely the duty of care that officers in the criminal justice system have to all the people with whom they come in contact (not just people in their custody); the complex human interactions involved in such incidents; and the fact that, although it is quite easy to point to breaches of duty of care with regard to some custodial deaths, very often we see exemplary behaviour on the part of the officers involved, even when a death ensues. In this case, where the officer shot and killed the 16-year-old Aboriginal boy in Tasmania, neither the coroner nor, probably, any other fair person would be able to fault the behaviour of the officers. Indeed, as the coroner pointed out:

I am positively satisfied that [the constable's] shooting of the deceased was justified as an act of self defence, and can only wonder that he had the courage to continue from one stage to yet another more critical stage in this confrontation until the final moment, when for him he was literally staring death in the face . . . Both officers showed remarkable, and in the case of constable [W] almost excessive, restraint, a dedication to preserving life at all but the expense of their own, and courage which was no less than heroic. Both officers deserve recognition by the highest possible commendation.

A particularly tragic aspect of this story is that the pistol used by the young man was only a replica, incapable of firing a projectile. There was no way that the police officers involved could have known that this was the case.

The Australian Royal Commission into Aboriginal Deaths in Custody
The Royal Commission commenced its work, nationally, with the appointment of the first Royal Commissioner, the Honourable J. H. Muirhead, on 16 October 1987 (Royal Commission into Aboriginal Deaths in Custody 1991). When it became apparent that the number of deaths was far higher than previously believed, and the scope of the inquiry far deeper than initially assumed, additional commissioners were appointed. Commissioner Muirhead resigned on 27 April 1989 and his place as the senior (national) commissioner was taken by Commissioner Elliott Johnston.

The Letters Patent (or terms of reference) under which the Royal Commission operated gave the commission responsibility for investigating both the 99 deaths in custody and, importantly, the broader issues which aid understanding of those deaths. The Royal Commission was authorised to investigate:

> The deaths in Australia since 1 January 1980 of Aboriginals and Torres Strait Islanders whilst in police custody, in prison or in any other place of detention, but not including such a death occurring in a hospital, mental institution, infirmary or medical treatment centre unless injuries suffered whilst in police custody, in prison or in any place of detention caused or contributed to that death.
>
> . . . for the purpose of reporting on any underlying issues associated with those deaths, you [the Commissioners] are authorised to take account of social, cultural and legal factors which, in your judgment, appear to have a bearing on those deaths.[2]

The final date for Commissioner Johnston to present his National Report was set at 26 April 1991; it was tabled in the Commonwealth Parliament by the minister for Aboriginal and Torres Strait Islander Affairs on 9 May of that year. The other Royal Commissioners contributed to the preparation of the National Report and released state-level reports and individual reports into the deaths of each Aboriginal person who died in custody during the relevant period.

The Royal Commission found that 99 Aboriginal people died in all forms of custody during the period 1 January 1980 to 31 May 1989, the cut-off date for deaths investigated. Sixty-three (or two-thirds) of these died in police custody, 33 in prison and three in juvenile detention. Of the 63 police custody deaths, 19 occurred in each of Queensland and Western Australia, nine in New South Wales, seven in South Australia, five in the Northern Territory, three in Victoria, and one in Tasmania (No deaths occurred in the Australian Capital Territory). The educational level of the people who died was generally low and more than half had been removed from their natural families as children as a result of interventions by government agencies, church mission organizations, or others. The adverse impacts of this forced separation and attempts at assimilation are deeply felt by many Aboriginal people today and have been identified by many as a contemporary source of individual and family dysfunction.[3]

Contrary to the expectations of many people, Aboriginal and non-Aboriginal alike, the Royal Commission did not find that any deaths were caused by culpable behaviour on the part of police officers. It did not recommend that any be charged with homicide. The central finding of the Royal Commission emphasised the duty of care considerations:

> The conclusions reached in this report will not accord with the expectations of those who anticipated that findings of foul play would be inevitable and frequent. That is not the conclusion which Commissioners reached. As reported in the individual case reports which have been released, Commissioners did not find that the deaths were the product of deliberate violence or brutality by police or prison officers.
>
> But Commissioners did find that, generally, there appeared to be little appreciation of and less dedication to the duty of care owed by custodial authorities and their officers to persons in custody. We found many system defects in relation to care, many failures to exercise proper care and in general a poor standard of care. In some cases the defects and failures were causally related to the deaths, in some cases they were not and in others it was open to debate . . . It can certainly be said that in many cases death was contributed to by system failures or absence of due care (Royal Commission into Aboriginal Deaths in Custody 1991, vol. 1, p. 3).

Epidemiological research conducted for the Royal Commission revealed an apparent anomaly with respect to the relative risks of deaths in police custody of Aboriginal and non-Aboriginal people.[4] After controlling for the different age distributions of the two populations, it is clear that, during the 1980s, Aboriginal people were heavily over-represented in deaths in custody (compared with non-Aboriginal people) when the number of deaths is compared with the number of Aboriginal and non-Aboriginal people, respectively, in the national population. However, when the number of deaths is compared with the number of people *in custody* (or more precisely the person/years spent in custody) the risks experienced by Aboriginal and non-Aboriginal people were similar. The explanation for this is the very high level of over-representation of Aboriginal people in custody: by a factor of 31 times in police custody in August 1995 (Carcach and McDonald 1997) and 18 times in prison (Australian Bureau of Statistics (quarterly)).

The Royal Commission investigated not only the deaths themselves, but also the underlying issues which contributed to the over-representation of Aboriginal people in custody and to the deaths in custody. These underlying issues reflected the breadth of the Letters Patent of the Royal Commission, which (as indicated above) empowered it to investigate and take account of not only the deaths, but also the 'social, cultural, and legal factors which (in the judgment of the Commissioners) appear to have a bearing on those deaths'.

Civil court actions for compensation

In the United States of America, almost every death in custody results in litigation by the family of the deceased against the officers involved and the authority which employs them. This litigation frequently results in court orders that plaintiffs be paid sums of money that are very large by Australian (and probably British) standards. I understand that this threat of litigation has been one of, if not the, most significant factor leading American prison and jail authorities to implement effective suicide prevention programmes. The position is quite different in Australia. In this country, it is rare that court actions are taken as a result of a death in custody. So far in only one death in custody case has a court found that officers and their employing authority were negligent and ordered that compensation payments be made. This case related to the death of Mark Quayle, an Aboriginal man who was found hanging from his cell door by a strip of blanket in the New South Wales country town of Wilcannia in June 1987. The Royal Commission into Aboriginal Deaths in Custody found that Mr Quayle was unlawfully in custody and that:

> While no other person intended or took part in his death it resulted from shocking and callous disregard for his welfare on behalf of a hospital sister, a doctor of the Royal Flying Doctor Service, and two police officers . . . Given Mark's disturbed and hallucinating condition and the effects of alcohol withdrawal, there is nothing surprising in his having hung himself in the conditions in which he was left [in the police cells] (Wootten 1990, pp. 1-2, 6).

Mr Quayle's family brought action in the District Court of New South Wales and the court found that the New South Wales Health Service and the New South Wales Police Service were both negligent in caring for him. The court awarded $56,000 to Mr Quayle's mother and $44,800 each to two of his brothers for 'pathological grief reaction' and 'nervous shock' (*Quayle v. New South Wales* (1995) Aust Torts Reports 62). While this unprecedented decision of the New South Wales District Court emphases the duty of care that people have to those in their custody, the level of the payments ordered to be made by the authorities to the family of the deceased were really quite small (particularly considering

48

the costs of legal fees) and is unlikely to be a large enough sum to have any significant impact on the authorities themselves. Nevertheless, a number of cases are currently before the Australian courts relating to custodial deaths and it could be that, in the future, litigation with become a more significant lever for change than it is at the moment.

The current position and trends with Australian custodial deaths[5]

During the 1996 calendar year 80 people were reported to have died in all forms of custody and custody-related police operations in the community throughout Australia (Dalton 1997). This figure is based upon the definition of deaths in custody and in custody-related police operations recommended by the Royal Commission to be used for the purposes of post-death investigations and for monitoring custodial deaths, namely:

(i) The death wherever occurring of a person who is in prison custody or police custody or detention as a juvenile;

(ii) the death wherever occurring of a person whose death is caused or contributed to by traumatic injuries sustained, or by lack of proper care whilst in such custody or detention;

(iii) the death wherever occurring of a person who dies or is fatally injured in the process of police or prison officers attempting to detain that person; and

(iv) the death wherever occurring of a person who dies or is fatally injured in the process of that person escaping or attempting to escape from prison custody or police custody or juvenile detention.

Deaths in Custody and Custody-related Police Operations Australia, 1996					
Cause	Prison	Police cells, etc.	Police operations	Juvenile detention	Total
Hanging	21	3	-	1	25
Natural causes	21	2	-	-	23
Injuries	5	-	11	-	16
Gunshot	-	-	7	-	7
Drugs	5	2	-	-	7
Alcohol	-	1	-	-	1
Other	-	1	-	-	1
Total	52	9	18	1	80

Table 1 Deaths reported for 1996 showing the causes of death and their settings.

It will be immediately apparent that 52 of the deaths, two-thirds of the total, occurred in prison custody. Nine deaths occurred in police cells or in hospital following transfer from police cells, 18 in police operations in community settings and one in a juvenile detention facility. Seventeen of these deaths were of Aboriginal or Torres Strait Islander people, 12 in prison, four in police operations in the community, and one in police in cells. The 17 deaths of Indigenous people represent some 21 per cent of the total although Indigenous make up less than two per cent of the Australian population. The heavy over-representation of Indigenous people, particularly among prison deaths is explained, almost entirely, by their over-representation in the prison population (Office of the Aboriginal and Torres Strait Islander Social Justice Commissioner 1996). All the deaths were of males excepting for one Aboriginal female. Their ages ranged from 13 to 75 years with a mean age of 36 years.

As indicated in *Table 1*, hanging was the most frequent cause of death with all but four of the hanging deaths occurring in prisons. This was followed, in frequency, by deaths from 'natural causes' (i.e. disease), again with most of those deaths occurring in prisons. Injury was the third most frequent cause of death. Although five injury deaths occurred in prison, it is important to note the eleven deaths from injuries in police operations. Ten of these were deaths that occurred in motor vehicle crashes in high speed police pursuits. Of the seven deaths in police operations from gunshot, two were cases of people shot and killed by police officers while attempting to detain them whereas the remaining five were instances where people shot and killed themselves, generally in siege situations. The remaining nine deaths included seven from drug overdoses, one from alcohol toxicity and one where a person choked on his vomit. Overall, 34 (or 44 per cent) of the 78 deaths in which responsibility was clear were self inflicted.

Trends and components of change

Data on Australian custodial deaths are available covering the period since 1980. Until the Royal Commission into Aboriginal Deaths in Custody placed emphasis on the full range of custodial situations in which deaths occur, it was generally assumed that the term 'deaths in custody' referred essentially to deaths in prisons, juvenile detention centres and police lock ups. Deaths in sieges or pursuits, for example, were generally not included in data collections. For the purposes of a long time series, it is necessary, then, to use only deaths in institutional forms of custody, i.e. prisons, police lock ups, police vehicles and in hospital following transfer from these types of institutional settings, and in juvenile detention centres. *Figure 1* applies this consistent time series.

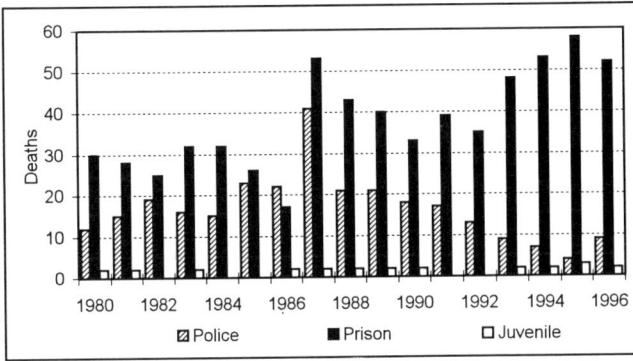

Figure 1 Deaths in Institutional forms of Custody, Australia 1980 - 1996

It is immediately apparent from *Figure 1* that the temporal pattern of deaths in prison is quite different from that of deaths in police custody. During the period 1980 to 1986 the number of deaths both in prison and police custody remained more or less stable with the number of prison deaths markedly exceeding the number of police custody deaths in the early part of the decade. The incidence of deaths in both police custody and prison custody doubled between 1986 and 1987. Although not shown in *Figure 1* this doubling occurred among both Aboriginal and non-Aboriginal custodial deaths. It was this huge increase, and the media publicity associated with it, that led to the establishment of the Royal Commission into Aboriginal Deaths in Custody in October 1987 (McDonald 1996a). At that stage, information was not generally available about the number of deaths of non-indigenous people in custody.

Following the peak of 1987, the number of deaths in prison fell until 1992 but has increased again since that year. (For completeness, the *Appendix* to this chapter contains a table of Australian prison death rates from all causes and from suicide alone, for the period 1985 to 1996.) In sharp contrast it can be observed that the number of deaths in institutional forms of police custody (as defined above) fell markedly from a 1987 peak of 41 to only four deaths nationally in 1995. The number increased to nine in 1996.

Data are available on deaths in police operations in community settings covering the period 1990 to 1996 only. Although not detailed here, these deaths (most of which are from high speed police pursuits and from sieges) average 18 per annum with little fluctuation over the seven years for which data are available (Dalton 1997).

The public policy issues here are clear. The pleasing reduction in the number of police custody deaths needs to be maintained, and more concerted action is needed to reverse the tragic upward trends in deaths in Australian prisons.

Deaths in police custody and police operations

Internationally, a great deal of excellent work has been done to prevent prison deaths, particularly deaths by suicide. In this section, however, I wish to place further emphasis on deaths in police custody, reviewing the circumstances in which such deaths occur, the reasons for the reduction in the incidence of police custody deaths in Australia and the continuing concerns about deaths in police operations in Australia.

Listed below are the main categories of deaths being treated in Australia as 'deaths in custody or in custody-related police operations'. Eight categories are differentiated.

1. *Cell suicides*

The most common form of death in police custody during the 1980s was the suicide, almost always by self-inflicted hanging, of people in police lock ups (Biles and McDonald 1992). Frequently people who die in this way are withdrawing from alcohol intoxication and have previously attempted suicide or given warnings or other indications that they are suicidal. These deaths raise concerns about the need to identify 'at-risk' detainees and the need to transfer them to more appropriate facilities or to supervise them closely. They also point to the need to consider cell design (e.g. removal of hanging points) and for the observation of people in the cells.

2. *Violence between detainees in a lock up*

From time to time, people die in police lock ups from violence inflicted there by other detainees or, it is sometimes alleged, by police officers. Many argue that John Pat's 1983 death that resulted in police officers being charged with his manslaughter and being acquitted, falls into this category (Johnston 1991). A second example is the death of Fay Yarrie who died from internal injuries as a result of being assaulted by another female prisoner in the police lock up in Brisbane (Wyvill 1990).

3. *Illness, death not preventable*

Some deaths in police custody are inevitable. A not uncommon example is a death from cerebrovascular disease (stroke) in an older person, a death which probably would have occurred wherever the person happened to be.

4. Illness, death possibly or probably preventable

Preventable deaths still occur in police custody. Cases still occur of people heavily intoxicated by alcohol and/or other drugs being simply treated as 'drunk' and locked in the cells, frequently in contravention of police standing instructions that people with impaired levels of consciousness (for example through alcohol intoxication) must be assessed by a medically trained person. Virtually every year there are deaths in Australian lock ups where the person had an injury, typically a head injury, but who received no treatment for this, being treated as 'drunk' rather than as at-risk.

Similarly, an intoxicated person placed in a cell and being allowed to roll onto his or her back can easily die from choking on vomit. The simple process of maintaining the person in the coma position with a clear airway removes much of this risk.

5. Sieges and raids

We turn now to deaths in police operations in community settings, in contrast to the deaths in police cells covered above. David Gundy was shot and killed by police officers raiding the house where he slept (Wootten 1991). A number of deaths occur each year when police mount siege on a premises with the aim of arresting an offender and/or preventing the commission of further offences. After a period they burst into the premises, killing the person in the process. Not all deaths in sieges and raids, however, are inflicted by police. Even more common, in Australia, is the situation where a person kills himself (almost all such cases are males) rather than allow the police to apprehend him.

6. Pursuits in motor vehicles and on foot—attempting to detain

Pursuits, on foot or (more commonly) in motor vehicles, frequently result in death. The duty of care which police must, in law, exercise at all times is too often overlooked in motor vehicle pursuits. The risks involved in a high speed pursuit through busy urban traffic of two 16-year-olds in a stolen car has been highlighted many times. Nevertheless, each year a number of such deaths occur.

7. Police shootings in community settings

A seventh category is where police officers shoot and kill a person, not in a raid or siege, but rather in a community setting such as a public street. This type of death received massive public attention in Australia during 1994: in that year nine people were shot and killed by police officers in the State of Victoria, compared with three such deaths in the whole of the rest of Australia. This resulted in all operational police in Victoria being retrained in alternatives to the use of lethal force. The aim was to ensure the implementation of the internationally accepted

53

principle that police must not use deadly force 'unless it is necessary to prevent the escape and the officer has probable cause to believe the suspect poses a significant threat of death or serious physical injury to the officer or others'.[6]

8. Detaining for health and/or welfare purposes

The final category to be listed here is deaths which occur when police are attempting to detain people not because they are offenders but, rather, for their own good, typically to prevent an act of suicide. A recent example was the death of a young woman in the Blue Mountains of New South Wales. She telephoned police who found her poised to jump from a cliff top. They negotiated with her, seeking to convince her not to jump, but to no avail (This type of incident is not included in the official Australian deaths in custody statistics as it is not a case where police were seeking to detain the person in conjunction with an offence). This categorisation has demonstrated the wide range of circumstances which fall under the heading of 'deaths in police custody or in police operations'. In each case we see police interacting with citizens in situations where police have a moral and legal responsibility for the well-being of the individuals concerned, while executing their responsibilities regarding the enforcement of law and the maintenance of order. The examples provided illustrate the fact that officers are frequently faced with extremely difficult circumstances where decisions about life and death have to be made almost instantaneously. On the other hand, they also demonstrate how some deaths in police custody are preventable through the careful application of best practice in caring for the citizens, convicted offenders or not, who find themselves in the hands of the authorities.

Why has there been a fall in deaths in police lock ups?

The Royal Commission into Aboriginal Deaths in Custody made recommendations aimed at reducing or eliminating Aboriginal disadvantage in the criminal justice system and in society generally and, by doing so, reducing or eliminating the gross over-representation of Aboriginal people in all forms of custody. Its National Report contained, in addition, some 43 recommendations addressing health and safety issues in police custody. The application of these is equally important for both Aboriginal and non-Aboriginal people. In my judgment, the Royal Commission's recommendations have been systematically implemented by most of Australia's eight police services and, significantly, the action taken has directly resulted in the substantial fall in the incidence of deaths in Australian police lock ups illustrated above. The following initiatives have been significant:

- fewer people being held in cells—this has fallen by 23 per cent from 1988 to 1995 (Carcach and McDonald 1997)
- pre-custody diversion of at-risk people—especially those who are severely intoxicated from alcohol or other drugs, are injured, ill or apparently suicidal
- screening on admission, including (in some states) computerised warnings of people known (from prior contacts with the police) to be at risk of drug use or suicide
- command systems to ensure that screening works, i.e. that decisions are made and appropriate action taken when at-risk detainees are identified; obtaining medical attention, diversion to hospital or sobering-up facilities and close supervision are options
- new procedures promulgated and staff training programmes to ensure that they are understood
- environmental changes: removal of hanging points, maintenance of visual contact between custodial officers and detainees and manipulating the social environment so as to minimise risk
- information on detainees at risk accompanies them as they move through the criminal justice system, e.g. between police stations, from police station to court and to prison.

It is clear that action in these areas has varied in intensity and impact but, overall, we can be pleased with the results. In most cases nowadays, when deaths occur in police lock ups they are either not preventable or demonstrate failure to follow the laid down procedures.

Duty of care

The Irish playwright Brendan Behan who died in 1994 apparently from alcohol dependence had a great deal of contact with the police as a result of his problematic drinking. Legend has it, in fact, that he was thrown out of 720 Dublin pubs! Behan is said to have summarised his attitudes towards the police in the following terms:

> I have never seen a situation so dismal that a policeman couldn't make it worse!

Much truth is to be found in this statement although it is probably preferable to express it in a positive way:

> Through their lawful exercise of discretion and the application of skills in people management, police officers have the capacity to determine, in very many cases, whether a high risk interaction between them and members of the community will result in positive or tragic outcomes.

The issue here is duty of care. It is widely accepted that policing is a social control process involving both surveillance and the threat of sanctions. It involves the prevention and control of crime and the preservation of good order. Researchers and the community are increasingly questioning, however, the effectiveness of our police services in achieving these goals.[7]

In finding that police officers frequently fail to meet acceptable standards of duty of care for detainees, the Royal Commission correctly emphasised that the duty of care is located in both individual custodial officers and the custodial authorities (the police services) themselves:

> It is settled law that a custodian owes a duty to a prisoner to take reasonable care for his or her safety. The existence and nature of that duty has been the subject of discussion in a number of cases both in Australian and common law jurisdictions overseas . . . On general principles, the duty of care would appear to extend to protection against risks which are reasonably foreseeable and the standard of care to be that which the reasonable person would regard as reasonable in all circumstances of the particular case.
>
> It is important to note that the duty of care attaches primarily to the custodial authority, that is to say, the corrections departments, the police services, and the child welfare departments (under whatever names they operate) which administer the prisons, the police cells and the juvenile detention centres. It is important, in my view, to stress that fact. It seemed to me that many of the discussions centred around the duty of the custodial officers involved in the given case. Any such tendency tends to obscure the primary responsibility of the relevant agency. . .
>
> Custodial officers, of course, also owe a duty to persons in custody. This duty should extend, at least, to putting into practice the precepts of their training, observing their orders and directions, and otherwise acting as would a reasonable person in the given circumstances (Royal Commission into Aboriginal Deaths in Custody 1991, vol. 1, pp. 78-79).

The Royal Commission did not agree with suggestions put to it that new legislation on duty of care was required. Rather, in recognising that duty of care is adequately encompassed within the common law and statute law approaches to negligence, the Royal Commission stressed the need for police regulations, training and staff supervisory processes to ensure that the duty of care is fully understood, accepted and implemented by all Australian police services.

Early in this paper I outlined the breadth of the concept of deaths in police custody. While many officers would understand and accept their duty of care with regard to people in police lock ups, it is crucial that this understanding be expanded to *all* interactions between police officers and members of the public. Raids, sieges, high speed motor vehicle pursuits and confrontations with armed offenders, all entail the risk of harm or even death to the alleged offenders, members of the general public and, of course, to the officers themselves. Recognising that what differentiates sworn police officers from others in society who have a policing role is the capacity of the former to use lawful lethal force, it is essential, I suggest, that duty of care considerations receive greater salience in the planning and execution of police operations. Just as police no longer have the authority to shoot and kill a 'fleeing felon', so they have a duty to act positively and proactively to maintain the well-being of the people with whom they interact. We are still seeing deaths each year, however, in which the necessity of giving precedence to duty of care considerations over law enforcement and social control is breached by Australian police officers.

Two special issues: 'Suicide by cop' and high speed police pursuits
Before leaving this discussion of deaths in police custody and police operations I wish to draw attention to two issues which are of particular concern in the contemporary Australian context. They are 'suicide by cop' and 'high speed police pursuits'. The story of the death of the young Aboriginal man in Tasmania with which I opened this paper illustrates the terrible dilemma that police officers sometimes face when confronted with an armed offender who apparently wishes to die and has a commitment to kill police officers in the process. As that young man said, while pointing his pistol at the officer: 'Go on, shoot me. I'll kill one of you then you can kill me. I don't care'. In fear of his life and seeing no alternative, the officer shot and killed the young man. No criticism is to be made of the officer for taking this extreme action in such a circumstance. Another example was a case in the city of Darwin in the Northern Territory of Australia where, to quote from a newspaper report:

> A man shot by police yesterday had been taunting them to blow his head off, witnesses said . . . Police said the man held the rifle to his chin while taunting them to kill him . . . a neighbour . . . said the man had yelled to police at the height of the siege 'Shoot me. Shoot me in the head, you wimps.' The witness said: 'The police were excellent. I can't fault them in trying to calm him down.' (*NT News*, 3 November 1996, p. 3)

Australian coroners have characterised this type of incident as 'suicide by cop'. It must be one of the most difficult situations in which police officers find themselves, one which calls on all their personal and professional capacities to attempt to defuse the situation. As evidenced by these two examples, however, it is inevitable that some of them will result in deaths.

The second issue to which I wish to draw particular attention is *high speed motor vehicle pursuits*. As noted above, ten of the 18 deaths in police operations in community settings during 1996 were deaths which occurred in just these circumstances: police were pursuing people in motor vehicles when the vehicle of the person being pursued crashed causing the death of the occupants. This particular circumstance highlights, most starkly, the issue of duty of care. A recent American study indicates that, in that nation, in deciding whether or not to initiate and continue a pursuit, police officers tend to concentrate more on the seriousness of the offence allegedly committed by the person pursued than they do on the risk to the person or the public (Alpert 1997). This, in my view, represents a straightforward breach of police officers' duty of care and highlights the type of problem that arises when officers place more salience on law enforcement than they do on their broader responsibilities to the wellbeing of alleged offenders and members of the community at large.

The Australian situation seems slightly different from the American one mentioned above. Reading the coroners' findings relating to deaths in high speed police pursuits, it can be seen over and over again that the offences which led to the pursuits were not really serious. Indeed, very often they are traffic offences such as failing to use a turning indicator, or speeding. One case was reported in the media with a newspaper headline 'Police killed son over $20 bill, parents say'. The article states that:

> The parents of a Sunshine Coast man killed during a police chase say their son needlessly died for a $20 petrol bill . . . The chase began after police received a complaint that a driver left a Nambour service station without paying for his petrol . . . 'They basically killed him for $20 worth of petrol', the father said (*Courier Mail*, 15 May 1996).

As it turned out, in this case the young man was driving a stolen vehicle; this was undoubtedly a factor in his attempting to flee from police and their initiating a high speed pursuit.

In recent years a number of Australian police services have reviewed their policies on high speed pursuits but it remains an issue of significant public policy in Australia and one which highlights the duty of care that police officers have to all the members of the public with whom they interact.

How far does the duty of care extend?

Some years ago a senior Australian federal police officer posed the question, 'How far does the police duty of care extend? To what degree are we (police officers) responsible for the well-being of a person after that person has left our custody?' His thinking about this issue was precipitated by the self-inflicted death of a middle-class man who had been in police custody for a day or two charged with a sex offence. Soon after release, apparently because of the shame that he felt about the offence and his involvement in the criminal justice system, the man killed himself. The police officer wondered if his staff should have been alert for signs of extreme distress in this man, including suicide potential, and should have made appropriate referrals to helping services as part of the process of releasing him on bail.

Little has been published on criminal offending as a risk factor for suicide. Perhaps this is because of the dominance of mental illness in the aetiology of suicide and the earlier perception of suicide being particularly a problem of the elderly, a low offending population. Although suicide is a frequent cause of death among people in custody, and among offenders serving non-custodial orders in the community (as discussed below), this tells us little about offending as a risk factor for suicide.

In a major literature review on suicide, Lester identified one case-control study which found that people who died by suicide in Sweden were more likely to have a criminal record than were the controls, and two studies of suicide attempters which showed the same relationship (Lester 1983) (Important differences appear to exist, however, in the risk factors for attempted and completed suicide). Lester concluded that 'research seems to find a consistent association between criminality and suicide but the ramifications of this association have not been explained yet'.

Fleming's unpublished descriptive epidemiological study of the Australian Capital Territory suicides which occurred between 1980 and 1988, suggested that legal matters were pending in 16 (8 per cent) of the 208 cases for which relevant data were available (Fleming 1989). In addition, a similar New Zealand study, using coroners' records, showed that of 320 suicide deaths which occurred in that country in 1981, 13 (4 per cent) were classified as having a 'main life related problem' of 'law infringement', referred to by the author as a predictor of suicide (Antoniadis 1988).

These indications that criminal offending and contact with the criminal justice system are (or at least, may be) risk factors for suicide have lead the New South Wales Police Academy to emphasise, as part of its custodial officers' training programme, the fact that police duty of care applies not only to people whilst they are in the custody of officers but beyond that custody. The training draws attention to the need for custodial officers to be conscious of the emotional state of detainees when they are released back into the community and, if the custodial officer is concerned that a person is particularly distressed upon release, then the officer should make efforts to ensure that the person is referred to helping services in the community. This initiative reinforces one of the central themes of this chapter, namely that the duty of care that criminal justice system personnel have extends far beyond the prison or the police cell.

Deaths in non-custodial correctional settings

I have discussed deaths in prison, deaths in police custody, deaths in police operations in the community and deaths of people having been released from custody. The final setting to receive attention here is the deaths of offenders in non-custodial correctional settings. This was investigated in a study of the extent and nature of mortality among men and women undertaking non-custodial correctional orders such as probation, parole, community service orders and pre-sentence supervision in Australia and New Zealand in the years 1987 and 1988 (Fleming, McDonald and Biles 1992). The study, which was exploratory in nature, noted that there were approximately 35,000 people on non-custodial correctional orders in Australia at that time. Over the two year period, 394 of those were reported to have died. This represents a crude mortality rate of 5.6 per 1,000 per annum. Eighty per cent of the people carrying out non-custodial correctional orders had a prior offence but the death rate of the first offenders appeared to be higher than those with a criminal record before the offence or offences which led to the current order.

Some 52 per cent (204 cases) of the deaths were from accidents, 21 per cent (84) were self inflicted, 20 per cent (75) from natural causes, five per cent (18) from homicide and two per cent (7) from other causes. The accidental deaths were reported to have been 64 per cent (128) from alcohol and/or other drugs, and 29 per cent (59) from motor vehicle crashes with the balance (seven per cent or 14 cases) from a variety of other forms of accident.

Significantly for this discussion, the crude death rate of 5.6 deaths per annum per 1,000 people on non-custodial orders was approximately twice the death rate in Australian prisons during the 1980-1988 period (2.6 per annum per 1,000 prisoners). The crude death rate of people on parole was twice that of people serving other types of non-custodial orders. The authors of the report on the study pointed to the fact that caution needs to be used in comparing the death rates for prison and non-custodial corrections orders as the denominators differ in some important respects. Although the age distributions of the prisoners and the people on non-custodial correctional orders were similar it is not clear that the number of people on orders actually represents the number of person/years of exposure during a 12 months period. Nevertheless, even accepting these difficulties in drawing comparisons, it is probably safe to conclude, as did the authors of the research report, that:

> . . . the mortality rate for people on non-custodial correctional orders is somewhat higher than that of prisoners. This accords, in fact, with common sense. Life in the general community . . . for young adult males with a criminal history is bound to be more dangerous, owing to the risk of death from drink driving, drug use, assaults, etc., than is life in prison (Fleming, McDonald and Biles 1992, p. 245).

What are the implications of these observations? I do not wish to take the matter too far, but they do highlight the fact that, when the court makes an order directing that a person's liberty be curtailed by having to undertake a non-custodial correctional order, then it can be argued that the state, through the work of the supervising officers, has a responsibility towards the well-being of such offenders. This responsibility could be discharged through supervising officers having a close understanding of the lifestyles of the people serving non-custodial correctional orders and seeking to institute remedial programmes when these lifestyles are characterised by high risks. Perhaps problematic use of alcohol and other drugs is the aspect of lifestyle which is most amenable to change in such settings. The general point, however, is that the non-custodial correctional environment is yet another part of the criminal justice system in which we find offenders at particularly high risk of death compared with others in the community and whose well-being is the responsibility, at least to some extent, of the agents of the state.

Conclusion

This chapter has addressed the conference theme of 'Deaths of Offenders: The Hidden Side of Justice' by looking at the deaths of offenders in a variety of settings in the criminal justice system. With regard to Australia in the late 1990s the conclusions to be drawn from the above discussion are, unfortunately, quite pessimistic. Although we have pointed to one positive feature, namely a reduction in deaths in Australian police lock ups, we are continuing to see a disturbingly high level of deaths in Australian prisons and in police operations in community settings.

The attitudes of Australian governments and the communities they represent appear to be becoming increasingly conservative in Australia with a lessening emphasis on the responsibility of governments to provide resources for the less well-off members of society. Attitudes on such issues as 'welfare cheats', the long-term unemployed and the terrible disadvantage experienced by Australia's Indigenous people appear to be becoming increasingly polarised (Adams 1997).

The title of this paper 'Man Passeth Away Like a Shadow' is a line from Brahms' German Requiem (which Brahms actually preferred to call his 'Human Requiem'). Sadly, we still see far too many lives of people in the criminal justice system 'passing away like shadows'. At the previous (1994) conference in this series (Liebling 1996, p. 68) Sir Louis Blom-Cooper quoted Voltaire stating (in translation from the French) 'To the living we owe respect; to the dead only truth'. But I argue that the truth is out: we *know* about the incidence of deaths in custody; we *know* that the incidence of deaths of offenders is too high in other parts of the criminal justice system; and we *know* how to prevent many of the deaths.

To prevent more lives of people in the hands of the State 'passing away like shadows' we need more action, and more effective action, to reduce the number of people in custody and to minimise the incidence of deaths in all components of the criminal justice system.

David McDonald is a social scientist with research interests in domains where public health and criminology interrelate, particularly deaths in custody, homicide, drugs policy and Aboriginal justice. He is currently at the Australian National University's National Centre for Epidemiology and Population Health, where he is developing a study of homicide and gun controls. Prior to this he was at the Australian Institute of Criminology where he lead the research team responsible for monitoring custodial deaths in Australia.

ENDNOTES

1. Some of this paper is a revised and updated version of McDonald 1996b
2. The information in this section is summarised from the final *National Report* of the Royal Commission. The Letters Patent are reproduced in that report at vol. 5, p. 158
3. This issue is of great significance in Australia at the moment. See Human Rights and Equal Opportunity Commission 1997
4. A discussion of this material is found in RCIADIC, *op. cit.,* vol. 3, pp. 142-148. A more detailed presentation is Thomson and McDonald 1993
5. The data presented here are drawn, in the main, from Dalton 1997. Ms Dalton's assistance in the preparation of this section is acknowledged with thanks
6. This is a quotation from the landmark case *Tennessee v. Garner*, 471 US 1 (1985) heard in the United States Supreme Court in 1985. See More 1992, p. 56. A United Nations perspective is contained in the statement: 'Basic principles on the use of force and firearms by law enforcement officials'

adopted by the Eighth UN Crime Congress, Havana, 27 August 1990 (7 September 1990)

7. See, e.g. Reiner 1994, pp. 705-772.

Appendix to *Chapter 3*

Prison Death Rates, Australia, 1985-1996 All Cases and Self-inflicted Deaths					
		All deaths		Self-inflicted deaths	
Year	Prisoners	Number	Rate per 1,000	Number	Rate per 1,000
1980	n.a.	30	n.a.	10	n.a.
1981	n.a.	28	n.a.	15	n.a.
1982	n.a.	25	n.a.	8	n.a.
1983	n.a.	31	n.a.	17	n.a.
1884	n.a.	31	n.a.	17	n.a.
1985	10,608	26	2.45	11	1.04
1986	11,243	17	1.51	7	0.62
1987	11,688	53	4.53	23	1.97
1988	11,841	42	3.55	18	1.52
1989	12,428	40	3.22	22	1.77
1990	13,322	33	2.48	17	1.28
1991	14,045	39	2.78	16	1.14
1992	14,323	36	2.51	20	1.40
1993	14,508	49	3.38	23	1.59
1994	15,576	53	3.40	22	1.41
1995	15,900	58	3.65	27	1.70
1996	16,429	52	3.17	23	1.40

- The 1980-1984 national prison population is not available in a form consistent with the data covering the subsequent years (shown as n.a.)
- The 1985-1994 prison populations shown are daily averages
- The 1995 prison population is the average of the number of prisoners on the first day of each month Jan-Dec 1995
- The 1996 prison population is an estimate based on counts on the first day of the month, Oct 1995 to Sep 1996.
- *Source*: Australian Institute of Criminology.

CHAPTER 4

Prison Suicide and the Nature of Imprisonment

Alison Liebling

> The general perception of the prison environment as relatively benevolent is particularly evident among individuals whose exposure to the imprisonment experience is superficial and far removed from other life experiences. The reason for this is that the pain of modern imprisonment is more often psychological than physical. The effects of the modern prison are merely more subtle . . . (Haley 1984: 494).

Introduction

Suicide in prison has been the subject of considerable international research in recent years (see Liebling and Ward 1994; Liebling 1992; and Liebling 1996 for a brief review). Prison suicide rates are relatively high and are increasing. In this chapter, I want to pose, and attempt to answer a single question: what does suicide tell us about the nature of the prison experience? I want to do this by looking at suicide, and at what suicide means, at what we know about vulnerability to suicide, at the significance of the subjectivity of experience, and finally at the nature of the prison experience, with these considerations about suicide in mind.

In England and Wales, there are about 60 prison suicides a year—about one every five days. Half of the prisons in the country can expect to experience a death by suicide each year—some will experience several. Many of those who die by suicide in prison are young—in the so-called 'prime of life'. The World Health Organization sees suicide rates as a visible and quantifiable reflection of the mental health of a nation. How far could prison suicide rates be taken to reflect the 'healthiness' of prison? The prison service is rightly cautious about developing a key performance indicator measuring suicide rates for individual prisons—but there might be a case for encouraging establishments as a whole to generate hope 'in the darkness', as it were. This is, after all, how the prison service is encouraged to think about tackling offending behaviour, assuming that change for the better is always possible.

Prison and the neglect of suicide

Many biographical and historical accounts of prison life refer to suicide: Foucault wrote an account of Pierre Riviere, who died by hanging; Foucault himself took an overdose in 1948, at the age of 22—leading to his hospitalisation where he encountered institutionalised psychiatry for the first time. Perhaps this experience, and his visit to Attica in 1972, which he described as a machine for elimination, gave him his interest in the destructive power of prisons. Bruno Bettleheim tells of prisoners who chose suicide as an escape from their experiences in captivity. The other prisoners would watch, thinking to themselves, will the next one be me? Yet those who write about prisons as a topic of academic inquiry rarely refer to suicide. Why is this?

Let us look for example at the studies we have available to us about the effects of imprisonment. Psychologists and criminologists have concluded their investigations with the following sorts of statements:

> Research in British prisons – chiefly by psychologists – has done much to deflate the sweeping exaggerations – chiefly by sociologists – about the ill-effects of normal incarceration. (Walker 1987)

Many detailed studies have been carried out on the effects of imprisonment. It has been established that the early period of confinement subjects prisoners to a great deal of stress and a feeling of disorientation. It is thought that in time, prisoners adjust and cope, and that they do not suffer from long-term deterioration, on the whole. Their styles of coping, and the social life which emerges in the process of coping has been the subject of interesting theoretical and sociological study. But several important omissions have been made. The most significant is that links between the suicide literature and studies on the effects of imprisonment have not been made. This is despite the existence of substantial evidence to illustrate, for example that suicides occur disproportionately early in confinement—when imprisonment is known to be most stressful. There are other similarities between, for example, patterns of absconding and patterns of suicide attempts. In a review article called 'Psychological Effects of Imprisonment on Confined Individuals', two psychologists found from the available evidence that

> confinement in penal isolation awaiting execution was quite stressful. (Bukstel and Kilmann, 1980:478)

These sort of conclusions—and understatements—illustrate the failure of research on the effects of prison life to ask the right questions, to look in the right places, or to ask in an appropriate kind of way what the

65

experience of imprisonment actually feels like. Answering the question 'is prison harmful?' is—at least in part—a matter of empathy, appreciation and understanding. These dimensions are essential to good research. They do not contradict the principles of rigour, care or the need for empirical evidence. Prison research (particularly prison suicide research, but also most of our major studies on the effects of imprisonment) have largely managed without sufficient appreciative understanding, in deference to scientific measurement. Such studies rarely follow prisoners up after release, and they rarely investigate psychological or emotional distress and disability (Grounds 1996). They look instead at skills and personality traits, omitting to consider those who have not survived the prison experience, either by suicide or by transfer to psychiatric hospital. It is by this route that such research has been able to conclude that imprisonment is not harmful.

Perhaps we should begin by asking, is prison painful? In his address to the Prison Chaplaincy Conference (September, 1989), Canon Eric James used a theme he applies to all human predicaments:

> We would all benefit from subjecting ourselves to what we subject them to
> . . . We could do with more sitting where they sit. (James 1989)

This comment conjured up a particular interview with a young woman who had injured herself repeatedly in prison. We sat in her cell, she had been stripped of her clothes, her furniture had been removed, and she was dressed only in an indestructible nylon tunic. We sat on her bare bed, the indestructible blanket on the floor. The room was cold, her skin was purple and red, broken by cuts all over her arms, legs and face. She was wearing bright blue eye shadow—this she had been allowed, and she had wanted to look more presentable before the interview. Even though I was clothed, and warm, I sat where she sat—and she apologised for the discomfort this might cause me. She, like others, talked of suicidal feelings, of desperate loneliness, and of despair.

The pains of imprisonment are many and varied. They are also, often, hidden. It is not to the visible eye or the measuring instrument that they are perceptible, but to the 'informed heart' (Bettleheim 1969).

Let us look for a moment at suicide; what is it, and how do individuals arrive at such a point?

Understanding suicide

Suicide seems to have at its root three main components. Suffering, lack of strong social bonds and support, and lack of meaning.

What else do we know about suicide? We know that there has been an almost universal increase in suicide amongst young males, mainly from lower social classes. We know that risk factors amongst young people include depression, conduct disorders, and substance misuse. Explanations for suicide include: the rising divorce rate and changes in family structure, geographical mobility (leading to lack of support, fragile relationships), unemployment, disempowerment, and decreased religious affiliation. These variables explain the lack of social bonds and the lack of meaning. Durkheim used the term 'anomie' to describe social 'detachment' or disintegration. The more strongly any individual is integrated into a social group (such as a close knit family, or religious group), the less likely they are to commit suicide. We are relatively knowledgeable about the lack of social bonds and the lack of social meaning—incidentally, also thought to be responsible for much crime.

But how much do we know (or wish to know) about suffering? There is evidence to suggest that some people can summon the resources to cope with adversity and others have limited access to resources. Likewise, some individuals may fail to realise or be able to sustain the bonds which connect them to other people, even if those bonds are there. It is the combination of poor circumstances and few resources to sustain the individual that leads to suicide. Prisoners may as a group be especially vulnerable to suicide, and to all the other risk factors which can lead to suicide, such as unemployment, family breakdown, etc. What is the connection between the known about risk factors and the less known about experience of despair?

Let us look more systematically at the risk factors, and remind ourselves how prevalent these are amongst prisoners. Factors found to predict suicide and suicide attempts include:

- previous suicide attempts
- a diagnosis of personality disorder
- alcohol misuse
- previous psychiatric treatment
- unemployment
- social class (V)
- drug abuse
- a criminal record
- violence
- being single, widowed or divorced
- being a white male
- problems of affective control (anger, impulsivity)
- suicide in the family.

Large groups amongst prisoner populations share those characteristics associated with increased suicide risk in the community: adverse life events, negative interpersonal relationships, social and economic disadvantage, alcohol and drug addiction, early contact with criminal justice agencies, poor educational and employment history, low self-esteem, poor problem-solving ability and low motivational drive (see for example, Zamble and Porporino 1988; Walmsley *et al* 1992; Liebling and Krarup 1993). Arguably, the prison population is carefully selected to be at risk of suicide.

The impact of these features of a life history on the psychological circumstances and emotional state of the individual is rarely addressed. We need to know more about what being in prison *feels like* and how far the prison experience exposes (or can repair) vulnerability.

The situational aspects of suicide in prison (such as bullying, lack of activity, isolation, the breakdown of relationships, parole refusal, an unexpected sentence or change in location, etc.) may be crucial in the onset of suicidal thoughts for particular groups. What matters in this presentation is how these experiences are interpreted and experienced subjectively by the prisoner. The most common idea verbalised after a suicide attempt is:

> The situation was so unbearable, I had to do something and I didn't know what else to do.

What is it to experience the 'unbearable'? Often there are multiple 'motivations' which can include the above, *and* wanting to die, *and* wanting to escape, wanting to get relief, communicating desperate feelings *and* trying to change a situation. These are not mutually exclusive.

A cry of pain
Mark Williams, a psychologist who has specialised in the understanding and treatment of depression, recently wrote in his book, *A Cry of Pain*, that people suffering from personality disorders, or borderline personality disorders, may be especially at risk of suicide. Borderline patients have affective instability (they may feel 'at the mercy' of powerful feelings), a history of self-damaging acts and damaging relationships, chronic feelings of emptiness and boredom, intolerance of being alone, and they may have brief dissociative episodes, often associated with flashbacks of physical or sexual abuse. Evidence shows that between four and ten per cent will eventually kill themselves, although up to half may attempt suicide at some stage in their lives.

The sort of suffering reported by those who go on to kill themselves, or who have made determined attempts, involves feelings of uncontrollability, helplessness, and powerlessness. This is one reason why changing circumstances (even a change in location) can be so devastating. These feelings—of upset mood, anger, anxiety and confusion—occur against a background condition of low self-esteem—or a feeling that one is not deserving of care; problems in integrating with others and in achieving a sense of fulfilment from life. Williams explains the pain of these acute feelings when they occur as like an animal caught in a trap, The animal lets out a squeal—the squeal is a cry of pain; it communicates pain; it represents an attempt to escape from the snare, but it is primarily an expression of pain and fear.

Mark Williams has found that those at risk of suicide are vulnerable to acute sensations of pain and despair for particular reasons. He found that suicide attempters attribute problems in their lives to global and stable causes—that is, they are pessimistic about themselves and their capacity to make life or their relationships better. This is consistent with a theory of learned helplessness, or external locus of control, where reactions to stressors may be especially negative. Their main problems in living are interpersonal as a result of underlying emotional and cognitive maps. Williams found that people who have made suicide attempts are more passive and less active in their problem-solving; they show more avoidance; they judge their problems more negatively than others might, and importantly, when asked to retrieve memories of events from their past, they tend to remember their past negatively and in a summarised, over-general way. They think far less into the future, and what little thinking about the future engaged in is devoid of positive events. Highly hopeless people tend to lack even short-term routines, as well as long-term plans and goals. Their emotions and their lives are experienced as chaotic, and full of anguish.

Their relationships with the world—especially with significant others; or those who come to represent significant others—tend to degenerate into hostility, demandingness and conflict—or eventually, into apathy. They are poor regulators of emotion, and experience instability, impulsivity and anger to intolerable degrees. They are prone to perceive abandonment and rejection even where it does not exist, and to react as though any abandonment were already complete at its first sign. Their behaviour with others may range from clinging to rejecting in a moment (Williams 1997: 91-99). Feelings of distress, aloneness and rage, and of wanting to punish others for abandoning them, are common. These feelings are usually linked to earlier experiences of loss and abandonment, when the vulnerability and aloneness were real, and were experienced as literally life-threatening. If individuals' self-perception is of low status, of being a failure, being 'rejectable', they may 'invent for themselves a punitive environment' (Williams 1997: 149). Such feelings, of worthlessness, uselessness, inferiority and powerlessness can lie behind lack of interest in engaging in activities or social relationships—the psychological 'anomie' of feeling isolated and excluded, different and unworthy. Inadequate.

Now let us return to prison.

Suicide and the pain of imprisonment

Prison is a 'critical situation' (Bettleheim 1960; Giddens 1984); a radical shattering of continuity and routine—both integral to the survival of the personality (Giddens 1984; p.60-61).[1] Prison disrupts accustomed forms of life, sweeping away an already fragile sense of trust, tearing apart families and friends, requiring a kind of psychological distancing from oneself that is in itself damaging. Prison has been described as a dislocation, shown to have similarities with those overwhelming dislocations experienced by victims of disaster or trauma, leading to severe problems of relatedness and identity (Grounds 1996).[2] Such trauma produces intense fear and helplessness, sometimes overwhelming an individual's psychological coping mechanisms. Traumatic experiences seem incomprehensible, shattering one's assumptions about the world; they can rupture attachments to others, and can leave individuals with a constant sense of threat. It has been shown that widely different kinds of trauma can produce a similar set of clinical symptoms, including severe difficulties in forming—or reforming—relationships. The key to traumatic experiences seems to be that they are uncontrollable, incomprehensible and intense; control over one's fate is swept away. It is this question of control, wielded by an unpredictable and external 'other' or 'others' that seems to do so much damage.

Control in prison, as we know, can be at once strictly routinised and erratic. The unpredictability of life in prison, under the deceptive aura of apparent (but highly selective) predictability, is one of its most acute pains. Prisoners prefer order, consistency and predictability to instability and change. Perhaps we have some beginning of an explanation for this deeply felt need for order, justice and consistency. Prisoners respond extremely negatively to sudden or unexplained changes to routines and rules. Giddens, in *The Constitution of Society*, describes a state of 'ontological insecurity', where the future is impossible to plan, and all tasks seem senseless. Giddens and Bettleheim, who shared Giddens' concern for order and freedom from arbitrary power, were writing about concentration camps. Anyone who has heard prisoners talk about recent radical changes in policy (e.g. the recent restrictions on temporary release), the changing of parole eligibility, the experience of sudden transfers and the discretion invested in staff, can surely recognise some analogy in this account. Prisoners describe separation from families as one of the greatest sources of distress. Another less clearly documented and articulated source of distress is the loss of the capacity to act, the loss of self brought about by regulation and discipline, the 'afflictive control' exerted in order to reform (Gallo and Ruggiero, 1991). Again, survivors of concentration camp experiences tell us that:

> Only prisoners who managed to maintain some small sphere of control in their daily lives, which they still regarded as their 'own', were able to survive. (Giddens 1984: 63)

It is significant that research has shown that those prisoners who find themselves able to exert control over their lives in prison are more likely to recover from suicidal feelings (Dexter 1993). Why would any prisoner forego parole? Because the experience of permitting unpredictable choices to be made about one's life is intolerable. It is especially intolerable if your life has exposed you to such threatening experiences before.

In order to survive, and to address the unbearable anxiety experienced at such a loss (of control), prisoners lose their orientation to the outside world and turn inwards, 'reconstituting themselves as agents' by integrating themselves deeply into prison life, participating in its rituals and even chastising the staff for not following the rules (cf. Mathiesen 1965). Psychological survival requires such adaptation. Is it so surprising that prisoners begin to exert control over each other, and that those over whom random violence and control is exerted find the experience catastrophic? It was Foucault who said that power can disguise itself as objectivity, as technology, as management. Power invests itself in people, and is transmitted through them, upon themselves and upon others. Surviving prison requires a form of self-regulation—a certain amount of distress is caused by 'the effort to keep distress itself under control' (Gallo and Ruggiero 1991: 280). Gallo and Ruggiero described custody as 'a factory for the manufacture of handicaps', a world of 'de-communication' and aggression (Gallo and Ruggiero 1991). Prisoners live in a constant state of anxiety, fearing violence or deterioration (Cohen and Taylor 1979), or more discipline. Why did Foucault, Giddens and others never apply their theoretical ideas to observational study of the inner life of prisons? Perhaps those who are theoretically sensitive to power are generally sensitive to power and can rarely bear to carry out research in prison.

Why do prisoners commit suicide?

> They do it because it's too much pressure on them, it gets to them and that, they're sick of being locked up, and they're sick of taking orders, and they're sick of no-one caring. (Suicide attempter)

It does your head in, doesn't it? Completely. (Suicide attempter)

Fear, anxiety, loneliness, trauma, depression, injustice, powerlessness, violence, rejection and uncertainty are all part of the experience of prison. It is this 'hidden', but everywhere apparent feature of prison life that psychologists have failed to measure or take seriously. Sociologists of prison life knew it was there, but have to date largely failed to convince others in a sufficiently methodologically convincing way that pain is *a harm*. It is increasingly recognised in other spheres (especially in psychoanalysis and psychiatry) that pain damages. Suicide is perhaps its most dramatic outcome, but there are many other consequences: increased aggression, bitterness, spiralling violence and the erosion of any capacity to love. How far there is a deep unwillingness to consider this unwelcome feature of imprisonment—it stands awkwardly next to the belief that 'prison works'—is a question I have asked myself often. It may be the apparent failure of the sociology of imprisonment to engage with relevant psychological research which has deprived critical sociological analysis of the prison of one of its most powerful tools. The deliberate infliction of pain needs a justification. The unintended infliction of pain should be remedied. That this harm is without any legitimate justification leaves staff, prisoners, and policy-makers confused and struggling. At least its existence should be acknowledged (as it constantly is by many prison governors known to me). Perhaps 'honest pain', and genuine efforts to minimise it, would be less damaging than covert, unconscious and unacknowledged pain.

In the debate over the existence of the lasting harms of imprisonment (see especially Walker 1983 and 1987; and the review by Bukstel and Kilmann 1980), it should be noted that those prisoners who have died by suicide have never had a voice in such studies. The operational measures of 'harm' in such studies have been inappropriate, failing to take into account the subjective world of the prisoner. We see that suicides are disproportionately likely early in custody (see Dooley 1990a; Backett 1987; Liebling 1992) just as absconding (see Sinclair 1971; Clarke and Martin 1971; Banks *et al* 1975; Laycock 1977) and extreme anxiety were found to be (Sapsford 1979; 1983; Erikson 1975). We see that the 'pains of imprisonment' may be acutely concentrated at particular points in time: arrival, parole refusal, following a visit, at weekends, at night, or amongst particular groups within the prison population (see Cohen and Taylor 1979; Home Office 1986; Erikson 1975; Clemmer 1940, etc.). All of these findings are illustrated in the suicide figures (see Lloyd 1990; Liebling 1992) and in what we know about suicide attempts (Liebling 1992; Liebling and Krarup 1993). Most important, we learn that most prisoners 'cope' (cf. Zamble and Porporino 1988; Sapsford 1983; Toch *et al* 1989; Johnson and

Toch 1982), but only just, and that not all prisoners are able to do so (Liebling 1992; Liebling and Krarup 1993). Prison is not a uniform experience—its effects have been underestimated by research which has taken average populations as its base line and insensitive measures of pain as its tools. The evidence suggests that the pains of imprisonment are tragically underestimated. We may not be asking the right questions, either of prison, or of those we imprison. For some, prisons may contain 'invitations to suicide' (Williams 1997: 196).

Responding to vulnerability in prison

Prisons differ. They differ in the extent to which they resemble the deliberately destructive institutions described by Bruno Bettleheim and others in the many powerful studies available to us. Prisons are less deliberately destructive; and their propensity to damage (or sometimes, to repair) may vary in important ways. It is surely important that we understand the nature of this difference between individual establishments and the reasons for it. We do not know enough about why some prisons offer fewer 'invitations to suicide' than others. Why is one prison better than another? Why do staff behave sensitively and professionally in one establishment, and with indifference in another? Prisons could learn more from each other, and from research on prisons which permit, or even encourage survival.

Prisoners may have distinct and individual needs. There seems to be a case for making available, for those who wish to undertake them, courses on problem-solving; coping skills; tackling offending behaviour; addressing motivation; and emotion control. If memory and the future are key problems, sensitive and realistic sentence planning could actually address the question of survival. A minimal requirement should be an orientation to prison life which respects and assists the individual. Building hope in impossible conditions requires that these ideas are communicated and heard; ultimately, that we 'sit where they sit', and re-build our prisons from there. Respect for the individual requires hope, for:

> We are not what we appear, but what we are becoming; and if that is truly what we are, no penal system is fully just which treats us as anything else. (Bedson in James 1990, pp. 43-4; see also Bottoms 1990)

Prisons, and prison staff, should be encouraged to develop a tolerance for anguish—to allow talk of despair. The best help for an individual feeling suicidal is not 'How do you, I or we make it all different?', since often we cannot, but 'How do you, I, we, take care of you just now?' (cf. Williams 1997: 227). Staff need careful training, support, and taking care of themselves.

To conclude

Let us remember that amongst those who have taken their own lives are Bruno Bettleheim, Arthur Koestler (in prison in Lisbon), Primo Levi, Virginia Woolf, Sylvia Plath, and Ernest Hemingway. All were gifted and creative commentators on the human condition, whose wisdom we acknowledge. As Bruno Bettleheim said after his experiences in concentration camps, to have survived is to be wealthy. Those who have attempted suicide in prison posses a wealth of knowledge about the prison experience. Their accounts constitute an important part of the truth about prison. We should listen very carefully to what they have to say.

ENDNOTES

1. Bettleheim describes the conscious efforts made by concentration camp survivors 'not to observe' or 'not to know' in situations where survival depended on such 'not knowing' (see Sutton, 1995: 147-149). Survivors of other forms of trauma (e.g. sexual abuse) describe the same mechanism, although the 'not knowing' process might be unconscious, a natural ego defence mechanism against unbearable attacks. Both processes have damaging consequences for future psychological health, leading to feelings of unreality and depression.

2. 'We find ourselves in an extreme situation when we are suddenly catapulted into a set of conditions where our old adaptive mechanisms and values do not apply any more and when some of them may even endanger the life they were meant to protect' (Bruno Bettleheim, *Surviving and Other Essays;* and in Sutton, 1995:153).

CHAPTER 5

Untoward Deaths in Special Hospital Care: Implications of These and Other Inquiries

Herschel Prins

Introductory note

When I was asked to speak at this conference, I expressed some misgivings. This was not because I did not wish to make a contribution to the Institute for the Study and Treatment of Delinquency's efforts— far from it, for I have had an association (sometimes very active) with ISTD going back nearly 50 years. This being the case, I must be about the 'oldest inhabitant' here today. No, my misgivings were based upon lack of extensive experience as to the matters being debated at this conference and I was not sure that the request to talk about the inquiry I chaired into Orville Blackwood's death in Broadmoor some several years ago was a sufficient basis for this. Eventually, we reached some kind of compromise, namely, that I would comment on the inquiry and then go on to say something about inquiries in general and their imperfections. This presentation is divided therefore into three overlapping parts: (1) The Avoidance of Scandal; (2) The 'Blackwood Inquiry' (as it has come to be known); and (3) Do Inquiries Serve Their Purposes? One final word by way of introduction. What I have to say about the detail of the Blackwood Inquiry can readily be taken to represent my views, and to that extent I represent the views of my three inquiry colleagues (Dr Ian Keitch, Mr Tony Backer-Holst and Mr Errol Francis), but as they are not here to speak for themselves I must not commit them to all the subsequent conclusions I draw.

THE AVOIDANCE OF SCANDAL

There is a tendency to think of the subject matter of this conference as a new phenomenon. Sadly, this is not the case, for the pages of our social history are littered with examples of the abuse and/or the neglect of the disadvantaged and the defenceless. In early times, 'defective' children were exposed to the elements to die, or were abused in other ways; for it is a well-known fact, that familial and allied child abuse have a much longer history than is commonly supposed. For example, Freud had to revise his original theory of the neuroses rather than face the opprobrium borne of the reality that what his female patients were telling him was actually true. The writings of socially conscious novelists all support this more general sordid history. Dickens, Zola and many many others, endeavoured to stir society's conscience. The later work of more academic explorers of such misery such as Mary Hopkirk and Ivy Pinchbeck did much to describe, for example, the fate of unwanted illegitimate children at the hands of the state; and of course John Howard, Elizabeth Fry and others were the forerunners of the Stephen Tumims of our own era. All these reminders of our lack of compassion have been compounded in recent times by the special discrimination shown against disadvantaged ethnic minority groups— one such example is given below. In our more thoughtful moments we may well ask whether such scandals are inevitable, for history seems to give a sharp reminder that this is so. In the final part of this presentation I shall return to this theme in the context of the purpose of inquiries more generally. But, now to Orville Blackwood and his death in Broadmoor.

THE 'BLACKWOOD INQUIRY'

In September, 1991, the Special Hospitals Service Authority, as it then was, set up an inquiry under my chairmanship to investigate the death of a young African-Caribbean patient, Orville Blackwood, and at the same time to review the reports of previous inquiries into two other deaths of African-Caribbean patients in Broadmoor, Michael Martin and Joseph Watts, in order to see if there were any common themes. It needs to be said that our inquiry was different from that going on contemporaneously at Ashworth Hospital under the chairmanship of my colleague Sir Louis Blom-Cooper (1992). We were not examining individual complaints or blame; instead, we were examining patterns of practice within Broadmoor which might have contributed to the deaths of the three patients. It is necessary to provide a pen-picture of Orville Blackwood in order to set the scene. I can do no better than quote from the summary that appeared in an article about our report written by Dr John Crichton for the *Psychiatric Bulletin* in 1994 (Crichton 1994: 236):

> Orville was a large Afro-Caribbean man born in Jamaica but who had moved to London at an early age. He had been in trouble with the police from an early age and by his twenties had convictions for several minor criminal offences and had served two sentences of a few weeks in prison. From 1982, at the age of 22, there was the start of a remitting and relapsing psychotic illness. Over the following two years Blackwood had nine, mostly compulsory, admissions to local psychiatric hospitals. His condition attracted several different diagnoses, including acute paranoid state, drug induced psychosis, acute situational psychosis and psychotic reaction in an inadequate personality.

76

In January 1986, shortly after serving a six month sentence for actual bodily harm and criminal damage, Blackwood was arrested for robbing a bookmaker's shop with a toy gun. It was suggested that he should have been admitted to the Denis Hill medium secure unit at Bethlem Royal Hospital, but since no bed was available he was sentenced to three years imprisonment. Within a year his mental state had deteriorated so seriously that he was transferred to the Denis Hill Unit.

In October 1987, after a settled period, Blackwood became disturbed after a trivial incident and seriously assaulted a nurse. The police were required to restrain him and transfer was arranged to Broadmoor. At Broadmoor he presented problems in management especially when he refused medication, but he did respond to fairly large doses of neuroleptics and when he was well was popular among staff and patients. He was always described as lacking insight and was bitter that he remained in hospital after the end of his custodial sentence. By 1991 there were moves for Blackwood to be transferred back to the Denis Hill Unit and a Mental Health Review Tribunal had adjourned to further consider his case.

At the beginning of August 1991, Blackwood became unsettled and demanding; he set off the fire alarm, blocked his sink and was abusive to his consultant. He was managed by being placed in seclusion where damage was done to the inside of the room. On 28 August the ward doctor prepared to review Blackwood in his side room. Blackwood was quietly lying on his bed when the doctor entered his room, allegedly without a knock or warning; there were nurses outside should he become violent. Blackwood allegedly tried to punch the doctor and was restrained. The doctor decided to administer Sparine 150 mg and Modecate 150 mg intramuscularly. The staff left the room after the administration of injections but soon observed from outside that Blackwood had stopped breathing. Cardio-pulmonary resuscitation was unsuccessful. Orville was subsequently found to be dead upon arrival at the local general hospital.

Our inquiry met in private and our proceedings were informal. Our witnesses were free to bring an adviser or advocate with them, and some did so. We met on 19 occasions to take oral evidence from 50 witnesses and on a further seven occasions to consider the issues and to formulate our report, the completion of which was delayed by a second inquest into Orville's death. The second inquest returned the same verdict as the first—'accidental death'. At the outset, we were under pressure in conducting the inquiry. When we began our work, it was clear that the Broadmoor nursing staff were anxious to participate in the inquiry; however it appeared that they were put under a good deal of pressure by their national association (the Prison Officers' Association (POA)) not to co-operate in this way. That they did so, and were greatly helped in the process by their local legal representative, is a credit to them all. We were also under pressure from the POA and Orville's family to conduct our inquiry in public, to let all parties have the right to hear oral evidence put before us and to cross-examine witnesses. We resisted these pressures. We were also aware of another pressure (as are all those who conduct inquiries of this kind), to concentrate on particular issues and to reach particular conclusions, and we were much aware of public expectations that were raised (or diminished) by the establishment of our inquiry. A final word about the sub-title to our report (Prins *et al* 1993). We chose the words 'Big, Black and Dangerous?' with a question mark because we felt it encapsulated some of the misconceptions that influenced Orville's treatment and the handling of such patients more generally. We made 47 recommendations and I have chosen to comment only on some of them in this presentation. (They occupy five pages of our 87 page report). I have tried to pull some of them together under two main headings: (a) Orville's death and (b) similarities between his death and those of Michael Martin and Joseph Watts.

The death of Orville Blackwood

We thought there had been something of a 'knee-jerk' reaction to Orville's behaviour, particularly on the fatal morning when he had not wished to go to occupational therapy. Seclusion and subsequently intramuscular medication were the responses. Orville's increasing tension and irritability had been increased by the adjournment of a Mental Health Review Tribunal, and, throughout, there seemed to be a tendency not to discriminate between his illness-driven behaviour and that which had a rational basis (for example, his concerns about his length of stay in special hospital and the way in which he and his fellow African-Caribbeans were treated). We concluded that Orville's treatment did not seem to be very sensitive and that his 'dangerousness' had been stressed unduly. We heard detailed and complicated evidence on the role of intramuscular injections in the sudden death of psychiatric patients, including the theory that the pharmaco-kinetics of phenothiazines are so effected when a patient is in an excited state (as Orville undoubtedly was) as to make them more cardio-toxic. We could not reach a definite specific conclusion on this issue but urged further research upon it as a matter of urgency. Events subsequent to Orville's death and their impact on the family caused us much concern. Due to a mistake, his family arrived at the local general hospital very late at night and eventually had to view his body in the refrigerated area of the mortuary where other bodies were stored. Normally, viewing would take place in an adjacent chapel of rest. It seems that a duty porter in the mortuary allowed the viewing to take place in the refrigerated area because of strict adherence to a coroner's ruling (that the body should not be disturbed). If such rules were so immutable, we urged that they be amended. Our own concerns about the insensitivity implicit in such an occurrence were confirmed when, as a result of my insistence, we visited and inspected the mortuary and 'viewing' arrangements. In our report, we made recommendations as to the best means of dealing with relatives in such a 'sudden death' situation. However we were not the first to do so, since Shirley Ritchie had made similar comments in her report into Michael Martin's death nearly ten years earlier (Ritchie 1985).

Similarities between the deaths of all three patients

All three patients died in, or following, seclusion, where they had been placed following disruptive and/or violent behaviour. All had been diagnosed as schizophrenic and in addition they were much over-weight and allowed, apparently, to consume large quantities of chocolate amongst other products. We recommended that the authorities do further work on healthier life-styles for such patients. All three patients were likable and popular when well but also they generated a fear of violence amongst the staff (hence my earlier comments). We endeavoured to determine whether staff had been racist in their behaviour. We considered that there was a racial institutional bias against ethnic minorities, but that this was by acts of omission rather than by commission. Our general view may be summed up as follows:

> The experience of Afro-Caribbean youngsters is not fully understood by Eurocentric psychiatry and those who work in the psychiatric system. It is important that differences are recognised and catered for. (Prins *et al* 1993: 51).

Aftermath

We suggested that we be asked to return to monitor the implementation of our recommendations; the offer was categorically rejected at the press conference that accompanied publication of our report. In addition, because the report attracted a good deal of media attention there was an initial fairly large demand for copies. These were quickly exhausted, and despite a very small further print-run, the report speedily became unavailable. Having had no sustained contact with Broadmoor since the time of our inquiry I am not able to be very specific about any improvements that may have occurred. It does seem that the use of seclusion has diminished, and that concerted attempts to address 'minority' issues are being made. I may know more later this year as I have been asked to visit Broadmoor to participate in an on-going seminar to evaluate progress concerning mental health and black issues. I shall have to wait and see.

DO INQUIRIES SERVE THEIR PURPOSES?

Now for the final part of my presentation. If numbers are an indicator, then mental health inquiries should have had a large impact upon practice. Sheppard (1996) has compiled an account of Mental Health Inquiry Reports published in England and Wales between 1969 and 1996; what sad repetitive reading they make. On a smaller, but no less important scale, Banerjee *et al* have reviewed the characteristics of the deaths of patients detained under the Mental Health Act 1983 who died while liable to be detained—between 1 April 1992 and 31 March 1994 and whose deaths resulted in an inquest (Banerjee *et al* 1995). These, and the large and continuing number of inquiries into allied matters, such as homicides committed by patients known to the psychiatric services fuel the impression that we live in an 'inquiry society', and, dare I say it, a 'blame culture' that may begin to have iatrogenic consequences.

I conclude this presentation with some general comments, which, in my view, are capable of wider extrapolation in relation to the theme of this conference and to my own contribution in particular. As already indicated, our own inquiry was held in private, as was for example, the inquiry into the case of Christopher Clunis (Ritchie *et al* 1994). There was no apparent evidence in the proceedings or the findings in the Clunis case that a decision to hold the hearings in private detracted in any way from either veracity or fairness. Two inquiries I have recently been engaged upon, one into a fairly high profile abscond from a medium secure unit of a detained offender patient, and the other, into a homicide have been in private—in my view to no-one's detriment.

Views differ on the most desirable course to adopt. Clothier (1996), who chaired the inquiry into the activities of the child killer, nurse Beverley Allitt, seems to favour private hearings. The key issue is one of achieving fairness to all parties involved; not least the personnel under scrutiny. At a recent public conference on the future of inquiries, the Responsible Medical Officer (RMO) in the 'Mitchell' case (Blom-Cooper *et al* 1996) gave a moving account of the impact of the inquiry on himself and his family; for him, it was clearly a traumatic experience, for even if no blame attaches, the professional is likely to feel, perhaps quite irrationally, that he or she is to blame. This is more likely to be the case if the hearings are public. Some feel that fairness also demands that the perpetrator of the homicide (who at the time of the inquiry will have been convicted and sentenced) should be asked to consent to all documentation in their case being made available to the inquiry team; and in a number of cases this has been done and consent obtained. An opposing view is that in such 'public interest' cases, consent is not required. Those taking this view cite the difficulties that would occur if the requested consent was to be withheld. Very few inquiries have had powers to compel witnesses to attend or to demand documents. However, it would be possible to compel the provision of such evidence by the somewhat laborious and costly route of a High Court hearing or an instruction from the central government department concerned. To achieve fairness, in the majority of inquiries—be they public or private—it is necessary to make clear to those being called before them the nature of the evidence they are likely to be required to give, the manner in which the proceedings will be conducted and give a clear undertaking to provide them with a 'transcript' of their evidence so that they can confirm its accuracy. They will also be told that any criticisms of substance of their professional conduct will be made available to them for comment before the final report is published.

Publication of inquiry reports is also a matter that needs further thought and the introduction of a degree of rationalisation. For example, some reports have been published (often in good quality 'glossy' format) by the commissioning authority (such as a Regional or District Health Authority, either alone, or in combination with a Social Services Authority), and some are published as 'Command' papers by authority of Parliament. One or two inquiry reports have been published commercially as books, two notable examples being the reports into the homicide committed by Andrew Robinson (Blom-Cooper et al 1995) and that of Jason Mitchell (Blom-Cooper et al 1996). It seems probable that such publication has ensured a wider readership. However, ensuring such a wide readership may encourage an inquiry team to go beyond their original remit and make much wider recommendations than were required. This appears to have occurred in the reports of the Robinson and Mitchell inquiries. Such tendencies are not new; Grounds (1997) makes the point that similar wide-ranging recommendations were being made into cases of alleged psychiatric hospital-patient abuse in the late 1960s. It is worth noting at this point, that accounts by well-informed and objective journalists of such events can also be very useful (see, for example, Masters' account of the 'serial killers' Nilsen, Dahmer, and more recently Rosemary West (Masters 1985, 1993, 1996) and Wansell's account of Frederick West's life (Wansell 1996)). Occasionally, reports are published 'in-house' in cyclostyled paper covers; these seem to do less than justice to the considerable work involved.

Most inquiry panels now give an assurance (with the approval of the commissioning authority) that the reports will be published in full, or if not in full that the substance will be imparted to 'interested parties'.

I now make brief reference to some of the purposes of inquiries. Blom-Cooper, who has chaired many and varied inquiries in the United Kingdom, concludes that the purpose is to '. . . examine the truth . . . what happened . . . how did it happen, and who, if anyone was responsible, culpably or otherwise, for it having happened?' (1993: 20). So far so good, but are there not difficulties in such a definition of purpose and are there not, indeed, other purposes, explicit or implicit? The search for truth is admirable, but is it readily ascertainable in the manner in which Sir Louis suggests? All workers in this field agree that it is very easy to be 'wise after the event', and that 'hindsight-bias' may lead one to draw erroneous conclusions. For example, as far as I am aware, no homicide inquiry has been able to state categorically that omissions or failures in practice could be shown *conclusively* to have caused the homicidal incident. The best that can be said is that such failures may have been contributory factors. This being the case, one must question the desirability of such complex and time-consuming procedures. However, it has been suggested that inquiries into homicides and similar matters are needed for additional and no less important purposes. Some experts have indicated that they are needed for public catharsis, most notably to help the families of the deceased cope with their grief (see Reder and Duncan 1996; Rock 1996). In this respect, Grounds (1997) suggests that 'Families have two overriding concerns; first, that they should know what happened, even if the process of learning is an ordeal; secondly that what happened to them should not happen to others in the future' (p.134). Eastman (1996) argues that 'The main purpose of inquiries should be pursued separately. This implies that inquiries should investigate only causal explanation and should always be explicitly excluded from expressing a judgment about *professional culpability*' (Eastman 1996: 1070—emphasis added). Eastman suggests that judgments about professional culpability should be made either through the professional's governing body or through the civil courts.

There is a further deficiency in the present system to be mentioned. Currently, each inquiry, whatever the focus, is a single event; the team carry out their required task and present their report. It is left to the authorities involved to accept or reject whatever recommendations are made and to act upon them as they see fit. As already indicated, rarely is a team asked to 'revisit' to ensure that their recommendations have been implemented. What direction should future policy take? There is little doubt, for example, that homicide inquiries are not only labour intensive and very costly, but they may contain inherent harmful elements—to both the perpetrator's victims and those responsible for his or her care. By way of conclusion, some suggestions are put forward concerning possible future policy directions.

1. Mandatory homicide inquiries should cease, or if not abandoned entirely, there should be some limit on the length of time that the perpetrator has been in prior contact with the relevant services. At present, there seems to be no time limitation in this respect.
2. Formal inquiries could usefully be replaced by more effective internal systems of monitoring and audit (notably in respect of risk assessment and management). There should still be a requirement for all homicide cases to be reported, perhaps to the Department of Health. This body would then make a decision as to whether an independent external inquiry was required.
3. Such 'residual' cases should then become the responsibility of a central inquiry body who could also maintain a list of possible inquiry team members. A body such as the Mental Health Act Commission for England and Wales could provide this service and also act as an Inquiry Secretariat.

Finally, the time for change is now upon us. Many inquiries that have been held, and those currently being undertaken, seem to produce very similar findings. The lessons from these are surely capable of being learned without the universal and somewhat cumbersome investigations just adverted to. However, we should remind ourselves of some of the positive benefits. Grounds in relation to homicide inquiries suggests that:

> Psychiatric scandals are important levers of longer-term reforms. The prevailing criticism of psychiatry in our age is not its excess of social control, but its failures of social control and public protection . . . at the present time it may be the voices of families and victims that are prophetic in showing where we need to move, as they articulate a need for services more sensitive to their concerns, and a need for changes in professional attitudes that may be taken for granted in a generation's time. (Grounds 1997: 135)

I am conscious that some of you may consider that I have strayed somewhat from my anticipated presentation. I apologise to those of you who take this view, but I considered that our current preoccupations with inquiries of one kind or another required me to expand somewhat upon my original and somewhat narrower brief. I hope I have earned your indulgence and perhaps even the approval of some of you.

Herschel Prins works part-time at the Midlands Centre for Criminology and Criminal Justice, Loughborough University and at Nottingham Trent University. He has served on the Parole Board, the Mental Health Act Commission and has been a lay member of the Mental Health Review Tribunal for 20 years. He has published widely in the fields of criminology and mental health. In addition to chairing the inquiry into Orville Blackwood's case he has chaired two other inquiries, one into the absconding of a patient on day leave from a secure unit and the other into a homicide committed by someone known to the mental health care and social services.

CHAPTER 6

The Coroner's Inquiry

Richard Whittington

To begin with, I will say the obvious: the coroner, like other judicial officers, must work within the confines of the law. The law in England and Wales gradually evolved over the centuries. I should explain; there are no coroners in Scotland. Change has occurred through the disuse of many of the original medieval powers, by statute expressing the will of our elected Parliament and by judge made law—as for instance through judicial review. The first coroners were appointed more than 800 years ago and we have travelled a long journey to where we stand today—a situation in which the coroner, as I have already stated, makes inquiries bound by the law and rules governing his or her judicial appointment. I make this important point early, as there may be a conflict between the constraints put on the coroner and the aspirations of those with a real and proper interest in one of his or her inquiries. There can be no better example than the sometimes differing and conflicting interests of people involved in 'a death in custody' inquest.

I speak from my own experience in the West Midlands, with one of the largest coroner's jurisdictions in the country, though with only one penal establishment, a large busy local prison, with a high proportion of remand prisoners, namely Birmingham Prison, commonly referred to as Winson Green Prison. This does not deter me from giving this paper. In fact I welcome the opportunity. Unfortunately after a death in custody, what the general public often see on television or read in the newspapers are the unverified allegations of the recently bereaved and angry family. Accompanying these are demands for an independent inquiry. I scarcely need to remind you there always is such an inquiry— the coroner's inquest; and coroners acquire therefore, a great deal of experience in this regard. I am grateful to the organizers of this conference for the invitation to talk to you about the coroner's role which also allows me to make some observations.

Nature of an inquest

A coroner's inquest is inquisitorial and not adversarial, as is the practice in most other English courts, i.e. there are no winners or losers. The purpose is to establish the truth. The coroner assumes jurisdiction under the section 8 Coroners Act 1988 when informed of:

(a) violent or unnatural death

(b) death of which the cause is unknown
(c) a person has died in prison.

For the purpose of this talk an inquest is held before the jury if the death occurred in prison, in police custody or due to injury caused by a police officer in the course of his or her duties.

When a death in custody occurs, the vicinity of the death is sealed. An immediate inquiry is initiated, headed by a senior C. I. D. officer acting on behalf of the coroner and in the case of police custody an independent senior police officer appointed and supervised by the Police Complaints Authority. Eventually, the police reports are placed before the coroner. These reports will contain the Home Office pathologist's report, toxicology results, statements, prison records, prison medical records, police custody sheets and a number of reports and forms, for example psychiatric reports or 'Prisoner at Exceptional Risk' forms (F1997), along with the comments of the investigating officer. It is the coroner alone who authorises the post mortem examination. He or she may also cause other inquiries to be made, for example with relatives, the deceased's general practitioner or at other prisons or hospitals with prior knowledge of the deceased person.

The coroner decides which witnesses to call at the inquest, in anticipation that their evidence is likely to be relevant. He or she may also allow the production of documents if of a non controversial nature. This does not preclude other people from giving evidence. An ancient proclamation may precede the inquest

> . . . and if anyone can give evidence, on behalf of our Sovereign Lady the Queen, when, how, and by what means A B came to his death, let him come forth, and he shall be heard . . .

The coroner performs the principal examination of witnesses who are duly summoned and give evidence on oath. Contempt applies in the coroner's court, as in any other court; and I had to impose a further prison sentence on a prisoner who shared a cell with another who died of an overdose and refused to give evidence. Perjury in the coroner's court, is, as might be expected, a criminal offence.

A not uncommon source of confusion lies within events prior to the inquest itself. This is the possible refusal by the coroner to grant disclosure of all documents and statements put before the coroner to an interested party, commonly the family. Contrary to the position in relation to most other, and mostly adversarial tribunals, no duty of disclosure, or to order disclosure, exists. This has been confirmed by judicial review (*R v. Hammersmith Coroner, ex p. Peach* (1980)). Statements are made and reports submitted in the knowledge that they are initially for the coroner's eyes only. If the makers believe that copies would be released to all parties they might well be submitted in an abbreviated and defensive form and much useful information might never be yielded to the coroner. Disclosure may, remarkably, diminish the effectiveness of the coroner's inquest. Further, documents may contain sensitive and confidential matters concerning other living people, for example, alleged child abuse by parents of the deceased. Release of this kind of information may be highly inflammatory.

The law and procedure at inquests
Today the law regarding coroners is contained in the Coroners Act 1988 and the Coroners Rules of 1984. Thus rule 36 states:

(1) The inquest shall solely determine, who the deceased was, how, when and where he came by his death and the particulars required to register the death.
(2) Neither the coroner nor the jury shall express any opinion on any other matter.

Following on from this, rule 42 states that no verdict is to appear to determine: (a) criminal liability on the part of a named person; or (b) civil liability.

The principal of a fact finding inquiry without establishing blame is reinforced by rule 22 which states that: no witness has to answer questions that may incriminate himself (s.22(1)); and that the coroner should advise (or caution) the witness not to answer such questions (s.22(2)).

The coroner will allow interested people either personally or through their legal representative to examine the witnesses. Such people may be relatives, an insurer, a someone whose act or admission may have contributed to the death, the deceased's trade union, a government inspector, for example a factory inspector or the chief officer of police, or any other person at the coroner's discretion. Similarly such people are entitled to have a suitable representative to attend the post mortem examination and to be notified of the time of the inquest. Members of the jury can also put questions or request that a particular witness be called.

At the conclusion of the evidence, the coroner will hear legal submissions as to the law, but according to rule 30 no person shall be allowed to address the jury as to the facts. The coroner will finally address the jury, first by summarising the evidence, and then by directing them as to the law and particularly drawing their attention to rule 36 (the constraints of the inquest, i.e. 'who, where, when and how') and rule 42 ('no blame'). The normal standard of proof by which the jury must judge the merits of the evidence is that of civil law—the balance of probabilities. There are two important exceptions. In the case of an unlawful killing or a suicide the criminal standard is used. The jury must be sure, i.e. satisfied beyond all reasonable doubt. For instance in the case of suicides, there must be evidence of intent by the deceased to bring about his or her own death and no other explanation can be entertained. When there *is* doubt, it is quite proper for a jury after thorough deliberation to return an open verdict.

If prior to or during the inquest the coroner acquires evidence that a person may have been killed unlawfully, he or she should refer the matter to the Crown Prosecution Service. On 18 August 1980 a prisoner died in Birmingham prison hospital of dreadful injuries, including rupture of the oesophagus and bone fractures. As a result of eight days of evidence heard in Birmingham coroner's court, three prison officers appeared in the Crown Court charged in relation to an alleged unlawful killing of the prisoner. This would never have occurred without the detailed consideration of the evidence at the inquest. They were eventually found not guilty.

Verdict
The findings of the jury must describe how the deceased died, in the common meaning of that word and can thus be described as in narrative form. When the possibility of neglect or lack of care is raised, as may often occur following deaths in custody, particular problems may arise. One instance is from one of my own inquests. A prisoner was found hanging in his cell, apparently as the result of suicide. The Divisional Court (*R v. Birmingham Coroner, ex p. Home Secretary* (1990) (Attwal)) ruled that it would be proper for the jury to consider a verdict that 'He killed himself, aggravated or brought about by lack of care', since he was allowed to remain alone in a cell when the prison authorities should have known that he posed a serious risk of suicide. The two aspects of the death were drawn together in one verdict. Another example of lack of care was of a young prisoner who deliberately starved and dehydrated himself and died in the hospital wing from dehydration in part due to the hospital officers failing to ensure he had sufficient fluid and to keep proper observation. I directed the jury to a lack of care verdict.

Lack of care has recently been replaced as a verdict. This arose in an appeal, concerning a death in custody in which Lord Bingham, then Master of the Rolls, stated in his judgment that lack of care was considered to be the obverse of self-neglect and therefore should be replaced by neglect, which refers to the failure of the provision of either the physical or medical needs of the deceased (*R v. Coroner for*

Humberside, ex p. Jamieson [1994] 3 WLR 82). Further, there must be a clear and causal connection between the death and the conduct in question, which, surpassing ordinary negligence, amounts to gross neglect.

Considerations for the coroner
A coroner has to consider a death in custody in the widest possible terms. Where an elderly convicted prisoner has died of natural causes, shall we say cancer, or the consequences of diabetes, even if this is in a general hospital, his death is still the subject of a jury inquest. When a prisoner on leave from prison dies, his death is the subject of an inquest. For instance, one such prisoner was found dead on the railway line from multiple injuries, but he was intoxicated with alcohol at the time. The jury returned an open verdict. Another died from the effects of drugs, to which he had lost his tolerance whilst in prison. I considered both to be 'prison deaths'. The circumstances of the arrest may be associated with death. An example from the West Midlands was a man who was arrested after a struggle with police officers, investigating a bank card fraud. He was black and this factor alone raises the profile of any subsequent inquest. Recently a man in Birmingham was shot dead when he refused to surrender to two armed police officers when he had handcuffed himself to the supermarket manager and was simultaneously thrusting a knife into this unfortunate man's back. He was white.

Coroners treat deaths in custody as part of a vast and extensive range of unnatural deaths. This is particularly true of suicide. A significant trend towards more suicides by young men is a great source of concern. Many suffer personality defects which are often brought about by home circumstances and upbringing and frequently aggravated by abuse of alcohol and drugs. Such inadequate individuals faced with the inevitable disintegration of their relationships and domestic arrangements and possibly expecting custodial sentences, develop a degree of despair that may lead them to take their own lives. The prison population contains many such people who have the same risk factors which may lead to successful suicide. That does not, however, mean that they do not deserve help and protection.

Examples within the general community of people who may take their own life include defendants shortly before a court appearance, when a custodial sentence is anticipated. Similarly a prisoner may kill himself or herself in prison if he or she expects a long sentence. A prime example was Fred West, charged with serial killings, who killed himself on 1 January 1996 in Birmingham Prison. Not infrequently a young man may kill himself if he believes his girlfriend or partner is abandoning him, whether or not he is in or out of prison. The effect of drugs has a powerful influence in either situation. For instance, a 29-year-old man was arrested by the police over a weekend and was brought to court on Monday, after 36 hours in custody. He was an amphetamine addict and being without his regular drug induced euphoria he rapidly became depressed and hanged himself one hour after his release from court on bail. A more generous use of bail does not necessarily prevent suicide. From my experience, men may kill themselves on bail and the relative freedom of a bail hostel does not prevent these deaths. We have in Birmingham a Home Office supported bail hostel for mentally ill offenders and residents have succeeded in killing themselves or dying from the effects of drug misuse. What I am saying is that there is a section of society, mostly young men, regardless of their custodial status, who are liable to suicide and drug (and alcohol) related deaths.

Those who are determined on suicide can be most devious and ingenious to achieve their ends. A person on admission to prison may deny any previous psychiatric condition or former suicidal behaviour at the primary medical screening. Even when under continuous observation, I have known of people who have succeeded in asphyxiating themselves, both in police custody or in hospital. Do not deceive yourselves, many suicides inquired into by coroners occur amongst hospital patients, whether or not voluntary patients or people detained under the Mental Health Act. It is often a matter of chance of circumstances that a person suffering from a mental disorder ends up in prison or in a psychiatric hospital. In either circumstances, they may be overcome by real or imagined guilt, depression or despair. Either way, they need society's help.

Young men have indeed always found loss of liberty and of contact with home and family hard to bear. In another context it is recounted in that book about British India, *Tales from the Raj*, that

Suicides among British other ranks in India were far from exceptional: besides these two shootings, we had a young boy who had only been out two weeks before he hanged himself, and another lad, only seventeen, who considered himself tormented by the NCOs and drove himself insane and blew his brains out.

These young men were sent to far off India on seven year postings and it was not uncommon for them to feign sickness at the time of the compulsory church parades and take the opportunity of shooting themselves with their own rifle. For these inexperienced lads it must have seemed like a seven year sentence.

It is beyond the brief of a coroner to contemplate the benefits of any alternatives to custodial sentences, the shortening of time on remand or more liberal structural organization of our penal system. There will always be difficulties; for example, when an arrested person with a head injury, but disguised by the effects of alcohol or drugs, makes detection of the injury extremely difficult, even for the experienced and trained police surgeon. This dilemma has, on occasions, led to loss of life. Prisoners will continue, no doubt, to deceive and manipulate the authorities, who are already burdened by numerous threats to self harm or actual instances of self harm. Fred West may have been a terrible abuser and murderer of young women, but was a model prisoner before his suicide. He hanged himself with the prison shirts that he was entrusted to repair, without giving any indication of his intention.

Please do not think I am complacent by saying that there is a significant group of people, mostly disadvantaged young men in and out of custody who are susceptible to violent or unnatural death of some sort. Clearly, one can only hope that the stability of family life will be restored and that standards of basic education will be raised so that young people will enter life with the necessary resources. In Birmingham, I have helped to get The Samaritans installed as an additional resource available to distressed or depressed prisoners. It takes time to train and make available suitable prisoner befrienders. I do believe in some respects the attitude of prison officers must change and the rigidity of the Prison Officers' Association must be modified. For instance, in Birmingham, Category A prisoners have a very high level of supervision—except at lunchtime when they are locked in their cells with one patrolling officer, the others being at their lunch. This has provided an opportunity for suicides. The inflexibility of shift patterns also has made it difficult to allocate personal officers to individual prisoners so that they can establish rapport with prisoners and have forewarning of serious worries and depression. Further, there seems, at least in Birmingham, a great reluctance or lack of determination to complete suicide prevention training by the prison officers and therefore to be more responsive to behavioural or psychiatric problems. I do sometimes ask myself—who is managing our prisons?

Although these days by recent legislation a jury is barred from adding a rider to its verdict, a coroner can by virtue of rule 43 report to the appropriate authority matters arising out of an inquest which may prevent a recurrence of fatalities in similar circumstances. Many years ago a middle aged prisoner threw himself to his death from one landing to another below (sustaining a fatal head injury). The police knew he suffered from a mental illness, since he thought his brain was controlled by his landlord. The prison authorities were unaware of this as the 'Prisoner at Exceptional Risk' form at the time only referred to physical illness, for example epilepsy or diabetes. I was able to make

91

recommendations to the Home Office so that the form additionally draws attention to behavioural or psychiatric problems which might put the prisoner at risk. Incidentally, I have also long advocated the integration of the Prison Medical Service with the National Health Service.

A coroner's experience does benefit from the diversity of his or her inquiries. I, for instance, had to hold an inquest on an elderly lady whose body was brought back from abroad. She had been strangled to death by her depressed husband who was charged with her murder and subsequently hanged himself in a foreign prison and his body was also returned, necessitating an inquest into a death in custody abroad.

A coroner's jurisdiction is open ended. Discussions are, in fact, in progress now to decide whether a coroner should also have to be informed of a death of a someone detained under the Mental Health Act in the same way as a death in custody, when restrictions of a patient's personal liberty are imposed in the same way as by an arrest or detention in prison.

In summary, I would like you to go away with the idea that coroners hold inquiries into all custodial deaths which lead to important fact finding inquests in which many parties can participate including an impartial jury. Such inquests are carried out with the sole intention of attempting to establish the truth as to how death came about.

Richard Whittington is President of the Coroners' Society of England and Wales. He is HM Coroner for Birmingham and Solihull and is an honorary teaching fellow in the Department of Biomedical Ethics at Birmingham University. He was formerly a general medical practitioner, police surgeon and university physician. He has published a number of papers relating to the causation of unnatural death.

PART TWO

Deaths of Offenders in Police Custody: Special Issues

CHAPTER 7

Investigating Deaths in Police Custody

John Cartwright, Police Complaints Authority

Thank you for giving me the opportunity to describe the Police Complaints Authority's role in investigating deaths in police custody. I would like to use the available time, firstly, by outlining the constitution and powers of the Authority, and by explaining how we come to be involved in this issue. I will then present the most recent analysis of the cases we have investigated and set out both our concerns and the steps which we believe could reduce the problems. Finally, I would like to touch on the vexed question of disclosure of evidence prior to the inquest when there has been a death in police custody.

CONSTITUTION AND POWERS

First, the constitution and statutory powers of the Police Complaints Authority (PCA). There are currently ten members, together with the chairman and the deputy chairman. All are appointed by the home secretary apart from the chairman whose formal appointment is by Her Majesty the Queen. We serve for an initial three year period with the possibility of a second term. That is the maximum permitted under the Nolan Rules.

Members have a wide variety of backgrounds and experiences. They come from industry, commerce, the professions, local government and the armed forces. There is even an occasional slot for an ex-politician who has turned over a new leaf and is trying to go straight and earn an honest living!

Our powers are drawn from the Police and Criminal Evidence Act 1984 (PACE). We supervise the investigation of the most serious complaints made against police officers. And we consider all completed complaint investigations, whether supervised or not, to determine whether officers should be charged with a disciplinary offence.

We also have a very useful power to supervise non-complaint matters referred to us by police forces or police authorities. These involve situations which are grave or unusual and in which a police officer *may* have committed an offence. These cases involve a high level of public interest or concern and it is under this aspect of PACE that deaths in police care or custody are referred to the Authority.

Complaints alleging that a police officer has caused death or serious injury must, by law, be the subject of a PCA supervised investigation. Complaints that an officer is guilty of assault, corruption, or any other serious arrestable offence must be referred to the Authority who have discretion over whether or not to supervise the inquiry.

The supervising member of the Authority has three statutory powers. He or she must approve the choice of the investigating officer who will lead the inquiry. He or she has power to impose requirements for the conduct of the investigation. And at the conclusion must issue a statutory certificate indicating whether or not he or she is satisfied with the way in which the investigation has been carried out.

In practice, the supervisor determines the strategy, sees all the evidence as it is obtained and has regular discussions with the investigating officer. In sensitive cases he or she will visit the scene and will meet complainants. Those of us who carry out this function are on call 24 hours a day, 7 days a week and 52 weeks a year. In high profile emergency situations we need to be at the scene of the incident as a matter of extreme urgency.

	1995/96	1996/97
Formal disciplinary charges	253	235
Informal discipline	860	1,018
Criminal prosecutions	16	16
TOTAL	1,129	1,269
Fully investigated cases	4,160	5,005

Disciplinary results

As for the disciplinary role, the figures for 1996/97 show that 5,005 fully investigated cases resulted in 235 formal charges against police officers, 1,018 less formal disciplinary actions and 16 criminal prosecutions. There was, therefore, some type of positive outcome in approximately 25 per cent of all the fully investigated cases.

DEATHS IN POLICE CARE OR CUSTODY

I now turn specifically to deaths in police care or custody. Until fairly recently there was a very broad definition of such cases which even incorporated people who had walked into police stations voluntarily to make a statement or to report a crime. However, following ministerial intervention, the definition was tightened up and from January 1996 it has been limited to two specific types of case, i.e. those in which the deceased person was:

- in police detention; or
- in the hands of the police or where death resulted from the actions of a police officer in the execution of his or her duty

As I mentioned earlier, these cases are voluntarily referred to the PCA by police forces, i.e. under section 88 of PACE. The history of such referrals is significant.

For the three years between 1991 and 1993 there were 153 deaths in custody notified to the Home Office. However, only 31 of these cases were referred to the PCA for an independently supervised inquiry. The Metropolitan Police Service seldom referred such deaths and a number of other forces took the same position.

However, a direct approach to Sir Paul Condon soon after he became commissioner resulted in a change of policy under which any case which fell into the Home Office definition was automatically to be referred to the Authority. Other forces have fallen into line and we now believe that all such deaths are referred to us.

The objectives of a PCA supervised investigation are threefold. First, we need to establish the facts. How did the deceased meet his or her death? This is essential because our report goes to the coroner, together with all the supporting evidence, and forms the basis for the public inquest.

Second, we must consider the conduct of the police officers involved. Is there any suggestion of a criminal or disciplinary offence? If so, all the evidence must be gathered so that the possibility of criminal or disciplinary action can be pursued.

Third, we need to determine what lessons can be learnt from this tragedy. Are there changes to police procedures, policies or working practices which could prevent another death occurring in similar circumstances? Such issues are then drawn to the attention of the individual police force or to the wider police service.

In analysing the recent cases dealt with by the Authority the first issue is the ethnic origin of the deceased. As you can see, both the number and the proportion of black deaths in the year ending 31 March 1997 was double that of the preceding year.

	1995/96	1996/97
White	41	39
Black	3	6
Asian	1	1
Other	1	2

Deaths in Custody — Ethnicity

Although the numbers may not be large, the deaths of black people have tended to be high profile, controversial and to raise disturbing issues. This has been particularly true when they have occurred as a result of street arrests.

An analysis of the location shows rather fewer deaths occurring at police stations in the most recent year but more in hospitals. This may reflect the growth in the numbers of deaths put down to a variety of natural causes. Most of these involved heart conditions of some sort, often aggravated by stress or exertion.

	1995/96	1996/97
Police station	26	21
Hospital	12	20
Elsewhere	8	7
TOTAL	46	48

Deaths in Custody — Location

Although the number of suicides has dropped from 15 in 1994/95 to seven in 1996/97, you will see that the level of deaths linked to alcohol or drug abuse remains disturbingly high.

	1994/95	1995/96	1996/97
Alcohol/drugs	19	14	20
Suicide	15	10	7
Natural causes	10	16	20
Traffic incidents	4	6	1
	48	46	48

Deaths in Custody — Causes

PROBLEMS AND CONCERNS

Having dealt with some 200 cases over recent years, the PCA's concern about deaths in police custody relates to three specific areas. The first is suicide. The second is the care of people who are, or appear to be, drunk. And the third arises from arrests made in the street.

Suicides
All the suicides considered over recent years took place in police cells and the overwhelming majority involved what we loosely term 'hanging'. By this we mean the use of some form of ligature placed around the throat and attached to a fixture or fitting either inside, or easily reached from within, the cell.

The ligature is usually created from an item of clothing. Laces and anorak cords are the most frequently employed but strips have also been torn from shirts. In one case, the detained person's clothes had been removed and he had been left in a paper suit. He still succeeded in tearing a strip from the paper suit to form a ligature.

Bedding also featured in some cases. Although the blankets provided in police cells are often supposed to be tear-proof, this has not prevented them from being torn into lethal strips. In two cases, toilet paper was used as a means of achieving suffocation.

Our main concern about the attachment of ligatures relates to open cell hatches. A Home Office circular, issued as long ago as 1968, requires hatches to be closed when cells are occupied. Nevertheless, some officers do leave them open—usually at the request of the detained person. An open hatch makes it very much easier to attach a ligature to the outside door handle or to some other fixed point outside the cell. Even with hatches closed, we have seen ligatures fixed to door hinges, bolt holes, window bars, ventilation grilles, pipes and even light fittings. In one case, a flush button of a low-level toilet was used.

People who are or appear to be drunk
Detainees who appear to be drunk pose particular problems. There is a tendency for custody officers simply to place them in the cell to 'sleep it off'—particularly when they are well known regular offenders. However, not all police stations have specific 'drunk tanks'. A drunken person placed on a normal cell bunk some distance above the floor may roll off and suffer serious head injuries.

Some people may appear to be simply drunk but are in fact in the last throes of alcohol poisoning. Others may have taken a lethal cocktail of alcohol and drugs. In some cases, the signs of drunkenness may conceal a life-threatening injury such as a fractured skull or brain damage. Occasionally the person is not drunk at all but is a diabetic.

In cases like these, the facts may not be discovered until it is too late and the detained person is dead. The Authority strongly endorses the view of the British Medical Association that a police cell can be a dangerous place for someone who is, or who appears to be, drunk. Moreover, it is unfair to expect police officers who are not medically trained to provide the care needed in such cases.

Arrest

Deaths which directly result from an arrest typically involve a violent struggle. This may include an officer's use of neck holds or batons. The police use of force must always be reasonable in the circumstances. However, if an officer believes a life to be at risk—whether his or her own or someone else's—he or she is entitled to use whatever force may be necessary and this includes life-threatening force. Officers must always be aware that they may subsequently have to justify their actions in a court of law.

The use of neck holds has been defended by some officers on the ground that they provide an effective means of restraining violent and dangerous people. The Authority's view, however, is that certain neck holds involve an unacceptably high element of risk. We have made our views clear to the Association of Chief Police Officers; we have called for the issue to be properly covered during police training; and we have set out our concerns in the 1993 annual report.

A more recent development has been the debate about positional asphyxia. Some pathologists have argued that this is a specific condition caused by restraining a person face down on the ground, with their arms handcuffed behind their back. It is claimed that this can cause serious breathing difficulties. These may be aggravated when the individual is seriously overweight.

The issue first arose in Britain following the 1994 death of Richard O'Brien in South East London. The inquest resulted in a verdict of unlawful killing and the coroner recommended regular retraining in restraint techniques and additional research into injuries resulting from physical restraint.

Similar concerns were raised at the inquest into the death of Wayne Douglas who died in 1995 after being arrested in Brixton. Two pathologists argued that the death was partly caused by positional asphyxia while a third believed that it was due to hypertensive heart disease. The jury determined that positional asphyxia had been a factor in the death and the coroner repeated the call for refresher training on restraint techniques. He also recommended that specific guidelines on positional asphyxia should be provided for all police officers.

It is fair to say that there are differing views in the medical profession about this issue of positional asphyxia. Nevertheless, restraining people in this way clearly involves risk and the Metropolitan Police Service has taken action as a result of the coroner's recommendations.

The introduction of new police batons has also caused us some concern. The old style baton was seldom used because it was singularly ineffective. It has been replaced by a wide variety of batons, all of which are more powerful and, therefore, carry a greater risk of serious injury. It was a baton blow, for example, which led to the controversial death of Brian Douglas in South London.

The Authority is closely monitoring complaints about the use of batons. We have so far been unable to establish any particular type of baton as being more likely to give rise to complaints. We can, however, see a link between the frequency of refresher training and the number of complaints. Those forces which retrain officers at two monthly intervals appear to have the lowest level of baton-related complaints.

CS spray is another area of concern. It was used during the arrest of Ibrahima Sey at Ilford in East London, although the inquest has yet to determine whether or not it was a factor in his death. The Authority is monitoring all complaints about the use of CS spray although it is fair to say that there have so far been comparatively few.

ACTION TO REDUCE DEATHS IN CUSTODY

I turn now to action which the Authority would like to see taken to reduce the number of deaths in police custody:

- first, we want to see more information made available about the record of detainees who may pose suicide risks. This means ensuring that all details are recorded on the Police National Computer and are accurate and up-to-date. It certainly means incorporating information from the Prison Service which may often be crucial. The Lancashire study on suicide and self-harm suggests a more questioning approach by custody officers to those in their care and we would certainly support that recommendation.
- custody officers do have power to remove items of clothing if they believe that these may be used for self-harm. This power should be exercised more frequently with obvious items such as

shoelaces and anorak cords. Similarly, blankets provided in cells should be genuinely tear-proof.

- perhaps most important of all is the installation of more closed-circuit television in custody suites. These systems provide crucial protection both for detained people and for police officers. We also believe that there is a powerful case for providing CCTV coverage of at least one cell so that particularly vulnerable prisoners can be properly monitored. There is a balance to be struck here between personal dignity and the protection of life.

- the Authority has been pressing for the redesign of police cells to remove as many risks as possible. The Home Office has been co-operative and architects have already produced proposals. However, it will obviously take many years before all cells can be brought up to a reasonable standard.

- in relation to arrest situations, we want to see more emphasis on regular refresher training in restraint techniques, with particular reference to the danger of neck holds and the risks of positional asphyxia. Officers may go for lengthy periods with no experience of having to restrain someone in the course of a violent struggle. Without regular refresher training there is a risk that they will react in an instinctive, rather than a controlled way.

- a more consistent approach to training is also needed in the use of batons. We currently have a patchwork quilt of differing forces using different types of baton, supported by a wide variety of training programmes.

- the role of the police surgeon is often critical and we want to see more of them having the necessary skill and experience to deal with the problems caused by detained people suffering from psychiatric illness or alcohol and/or drug abuse.

- we also believe that the police surgeon should specify the level of care needed by a detained person rather than simply describe someone as 'fit to be detained'.

- similarly, there must be effective communication between surgeons and custody officers so that each understands the situation. When someone is held for longer periods both doctors and custody officers need to ensure that those to whom they hand over responsibility are fully aware of all relevant facts. This may sound elementary but it does not always happen and it can lead to tragedy.

- it also seems simple commonsense that custody officers should have a basic knowledge of first-aid, should be trained in suicide awareness and should have swift access to a comprehensive first-aid kit.

The PCA has for some time been pressing for more research into deaths in police custody. We had agreed to sponsor a specific project to be undertaken jointly with the Association of Police Surgeons. Unfortunately, the necessary Home Office funding was not forthcoming and a more general study is now being carried out by the Police Research Group at the Home Office. We hope that this will identify common factors and suggest changes to police procedures which lead to a reduction in the numbers of deaths.

DISCLOSURE OF STATEMENTS

I would now like to spend a few moments on the issue of disclosure of statements before the opening of an inquest. The Authority is sometimes subjected to perfectly understandable criticism because there is often a lengthy gap between the completion of our inquiry and the opening of the coroner's inquest.

The family of the deceased person naturally wants to know what we have discovered. But we have no power to disclose documents or findings. Our statutory role is, firstly, to ensure a fair and thorough investigation and then, after the inquest, to consider whether disciplinary action should be taken against any police officer.

The conduct of the inquest is entirely a matter for the coroner and it is not our job to usurp his or her functions by releasing information beforehand. However, we have been concerned to find that police legal representatives at inquests have had full prior access to our investigation files when these have been denied to the families of the deceased.

In our view, this does not constitute a level playing field. The families have a legitimate interest in knowing how a loved one came to die. They are placed at a severe disadvantage if they are prevented from seeing the evidence before the inquest. The PCA has been pressing this issue for several years. We have drawn attention to it in our annual reports. We have discussed it with the Coroners' Society and with the police. We have also taken legal advice which makes it clear that statements taken in the course of our supervised investigations remain the property of the police.

The police refuse to disclose the material, citing previous decisions of the courts. These have laid down that the purpose of an inquest is to establish facts not to apportion blame. Since there are no parties at an inquest there is no question of disclosure.

Nevertheless, the Authority would argue that by briefing counsel and using the material from the PCA's supervised investigation the police have made themselves a party. Why should they deny similar status and so documentation to the family of the deceased person? Unless there is a change in police thinking an alteration in the law will be necessary to resolve this matter. This is an issue about which we feel strongly and the Authority intends to pursue it.

CONCLUSION

As I have explained, the PCA's involvement with deaths in custody has expanded dramatically over recent years. As our experience has grown so has our concern. We believe that a number of the tragedies with which we have been associated could have been prevented.

Perhaps the biggest worry is that the whole issue is not being given sufficient attention. There appears to be no real co-ordinated attempt to reduce the number of those who die in police custody. There are 43 individual police forces, with differing policies and procedures. Police surgeons are hard to recruit in some parts of the country and not all have access to the training provided by the Association of Police Surgeons.

The only body able to pull all the various strands together into a concerted strategy is probably the Home Office. But sadly there is little evidence that the seriousness of the problem has yet been recognised. I very much hope that this conference will help to concentrate attention on ways of reducing the tragic and needless death toll which could undermine the public standing of the police service.

John Cartwright joined the Police Complaints Authority in 1992 and became Deputy Chairman in 1993. He was MP for Woolwich from 1974 to 1992 and Leader of the Council for the London Borough of Greenwich between 1971 and 1974. He was a founder member of the SDP, serving both as parliamentary whip and party president.

CHAPTER 8

Investigating Suspicious Deaths in Police Custody

Tony Ward and Deborah Coles

In the month that has elapsed between the presentation of this paper at the ISTD conference and its submission for publication at the beginning of August 1997, there have been dramatic developments relating to our theme of the investigation of death and ill-treatment in police custody. Three decisions of the Director of Public Prosecutions (DPP) not to prosecute police officers have been quashed (*R v. DPP, ex p. Jones, O'Brien and Treadway* (1997)). Two of these concerned people who were asphyxiated while being arrested and restrained. Both Shiji Lapite and Richard O'Brien suffered numerous injuries which were unaccounted for by police evidence; both were found by coroners' juries to have been unlawfully killed; yet no officer involved was charged with any crime. The third case concerned the CPS's failure to prosecute West Midlands Serious Crime Squad officers who had been found by a High Court judge (in *Treadaway v. Chief Constable of West Midlands Police*, *The Times*, 25 October 1994, *The Independent*, 23 September, 1994) to have extracted a confession under torture from Derek Treadaway. These three cases overlapped with the hearing by another High Court judge of an application for judicial review of the coroner's summing-up in the case of Wayne Douglas who, like Richard O'Brien, died from positional asphyxia because of the way in which he was restrained by Metropolitan Police officers (*R v. Inner London Coroner*, ex p. Douglas-Williams, 31 July 1997). All four cases have presented disturbing images of police violence and have confirmed what INQUEST's 17 years of monitoring deaths in custody has taught us about the reluctance of the Crown Prosecution Service (CPS) to prosecute officers who cause death or serious injury. They have also exposed the inadequacies of the way such deaths are investigated.

The CPS now faces two inquiries into its work. One, conducted by Gerald Butler QC (a retired Crown Court judge) will look at the work of CPS Central Casework in dealing with complaints against the police and deaths in custody. The other, headed by Sir William Macpherson (a retired High Court judge), is to inquire into matters arising from the racist murder of Stephen Lawrence in 1993, and 'the lessons to be learnt for the investigation and prosecution of racially motivated crime' (It is not clear whether this will include racially motivated crimes by police officers). In addition, the House of Commons Select Committee on Home Affairs has announced an inquiry into police complaints procedures.

In this chapter we are concerned with the lessons to be learnt about the investigation and prosecution of possible police crimes from the three deaths in custody we have mentioned: Shiji Lapite, Richard O'Brien and Wayne Douglas.

THE CASES

We begin by outlining the facts of the three cases. We will then comment briefly on the question of police racism before turning to a discussion of the investigative process.

Richard O'Brien

Richard O'Brien, an Irish market trader and father of seven children, was arrested for being drunk and disorderly following a disturbance at a social club in Walworth, South London on 4 April 1994. He was not involved in the disturbance and witnesses say that he was neither drunk nor disorderly, but retaliated when he was pushed and insulted by an officer. Police claimed that he was drunk and struggling violently. He was pushed to the ground and held face down by three officers, with his wrists handcuffed behind his back. One officer had his knee on Mr O'Brien's back, just behind the neck. Another held his legs bent up behind him, while a third restrained his middle and back. He was restrained in this way for at least five minutes and possibly nearer ten. His wife, son and other witnesses heard Mr O'Brien say words to the effect of 'Let me up! I can't breathe! You win!', and an officer reply: 'We always win!' Together with his wife and 14-year-old son, who had also been arrested, Mr O'Brien was driven away in a police van. By now, as the inquest jury later determined, he was probably already dead. His wife and son described him being dragged into the van by his head or hair, and their account is supported by forensic evidence of a pool of blood mixed with human hair inside the van. When the son complained about his father's treatment he was slapped across the face. Mr O'Brien was placed face down on the floor of the police van; when they arrived at Walworth police station, his wife and son had to clamber out over his body. Mr O'Brien was carried face down into the police station and placed face down on the charge room floor. Officers realised he had turned blue and tried unsuccessfully to resuscitate him. The pathologist found 30 separate areas of injury on his body, including numerous cuts and bruises sustained shortly before death, for which the officers who testified at the inquest could offer no explanation. The cause of death was positional asphyxia: he had been unable to breathe in the position in which he had been restrained. The inquest jury returned a unanimous verdict of unlawful killing.

The DPP's decision not to prosecute any of the officers involved was quashed by the High Court. In the O'Brien case the Police Complaints Authority (PCA) recommended, and the Metropolitan Police accepted, that disciplinary charges of neglect of duty should be brought against two officers. The PCA will have to reconsider this in light of the further consideration of the case by the DPP.

Shiji Lapite

Shiji Lapite was a 34-year-old Nigerian decorator who had been seeking political asylum in Britain. He died on 16 December 1994 after a struggle outside a club in Stoke Newington with two police officers who had stopped him for 'acting suspiciously'. He received between 35 and 45 injuries; his larynx and neck were found to be bruised and his voice box fractured in a way which was consistent with the use of a neckhold. At the inquest the officers admitted to applying a neckhold twice to Mr Lapite, kicking him in the head twice and biting him but said they did so because they feared for their safety. But when the officers were medically examined shortly afterwards no significant injuries were found. One of the officers claimed that Mr Lapite had tried to strangle him but there were no marks on his neck, which, as the pathologist confirmed at the inquest, threw serious doubt on that part of his story and the whole account of the police version of events. The coroner's jury clearly did not believe the officers, and returned a verdict of unlawful killing.

In the recent High Court proceedings, the DPP's decision not to prosecute either of the arresting officers was quashed, as was the PCA's decision to bring no disciplinary charges against them. An application for judicial review of the PCA's decision not to bring disciplinary charges against officers responsible for training, for their neglect of duty in failing to act on warnings about the use of neckholds from the PCA (1994: 34) and the Association of Chief Police Officers, was adjourned.

Wayne Douglas

Wayne Douglas was a 25-year-old black man who was found dead in his cell at Brixton police station on 5 December 1995. He had been arrested on suspicion of carrying out a burglary shortly before, during which the victims were threatened with a knife. Eye-witnesses claimed he had been beaten by the police, while the police claimed he had died from a heart attack. At the inquest it emerged that he did not have injuries consistent with a serious beating but had died from heart failure as a result of a combination of stress, exhaustion, and positional asphyxia resulting from being restrained face down with his hands behind his back. The inquest jury found that this reflected current police methods, and returned a verdict of accidental death. The coroner made six recommendations, among them the need for police officers to receive specific training and guidelines in positional asphyxia from experts in this field. As in Shiji Lapite's case above, the inquest revealed a failure by police to act on warnings and recommendations made after earlier deaths from positional asphyxia.

At the inquest there was conflicting evidence from police officers as to whether Mr Douglas was left lying face down after he showed signs of breathing difficulties, or whether he was turned over on to his back. His family's lawyers argued at the inquest and in the High Court that restraining him and then leaving him in that position when he was in obvious distress could constitute manslaughter. The basis of their application for judicial review was that the coroner had not made the complex criminal law on this point sufficiently clear to the jury, and had not left them the alternative verdict that neglect contributed to the death.

Mr Justice Laws accepted that there had been a misdirection but did not consider that the jury could properly have returned an unlawful killing verdict on the evidence. He considered that no one officer had participated sufficiently in the various stages of the incident to be guilty of manslaughter on the basis of unreasonable force; and that it was 'unreal' to think that a jury would find individual officers to be grossly negligent in acting in accordance with current police methods. He also considered the 'neglect' verdict inappropriate in the circumstances of the case (see below).

RACISM AND DEATHS IN POLICE CUSTODY

One of the disturbing questions raised by these cases is: would any of the three men have died had their ethnic background been different? The case in which police racism was most blatant was that of Richard O'Brien, who was not black but Irish. Immediately before his arrest an officer told him to 'Fuck off back to Fishguard' (similar remarks were directed to other Irish people present). When his son asked the police if he was all right as he wasn't moving, the police response sounded to him like 'It's all right, he's a Paddy'. An officer was heard to complain, 'We can't get the big, fat Paddy into the van'.

In Shiji Lapite's case the allegations made by the police about his alleged violence echoed similar allegations made in police evidence at the inquests on Oliver Pryce ('unlawfully killed' by a police neckhold in 1990) and Joy Gardner (asphyxiated by being gagged with adhesive tape in 1993) ascribing to black people stereotypical characteristics of extraordinary strength and dangerousness (Two police officers were acquitted of manslaughter in Joy Gardner's case but no criminal or disciplinary charges were brought over the death of Mr Pryce).

The anger of many black people at Wayne Douglas's death, which lead to public disorder in the streets of Brixton, reflected a long-standing mistrust of the police which had been exacerbated by the death the previous May of another black man, Brian Douglas (no relation), who died from a fractured skull after being struck on the head with a long handled baton less than 300 yards from where Wayne was arrested.

Until recently there was no official breakdown of the ethnic origin of people who die in custody. INQUEST argued in 1990, and again in its 1996 report to the United Nations Committee on the Elimination Racial Discrimination (CERD), that while the proportion of black deaths is not particularly high considering the over-representation of black people among those arrested, there is an alarming preponderance of black people among those who die following violent incidents involving the police. Since 1990 those who have died as a result of police restraints or physical force (other than the use of guns) have been almost exclusively drawn from ethnic minority groups. This has been acknowledged by the PCA (1997:20) and by CERD whose report on the UK identified deaths in police custody as a cause for 'serious concern' (CERD, 1996, para. 14). Since April 1996 the police service has monitored the ethnic origin of those who die in custody. Of 48 people whose deaths in custody in 1996/7 were investigated under PCA supervision, six were African-Caribbean, one Arab, one Turkish and 39 white (PCA, 1997: 20).

THE INVESTIGATIVE PROCESS

Responsibility for investigating deaths in police custody rests primarily with the police themselves. The Police Complaints Authority (PCA) must supervise the investigation if a complaint is made. Where no complaint is made the usual practice is for the police to refer the matter voluntarily to the PCA under section 88 Police and Criminal Evidence Act 1984. The wording of section 88 limits such matters to grave or exceptional circumstances where a criminal or disciplinary offence may have been committed. In recent years, however, it has been the practice of the Metropolitan Police and many other forces to make a voluntary referral to the PCA in all cases of death in custody.

When a case is referred a member of the PCA supervises the police investigation, and must approve the appointment of the investigating officer who leads it. The PCA can require an outside force to be called in, but the only two recent cases where it has done so are those that of Ibrahima Sey, who died after being sprayed with CS gas in Ilford police station in 1996, and Shiji Lapite above. These cases have been investigated by Hertfordshire and City of London police respectively. The Brian Douglas, Wayne Douglas and Richard O'Brien cases were all dealt with by the Metropolitan Police's own Complaints Investigation Bureau.

At the end of the investigation, the PCA issues an interim certificate expressing satisfaction (or, in theory, dissatisfaction) with the police investigation. Subject to this certificate the chief officer of the force under investigation must decide whether there is evidence that a police officer may have committed a criminal offence with which he or she could be charged. If so the file on the investigation is sent to the DPP. This normally happens as a matter of routine. The DPP is required to apply a two-stage test in deciding whether to prosecute: is the evidence such 'that a jury . . . properly directed . . . is more likely than not to convict' (Code for Crown Prosecutors, 1994, para. 5.2); and would a prosecution be in the public interest? Decisions about the prosecution of police officers have until now been taken within a branch of the Prosecution Division of CPS Central Casework (which took over from the CPS Police Complaints Division in 1995) and reviewed in seemingly minimal fashion by more senior officials including, apparently, the DPP herself. The inconsistent evidence about the Director's role in the O'Brien case was one of the reasons why her case collapsed.

Following the Lapite and O'Brien debacles, judge Gerald Butler was appointed to inquire into the role of CPS Central Casework in the two cases and decisions on deaths in custody generally; and a meeting was held between the DPP and attorney-general after which it was announced that, pending the result of the inquiry, no prosecution decisions about deaths in custody would be made without advice from Treasury Counsel. Where the DPP and Treasury Counsel disagree, the attorney-general and solicitor-general will be consulted (CPS Statement, 28 July 1997).

If the CPS decides against prosecution, the chief officer of the force under investigation has to determine whether the officer may be charged with a disciplinary offence. The PCA has power to recommend, or require, that disciplinary charges be brought. An officer who has been acquitted of a criminal offence may not be charged with a disciplinary offence which is in substance the same, but this 'double jeopardy' rule does not apply where the CPS decides against criminal charges (section 104 Police and Criminal Evidence Act 1984; *R v. Chief Constable of Thames Valley Police ex p. PCA*, (1994)).

Until a decision is reached on prosecution, the coroner's inquest, having been formally opened a few days after the death, stands adjourned. Where charges are brought the inquest is not normally resumed, and cannot return a verdict inconsistent with the result of any trial. If there is no prosecution the coroner must hold a full inquest with a jury. The jury must not name any individual as being responsible for the death but can return a verdict of 'unlawful killing' if satisfied beyond reasonable doubt that murder or manslaughter has been committed. It must not return a verdict which appears to imply civil liability (such as 'death by negligence') but can in limited circumstances record that 'lack of care' or 'neglect' contributed to the death (see below). In the event of an 'unlawful killing' verdict the coroner refers the case back to the DPP to reconsider whether charges should be brought.

The High Court proceedings in the Lapite and O'Brien cases have highlighted the role played by the CPS and the DPP. In the Lapite case, after the DPP decided not to prosecute either of the arresting officers for manslaughter, the commander of the Complaints Investigation Bureau of the Metropolitan Police notified the relevant PCA member that he was not minded to bring any disciplinary charges against either of the officers. The PCA member was on the brink of recommending disciplinary charges but felt bound to offer the commander an opportunity to make representations on concerns that she had about the evidence. On the basis of the recommendations she then received from the commander and after consultation with her chairman and deputy she felt compelled to change her initial view and decided not to press disciplinary charges. On the eve of the hearing of the judicial review proceedings brought against the PCA by Mr Lapite's widow the PCA conceded that they could no longer justify their decision. The reason why the CPS decided not to press criminal charges was their claim that it would be impossible to refute the explanation for Mr Lapite's death put forward by the officers involved, namely that he had been accidentally strangled by his own clothing while struggling with them.

Lapite's case illustrates a general feature of the prosecution process, which is that decision-makers are heavily dependent on the way that a case is 'constructed' in the file compiled by investigating police officers (McConville et al 1991). If the police select and present information in a way which discourages prosecution it is easy to see how that then shapes the way in which the CPS and PCA are bound to approach their task. Similarly, the dependence of the PCA on police investigators means that even where, as appears often to be the case following deaths in custody, its members take a very active interest in the case, they probably exert little influence on the conduct of the investigation. Certainly that is the impression which emerges from the (admittedly somewhat dated) interviews conducted by Maguire and Corbett (1991:

145) with 19 senior police officers involved in investigating complaints:

> About a third felt that the main value was to reassure the public of the integrity of the investigation—some alluding to this as 'useful for P R purposes'—another third believed that supervision might be useful to them in a high profile case to divert media attention away from themselves . . . Another third could see no value at all in supervision, one referring to it, for example, as 'a complete and utter waste of time'.

None of those who had been supervised felt that this had made any difference to the result, nor—except in unimportant respects—to the lines of inquiry they had pursued.

The fact that the police are investigating themselves makes it very difficult for them to win the trust of the deceased person's family and the local community, especially where the death occurs against a background of mistrust of the police. In seeking to reassure the public and the media the police have two conflicting messages to communicate: that they are not responsible for the death, and that they are carrying out the investigation with an open mind. In the Wayne Douglas case the former message took precedence. The first post-mortem on Mr Douglas was carried out before his family knew he was dead. The police put out the information that he had died of a heart attack long before they had the pathologist's final report, which took nine months to be disclosed. In their anxiety to pacify the local community, the police put pressure on the Douglas family to issue a statement saying that the second post-mortem also indicated a heart attack: a statement which, as medical evidence subsequently provided for the family showed, would have been both premature and inaccurate.

The PCA also plays an important role in communicating with the press and the deceased person's family; its ability to deflect media attention from the police themselves appears to be one of the main benefits for the police of referring cases to the PCA (Maguire and Corbett 1991: 121). Again, the same dilemma arises: offering reassurance about the death undermines confidence in the integrity of the investigation. This was vividly illustrated in our workshop at the ISTD conference by Mrs Downes, who described the efforts the PCA member supervising the investigation into her son's death made in trying to persuade her that her son had committed suicide. This was hardly calculated to assure her that the PCA member had an open mind about the cause of death.

One effect of public mistrust of the police investigation, which was evident in both the Douglas and O'Brien cases, is a reluctance of witnesses to come forward. One witness in the Wayne Douglas case chose to make a statement anonymously to a solicitor (*The Guardian*, 16 December 1995). In this case, the deputy chair of the PCA, John Cartwright, issued a statement that he would 'personally guarantee that everything possible will be done to ensure that the investigation is thorough and fair'. (Press Release, 5 December 1995). His personal assurance may have counted for less than the fact the investigation was carried out by the Metropolitan Police.

The case of Richard O'Brien gives a particularly disturbing insight into the role of the DPP, such that Paddy O'Connor QC was compelled to remark during the High Court hearing that decisions were based on unfounded and offensive speculation, which ignored the blood and hair found on the pavement where Mr O'Brien was arrested and exemplified the 'manifest efforts of the decision-maker to avoid the obvious implications of the evidence.' Because the content of the police investigator's report was not revealed in court it is not clear how far this shaped the attitude of the principal Crown prosecutor who reviewed the case. What is clear is that he consistently preferred the evidence of police officers to that of other witnesses and to that of Mr O'Brien's wife and son, whose evidence he sought to discredit with a theory that the injuries might have been caused accidentally in the van during a scuffle between Mr O'Brien's young son and one of the officers.[1]

THE CORONER'S INQUEST

The three cases which we focus on in this chapter may appear to show the inquest procedure in a relatively favourable light. In the Lapite and O'Brien cases it was the inquests which brought out the evidence which suggested that officers might have been guilty of manslaughter, and which in each case persuaded the jury to return a verdict of unlawful killing. At the end of the O'Brien inquest the family's lawyer told the coroner on their behalf that they would never forget the contribution he had made to securing justice in their case. The same (now retired) coroner, Sir Montague Levine, conducted the Wayne Douglas inquest, and although his summing-up has been challenged in the High Court for failing to explain clearly to the jury a complex aspect of the law of manslaughter, it is not disputed that the proceedings were generally fair. Nevertheless, these cases do reveal significant defects in the inquest system.

The coroner is in a similar position to the PCA and CPS in the sense that his (or, rarely, her) investigation is dependent on that carried out by the police. The file compiled during the police investigation, having formed the basis of the decision not to prosecute any officer, is passed to the coroner and provides a basis for the selection and questioning of witnesses at the inquest. The inquest, however, provides a forum in which the case constructed by the police investigation can be challenged both by the family of the deceased and by any officers who may be subject to criticism. The jury introduces an important element of independence and public participation into the proceedings, which is particularly vital in cases involving the possibility of unreasonable force or gross negligence, the limits of which are matters of moral judgment which a jury is pre-eminently qualified to decide.

The inquest is an uneasy hybrid of inquisitorial and adversarial procedures (see Scraton and Chadwick 1987). It is not a dispute between parties but an inquiry into facts, and to that extent it is and must be an essentially inquisitorial process, in which the coroner plays an active fact-finding role rather than acting as an umpire between parties to a dispute. But in those cases where the inquest works at all effectively to investigate complex and contentious events it relies heavily on the key truth-finding mechanism of the adversarial system, the questioning of witnesses on behalf of those with the strongest interest in challenging what they say. It is very rare indeed for a coroner, in the absence of legal representation, to conduct the kind of searching questioning that occurs when interested parties are represented

Lawyers appearing on behalf of the deceased person's family therefore make a vital contribution to discovering the truth. But there are a number of obstacles in the way of effective legal representation. For a start, not everyone has a family; in some cases there is no-one who qualifies as a 'properly interested person' under the Coroners' Rules. Then there is no legal aid (provision for it was made in the Legal Aid Act 1949 but never brought into force; it was repealed in 1988). Even where lawyers can be found to represent the family for free or for a reduced fee, it may be necessary to pay an independent pathologist or other expert, who may make a vital contribution as the Wayne Douglas case illustrates. The financial burden placed on the family appears all the more unfair when they are confronted at the inquest by lawyers representing the police force, paid for out of public funds, and additional lawyers for individual officers paid for by the Police Federation.

Another frequent cause of complaint is unequal access to documents. The witness statements taken in the course of the police investigation remain the property of the investigating police force, and the coroner has no power to disclose them without the consent of the police (*R v. Hammersmith Coroner, ex p. Peach* (1980)). Without access to the witness statements, the representatives of the deceased's family have no way of knowing whether all witnesses have been called. The importance of this was illustrated by the O'Brien case where, very unusually, the Complaints Investigation Bureau acceded to the coroner's request to allow the family's solicitor to see the statements. She found crucially important forensic reports on the blood and hair found at the scene which the coroner, by an oversight, had omitted from the evidence to be called at the inquest.

In the case of Brian Douglas, the Metropolitan Police Commissioner was asked to consent to disclosure statements taken by the investigating officers, but refused on the grounds that 'It is essential if [criminal and disciplinary] investigations of this sort are to be conducted effectively that witnesses should be able to give evidence to investigating officers on the basis that the information they provide will be treated with the utmost confidentiality'; and that disclosure was unnecessary to enable the inquest to fulfil its 'very limited statutory objective' (letter to Deborah Coles, 17 July 1996). The first argument is absurd. Police officers interviewing witnesses to a possible crime are never in a position to guarantee confidentiality; and even if disclosure at the inquest is limited to the coroner, the result may be that the content of the witness's statement are revealed in open court through the coroner's questioning. Any notion of confidentiality is further undermined by the House of Lords' ruling (*R v. Chief Constable of the West Midlands Police, ex p. Wiley* [1994] 3 WLR 433) that the statements taken during the investigation of a complaint (though not the investigating officer's report: see *Taylor v. Anderton*, [1995 2 All ER 420] may be disclosed in a civil action against the police. As for the 'very limited statutory objective' of the inquest, the Court of Appeal has stressed that the narrowness of the objective should not detract from:

> the duty of the coroner . . . to ensure that the relevant facts are fully, frankly and fearlessly investigated. He is bound to recognise the acute public concern rightly aroused where deaths in custody. He must ensure that the relevant facts are exposed to public scrutiny, particularly if there is evidence of foul play, abuse or inhumanity. (*R v. Humberside Coroner, ex p. Jamieson* [1994] 3 WLR 82: 101)

Disclosure of the statements to the family's lawyers would help to ensure (and to assure the public) that all the relevant facts are so exposed.

In its Annual Report for 1995/6, the PCA expressed concern at the unfairness of the statements and documents taken by the investigating officers being used at the inquest by lawyers representing the police but denied to those representing the family. But by indicating that they were taking the matter up with the Coroners' Society, the PCA appeared to be confused as to where the responsibility lay for this state of affairs. In its 1996/7 report, however, the PCA correctly treats the matter as one of police discretion:

> . . . it cannot be denied that the family of the deceased have a legitimate interest in discovering how he or she died. They are placed at a severe disadvantage by their lack of documents . . . there is nothing to prevent [the police] from simply agreeing to the disclosure of their documents. If this consent is not forthcoming, it would appear that the issue can only be resolved by a change in the law. In the meantime, the Authority remains concerned that all those at an inquest should be seen to have been treated fairly and equally. We shall continue to pursue the matter.

The PCA has indeed continued to pursue the matter, but despite its representations the Metropolitan Police has refused to alter its policy of refusing disclosure in relation to the forthcoming inquest on Mr Ahmed El-Gamal, who died in Leyton police station on 13 August 1996 after being restrained by police.

Interested parties and their legal representatives have no right to call witnesses at an inquest: they can only bring potential witnesses to the attention of the coroner who decides whether or not to call them. The initial questioning of each witness is conducted by the coroner, who often leads the witness through the statement taken during the police investigation. Here again access to the witness statements is crucial. If the police lawyers have the witness statements they can cross-examine anyone whose testimony is unfavourable to the police on any discrepancy between their evidence in court and their previous statement. The family's lawyers have no such opportunity. The scope of questioning which is permitted is ill-defined and largely dependent on the coroner's discretion.

At the end of the inquest the coroner has to decide what verdicts the jury may consider. These should be limited to the verdicts which a reasonable jury could reach. At this stage the coroner sometimes invites the legal representatives present to make submissions as to the law. During the High Court hearing in the Wayne Douglas case, Mr Justice Laws expressed the view that this should always be done. The coroner's decision at this stage may be a very difficult one, as in the Douglas case where counsel for the police argued in the High Court that he ought not to have left unlawful killing to the jury, and counsel for the family argued that he wrongly omitted to leave neglect.

The Coroners' Rules prohibit anyone from addressing the coroner or jury as to the facts. Thus, in contrast to a trial where the jury hears the competing interpretations of the evidence put forward by the prosecution and defence, an inquest jury hears only the coroner's interpretation. Some coroners' summings-up are much more even-handed than others.

When it comes to the verdict the jury is subject to a restriction we have already mentioned: it must not 'appear to determine any question of criminal responsibility by a named person, or civil liability' (Coroners' Rules 1984, r. 42). In cases of alleged police negligence this puts the jury in a very difficult position. They can return a verdict of unlawful killing if they decide the negligence involved was 'so gross . . . as to amount to a crime' (*R v. Adomako*, [1995] 1 AC 171:187). The jury can also find that neglect contributed to the death, but the Court of Appeal has defined 'neglect' in this context as limited to 'gross failure to provide adequate nourishment or liquid . . . basic medical attention or shelter or warmth for someone in a dependent position' (*R v. Humberside Coroner*, above). This definition is so restrictive that Mr Justice Laws remarked that it would be difficult to envisage conduct in a case like Wayne Douglas' that would amount to 'neglect' but not to manslaughter by gross negligence. Unless they find either of these very high degrees of negligence proved the jury can only do what they did in the Douglas case and bring in a verdict of accidental death. It must often be the case that none of these verdicts adequately reflects the jury's view of what happened. The jury cannot, as it once could, add riders to its verdict recommending steps to avoid future deaths. The coroner can, however, make such recommendations and announce them in open court; sometimes, as in the Douglas case, these amount to implied criticisms of the police. The only way the jury can hint at its views is through a carefully-worded statement of the circumstances of the death, as in the Douglas case where it found that death was due to 'stress and exhaustion and positional asphyxia . . . following a chase and a series of restraints in the prone position face down as used in current police methods'.

In the rare cases where an unlawful killing verdict is recorded, the jury must be satisfied beyond reasonable doubt that someone is guilty of an offence of homicide. In applying the law of manslaughter in a case like O'Brien or Lapite, the jury is bound to consider the culpability and mental state of particular individuals, even though it cannot name them. It is this which makes it hard to understand how a Crown prosecutor can decide that there is no reasonable prospect of conviction where a jury has found murder or manslaughter proved to such a high standard. At the very least, such a verdict gives a strong indication of the view a jury is likely to take of the testimony of the various witnesses, but one which the Crown prosecutor in the O'Brien and Lapite cases chose to ignore

117

CONCLUSION

There are two lessons to be drawn from the recent High Court cases. One is that those affected by police misconduct have good reason to be sceptical of the investigation of state officials by other state officials. The other is that the court system can sometimes provide a measure of accountability, but at great personal cost to those who have to fight for it. As Richard O'Brien's widow Alison describes it, 'I go home and live normal life for a while and then there are hearings—like this High Court case—and I have to relive the whole thing over again' (quoted by Mills 1997). But, she says, 'I will not stop fighting until those responsible for my husband's death are made accountable for their actions. I will fight and fight, not only for ourselves but for other people' (INQUEST Press Release).

One approach to improving the investigation of suspicious deaths in police custody is to build on the element of openness and adversarial procedure which is already present in the coroner's inquest system. The changes that are needed are implicit in our criticism of the inquest system: legal aid; disclosure of witness statements; the right of interested parties to call witnesses and address the jury on the facts; a broader range of verdicts. But the burden of ensuring a thorough investigation of deaths in custody cannot be placed solely on families: it is also necessary to strengthen the official mechanisms. Referral of deaths in custody to the PCA should be mandatory, and the PCA should be able (like the new Criminal Cases Review Commission, which in other respects is modelled on the PCA) to call on its own independent investigators rather than relying on the police to investigate themselves. The Lapite and O'Brien cases point to a need for internal reorganization in the Crown Prosecution Service and greater objectivity and distance from the police to ensure the thorough scrutiny of major cases. The appointment in major inquests of a 'counsel to the coroner' to question witnesses on behalf of the court could improve the quality of the inquest even where there is no family represented.

Even if the inquest is reformed, the most serious cases will raise questions which go beyond its narrow remit and require some form of public inquiry. As in the case of disaster inquiries which have recently been considered by the Home Office (1997), there needs to be some mechanism to avoid unnecessary duplication between inquests and public inquiries. There also needs to be a mechanism to monitor the implementation of recommendations made by inquests and inquiries, such as those concerning police restraints and training which Sir Montague Levine made after the O'Brien and Wayne Douglas inquests. This suggests that some form of standing commission, rather than a series of *ad hoc* inquiries, is called for.

We write at a time when a series of tragic events has placed these issues probably higher on the political agenda than they have ever been. The Lapite and O'Brien cases have called into question decision-making of the CPS and the PCA at the culmination of the police complaints process. The home secretary's acceptance of the need for an inquiry in the Stephen Lawrence case raises further issues about the CPS and about the relationship between the black community and the police. The re-opening of the Hillsborough inquiry (and the possibility of a further inquiry into the Marchioness disaster) has revived the concerns raised by those cases about inquests, public inquiries and the relationship between them. If the ISTD conference is anything to go by, there is recognition in some sections of the police service and the PCA of the need for change but that recognition does not appear to be shared by many within the Police Federation and Association of Chief Police Officers (ACPO) alike. When such a catalogue of terrible events creates such an opportunity for reform, it would be tragic indeed if the opportunity were missed.

Tony Ward is a senior lecturer in law at de Montfort University, Leicester. He is a barrister and from 1982 to 1990 was Co-director of INQUEST. With Alison Liebling, he co-edited *Deaths in Custody: International Perspectives*, based on the proceedings of the ISTD's first conference on deaths in custody. His other publications include *Privatisation and the Penal System* (with Mick Ryan).

Deborah Coles has been Co-director of INQUEST since 1990. She previously worked in the field of penal reform and is on the management committees of Women in Prison and the Prisoners' Advice Service. She is co-author of *Failure Stories: Prison Suicides and How Not to Prevent Them* (with Tony Ward) and *Racial Discrimination and Deaths in Custody*, the INQUEST report to the United Nations Committee on the Elimination of Racial Discrimination (with Helen Shaw).

Acknowledgement
We are indebted to Raju Bhatt for his comments on a draft of this chapter. Any remaining errors are our responsibility.

ENDNOTE

---

[1] Further details of the O'Brien case and of concerns about prosecution decision-making in the proceedings can be obtained by contacting INQUEST.

CHAPTER 9

What Are The Lessons From Tragedies?

Nicholas Long

INTRODUCTION

This presentation is concerned with examining whether any lessons have been learned from the tragedies of deaths in police custody, in particular those of Brian Douglas, who died on 8 May 1995 and Wayne Douglas (no relation) on 5 December 1995. Both deaths occurred following arrests in the south London borough of Lambeth, where I am chairperson of the Community-Police Consultative Group.

Following Wayne's death, the group's response was to establish a working group to examine the circumstances of the deaths and what might be done both to throw more light on what happens after a death in custody occurs and to make proposals for improvements.

I aim to review progress since the publication ten months ago, in September 1996, of the report 'Lessons From Tragedies'. I chaired the Deaths in Custody Working Group which produced the report and, in my capacity as chairperson of the Community-Police Consultative Group, I have been closely involved with many aspects of the aftermath of the deaths of Brian Douglas and Wayne Douglas and, more recently Oscar Okoye, who died in November 1996.

LESSONS FROM TRAGEDIES

This report was commissioned in January 1996 by the Community-Police Consultative Group for Lambeth (CPCG) with the aim of seeking greater understanding of the processes which occur when someone dies in custody and how the death is investigated. It was directly prompted by the deaths during 1995, while in police custody, of Brian Douglas and Wayne Douglas. It became apparent to the CPCG that little had been published and not much was available to the public about the topic of deaths in police custody. In the course of its reporting, the working group made recommendations for improvements to the present arrangements.

A further important aim was the urgent need to review the question of the circumstances in which a police officer might be suspended following a death in custody. The working group considered this issue in some detail, and the report made recommendations as to how this might be achieved.

The terms of reference of the working group were:

- to review existing procedures for the investigation of deaths in police custody, taking into account the views of the community and the current statutory framework
- to make the procedures better known and understood in the community
- to consider the matter of the suspension of police officers following a death in custody.

Although the group was looking at the circumstances of the deaths in custody of Brian Douglas and Wayne Douglas it could not be concerned directly with those investigations. It was agreed that the working group would report by 31 May 1996. The members of the Working Group were:

Mike Franklin (chairperson of the CPCG Racial Harassment Panel)
Lloyd Leon (CPCG vice-chairperson)
Nicholas Long (CPCG chairperson)
Paul Manning (assistant commissioner, Metropolitan Police)
Dr Uvanney Maylor (CPCG member)
Peter Moorhouse (acting chairman, Police Complaints Authority).

The report was presented to the CPCG on 2 June 1996 but publication was delayed until after the conclusion of the inquest into the circumstances of the death of Brian Douglas. It is 54 pages long and comprises six chapters and four appendices. It contains data relating to the 213 deaths in police custody *or otherwise*, as recorded in the Commissioner's Annual Reports for the ten years 1986-1995. The report concluded with 22 recommendations. I do not intend to review the report in any detail but will examine two aspects closely:

- what progress with the 22 recommendations has been made following publication
- the subsequent availability of data indicating the ethnic origin of people who have died in police custody between 1 January 1990 and 31 December 1996.

The 'Lambeth Index'
Appended to 'Lessons From Tragedies' was a schedule of the 213 deaths in police custody or otherwise that had been recorded in the

Metropolitan Police Commissioner's Annual Reports between 1 January 1986 and 31 December 1995. Great care has to be taken with the data as many of the deaths recorded in those appendices refer to cases where police officers were involved, often in differing circumstances, at the time of the death of a member of the public not in police custody. Examples include attendance at the scene of a collapse in the street by someone who subsequently dies, conveyance to hospital in a police vehicle of a person who dies in transit or shortly thereafter, and people who attend at a police station—not in custody—and die while they are there at the police station.

The CPCG will in future publish annually a list of all recorded deaths in police custody or otherwise (as in the Commissioner's Annual Report.) These will be in numerical sequence from 1 January 1986. The sequence will be called the 'Lambeth Index' and is intended as a reference guide for research purposes.

A supplement to the schedule in 'Lessons From Tragedies', with deaths recorded for 1996, is appended to this report. There are 20 deaths recorded, numbered 214-233, of which 16 are considered to be 'Deaths while in custody'. The four not considered as deaths while in custody are:

- 214 the deceased was the victim of a robbery who collapsed while being taken by police to look for a suspect. He was taken to hospital by ambulance where he was pronounced dead
- 225 the deceased was seen brandishing a kitchen knife and was pursued by police. Before police were able to reach her, she stabbed herself twice. She was not under arrest. She was taken to hospital where she died a short while later
- 228 while in his garden the deceased saw four youths tampering with his car. Police were called and found four suspects. The deceased agreed to go with police to identify the suspected persons and collapsed while in a police vehicle. He was taken to hospital by ambulance where he was pronounced dead
- 231 police were called to assist a man who had collapsed in the street. While speaking to him he became unwell; police attempted to resuscitate him. He was taken to hospital by ambulance where he was pronounced dead.

DEATHS WHILE IN CUSTODY (1990-1996)

In order to assess whether there are trends in the pattern of deaths while in police custody, I have reviewed the available data for the period 1 January 1990 to 31 December 1996. I would stress that this is not, and cannot be, a full research project and the results should be treated as indicative only. I would welcome the establishment of a funded research project to examine deaths in police custody nationally. The significance of the period is simply that for which details of ethnic origin data is available.

During that period I believe there were 83 (out of 111 recorded) deaths that qualify for consideration as deaths while in police custody. There were three further deaths (one each in 1990, 1991 and 1992) of people while in police custody at magistrates' courts but this is no longer a police function and for the purposes of year-on-year comparison I have excluded them.

Of the 83 highlighted deaths, 79 were men and four were women. There are no readily discernible patterns based on an analysis of the ages (where known) of the deceased. The breakdown by year is as follows:

		1990	1991	1992	1993	1994	1995	1996	Total
Male	White	7	8	8	9	6	7	10	55
	Black	-	2	1	1	3	2	5	14
	Asian	1	2	1	1	2	-	-	7
	Unknown	3	-	-	-	-	-	-	3
Total Male									79
Female	White	1	1	-	-	-	-	1	3
	Black	-	-	-	1	-	-	-	1
	Asian	-	-	-	-	-	-	-	-
	Unknown	-	-	-	-	-	-	-	-
Total Female									4
TOTAL									83

Deaths in Police Custody 1990-1996 by Sex

My analysis—see *Appendix* (*Tables 1 to 4*)—shows a significant increase in the number of deaths in 1996 (16) by comparison with the earlier years (between nine and 13, an average of eleven a year). There are no discernible reasons for the increase.

The largest single cause of deaths in custody, i.e. 22 (or 26.5 per cent) is found (by coroners' courts) to be accidental death. Natural causes and misadventure each claim 16 (or 19.3 per cent). There were three suicide and two unlawful killing verdicts.

These verdicts appear consistent with my attempt to place each death in a category. By far the greatest number of deaths are alcohol related, following arrests for being drunk and disorderly or drunk and incapable. Of the 83 deaths, no fewer than 50 (or 60 per cent) were attributable to being alcohol related, an alarming proportion.

Twenty-one deaths followed arrest in other circumstances. The circumstances were varied and defied improved categorisation without much more detail about each case. These cases require much more research in order to establish linkages or patterns.

A particularly worrying concern were the seven deaths in respect of people taken into police custody on account of mental health or place of safety considerations. They can be identified as 'Lambeth Index' numbers 119, 131, 160, 168, 190, 197 and 201. The victims were six men and one woman. Three of those deaths are black, three white and one Asian.

The ethnic origin data reflects a marked change during 1996 over previous years. As percentages over the seven year period, the figures are:

White	70.0 per cent
Black	18.0
Asian	8.5
Unknown	3.5
	100.0 per cent

Deaths in police Custody by ethnic origin

However, during 1996 the proportion of black deaths rose in 1996 to just over 31 per cent. More research is needed to establish whether a correlation exists between the drop in alcohol related deaths during that year and the rise in 'other circumstances' deaths.

Recommendations

'Lessons From Tragedies' concluded with 22 recommendations. The Deputy Commissioner provided the Metropolitan Police's formal response on the day of the launch of the report, 2 September 1996. Those responses appear as *MPS Response* in the summary below. The CPCG debated the responses at its meeting on 1 October 1996 and the consensus view of the CPCG appears as *CPCG Reply*. A meeting followed on 10 December 1996 between CPCG representatives and the deputy commissioner and other senior officers. The agreement at that meeting is recorded as *10 Dec Minute*.

The then home secretary, Michael Howard, was provided with a copy of the report on 4 September 1996. He did not acknowledge or respond to the report or the recommendations. However, Sir John Quinton, chairman of the Metropolitan Police Committee (MPC) did respond, acknowledging receipt and stating that the MPC would wish to consider the report and that he would write further at that time. No further communication on the subject of 'Lessons From Tragedies' has been received from the MPC.

The present home secretary, Jack Straw, received a copy of the report while in Opposition and a further copy was sent to him on 5 May 1997. At the same time his attention was drawn particularly to recommendations 11, 14, 20 and 21. The matter was discussed briefly at a meeting between Kate Hoey MP, the home secretary and Nicholas Long on 27 June 1997. The home secretary indicated that the matters would be considered.

Recommendations 1, 2, 5, 12, 15, 18, 19 and 22 are considered to have been satisfactorily met and no further action is proposed. The actions of the MPS in response to recommendations 6, 7, 8, 9, 10 and 17 will continue to be monitored. Recommendations 3, 4, 11, 13, 14, 16, 20 and 21 require further action to be taken. The recommendations and the various responses were:

Recommendation 1

Ethnic Origin of Recorded Deaths in Police Custody 1986-1995: . . . that the Metropolitan Police Service publish as soon as possible a full breakdown of ethnic origin of all recorded deaths in police custody 1986-1995, when the information becomes available.

MPS Response: We are publishing the ethnic origins of all recorded deaths in custody for the last six years (1990-1996). Such detailed information has not been recorded for the previous four years and as such would be difficult to obtain. However, we feel that the figures from the last six years will give a clear enough indication of the situation.

10 Dec Minute: The deputy commissioner confirmed the ethnic origin or recorded deaths in custody for 1995/6 had been included in the commissioner's Annual Report. Commander Quinn undertook to provide figures for 1990-95.

Comment: The data has been provided and has been incorporated as *Table 4* of the *Appendix* to this paper.

Recommendation 2

Criteria for Metropolitan Police Service Statistical Recording: . . . that the commissioner publish the criteria used in the compilation of the Appendix

'Deaths in police custody or otherwise' in his Annual Report and note amendments when they occur.

MPS Response: This recommendation has been accepted. The latest commissioner's Annual Report included the Home Office definition of deaths in custody.

Recommendation 3

Persons Arrested for Being Drunk and Disorderly (i): . . . that members of the Lambeth Community-Police Consultative Group jointly with the Panel of Lay Visitors for Lambeth establish a separate, more detailed, study of alternatives to police custody for persons arrested for being drunk and disorderly.

MPS Response: This recommendation is a matter for members of the Lambeth Community-Police Consultative Group and Lay Visitors of Lambeth. However, should they decide to embark on this further research assistant commissioner Dunn, who has responsibility for criminal justice will be a point of contact for them.

10 Dec Minute: Mr Long reported that he had discussed with representatives of Ealing and Southwark PCCGs the possibility of their follow up to this recommendation.

Comment: Discussions with the Ealing and Southwark PCCGs have been inconclusive. A partner PCCG is required to assist with the preparation of a study.

Recommendation 4

Persons Arrested for Being Drunk and Disorderly (ii): . . . that under no circumstances should a person arrested for being drunk and disorderly or drunk and incapable be placed in a cell with another detained person.

MPS Response: We already have a policy which is that wherever possible people arrested for drunk and disorderly behaviour should be kept in separate cells, although the number of prisoners and lack of cell space has occasionally caused us difficulties. This problem highlights the social care role of the police but also highlights that the police are not necessarily always the most appropriate agencies to deal with the problem of people who may do — or have done — damage to themselves or others as a result of taking drink or drugs.

CPCG Reply: The Group noted that the recommendation was prefaced with the statement 'Under no circumstances . . .'. It felt the response was unsatisfactory because it failed to address the issue. The lack of cell accommodation and the occasional need to 'double up' is not the issue; the response sought by the Group is prohibition of the practice.

10 Dec Minute: The deputy commissioner pointed out the advantages of having another (sober) detainee in a cell with an intoxicated person, particularly the ability to summon urgent assistance if difficulties arose. Assistant commissioner Dunn said he felt that caring for intoxicated people should not be a police function, but be dealt with by a detoxification unit. The CPCG members endorsed this view and would continue their drive locally in Lambeth for detoxification units to be opened. The Lambeth CPCG wished to see a more co-ordinated multi-agency approach to the problems of persons arrested for being drunk and disorderly as part of the proposed Clapham Criminal Justice Facility.

Comment: A Criminal Justice Facility (CJF) is proposed for Grafton Square at Clapham. If built, it would consolidate the existing custody facilities at Brixton, Streatham and Vauxhall Divisions into a single borough facility. At the CPCG meeting on 8 April 1997, the group agreed to participate in a 'Concept Group' aimed at bringing together representatives of agencies concerned with people in custody in order that detailed proposals might be discussed prior to the scheme being tendered for contract. Alcoholism is a concern falling within the remit of the Drugs Action Team, and the CPCG is anxious to see a new initiative started in Lambeth (in conjunction with the creation of the CJF) diverting people regularly arrested for alcohol-related offences into a specialist unit.

Recommendation 5

Suicides in Custody: . . . that the Metropolitan Police Service note the steps recently taken by HM Prison Service to reduce the number of suicides in prison and adopt appropriate practices.

MPS Response: We accept this recommendation and will examine the steps the Prison Service have taken to prevent suicides in cells. Where appropriate we will adopt these measures. As a matter of course, however, we already take away any items which we think could be used by prisoners to harm themselves. However, we do have to take into account the fact that prisoners have certain rights to retain some belongings. It is a delicate balance.

Recommendation 6

CCTV in Custody Areas: . . . that all Metropolitan Police Service designated custody centres be equipped with CCTV and that it cover the charge room, cell passage(s), van bay, fingerprint room and interview room(s). We do not recommend installation (in the initial phase) of cameras in every cell or in the Forensic Medical Examiner's room until more research has been undertaken and the civil rights considerations fully explored.

MPS Response: (including response to recommendation 8 below). In principle we agree with these recommendations. However, the cost means that we need to look very carefully at the implications on our resources. There is already a pilot scheme in Islington which members of the working group went to see. There are now plans to extend this pilot to Brixton, in September. The commissioner is on record as saying he fully accepts the concept of CCTV in police stations and—subject to resources being available—we fully intend to implement this as far as possible. Having CCTV in police stations and in certain police vehicles is in the interests of both police and the public. The public may feel more reassured and the police can carry out their duties knowing that false allegations on their part will be avoided.

CPCG Reply: The Group was aided by superintendent O'Brien's helpful account of progress on the installation of CCTV at Brixton. It was noted that the installation will not be as extensive as envisaged in the recommendation.

The Group was anxious that Vauxhall and Streatham police station custody areas (in that order of priority) be equipped with CCTV as soon as practicable.

10 Dec Minute: Members of the CPCG were informed that the MPS aimed to install CCTV across the Metropolitan district. The cost of £60,000 per police station for installing the system would affect timescales. Islington had been piloting CCTV in the custody area for a long time with substantial success. Assistant commissioner Manning confirmed that a system had now been installed in Brixton and would go live early in the New Year. Brixton was also to fit a video system to their van for transporting prisoners. It would go live imminently and be used as a pilot for other stations. Assistant commissioner Manning confirmed that video would be installed in Vauxhall and Streatham police stations in the New Year.

Comment: The CCTV installations in the custody areas of Brixton, Streatham and Vauxhall police stations are now in operation. The extension of CCTV to custody areas in other police stations in the MPS area will occur as funding permits (the CPCG has been informed).

Recommendation 7

CCTV in Custody Areas and Lay Visitors: . . . that lay visitors be given the right to request and review any videotape not required for evidential purposes, for viewing at a police station.

MPS Response: In principle we have no objections to lay visitors viewing any videotape that is not required for evidential purposes. However, this would also have to be approved by any prisoners who have been recorded.

CPCG Reply: This response was considered to be unnecesarily obstructive. The envisaged right of lay visitors would, subject to further discussion, be limited to the period during which a detained person seen by the visitors had been in custody. It was not considered to be a general right to view and, in all probability, would only be exercised in instances where concern arose in respect of alleged ill-treatment or omission. The response was judged to have the effect of making such a right unworkable (as it was felt that obtaining the consent of all prisoners, some perhaps after release from custody, would be too time-consuming).

It was suggested that the difficulty could be overcome by inclusion of a statement relating to the presence of CCTV on the custody record with an action required if the detainee did *not* wish the videotape to be viewed by lay visitors.

10 Dec Minute: Assistant commissioner Manning endorsed the recommendation to include a section on the custody record for the arrested person to sign. It would give their approval for lay visitors to view any videotape not required for evidential purposes. He recommended that Brixton be used as a pilot site.

Comment: This issue remains unresolved. It is more for the Panel of Lay Visitors to take forward and negotiate with police on practice. The Group will assist with issues of policy.

Recommendation 8

CCTV in Custody Areas (individual cells): . . . that one designated and clearly marked cell in each custody area be equipped with CCTV for occupation by detained persons believed to be at risk.

MPS Response: (see response to *Recommendation 6* above)

CPCG Reply: The Group was informed that no cell at Brixton was being equipped with CCTV. The Group wished to keep this under review.

10 Dec Minute: see note at *Recommendation 6.*

Comment: Many members of the CPCG felt that each cell should be equipped with a camera, regardless of civil liberties considerations.

Recommendation 9

CCTV in Police Vehicles: . . . that CCTV be fitted in all police vehicles used primarily for the conveyance of detained persons.

MPS Response: We accept this recommendation in principle and are supportive of it not just because it will give reassurance to members of the public. It would also prevent potential false allegations of misconduct. The MPS are already considering a pilot scheme of CCTV in police vehicles in Brixton, subject to resources being available.

10 Dec Minute: see note at *Recommendation 6.*

Comment: The van used by officers of Brixton Division for the transport of detained people was experimentally fitted with a CCTV camera and microphone in February 1997. The experiment continues.

Recommendation 10

Stereotyping of Behaviour: . . . that Metropolitan Police Service training policies be reviewed, and amended where necessary, to ensure that police officers avoid stereotyping behaviour and be made fully aware of the more common conditions likely to give rise to erratic behaviour, and how to deal with it.

MPS Response: We accept this recommendation although a great deal of training is already in existence, which includes raising awareness of certain medical conditions. We now intend to look at the training provided again and shall include this aspect in it.

CPCG Reply: There was a wish expressed to keep the issue of training under review. Members felt strongly about this issue and would welcome more information of actions taken.

10 Dec Minute: Members of the CPCG were informed that the MPS director of personnel was examining this issue. Mr Franklin raised concerns about pressures on OCU commanders under Total Resource Budgets and whether training might suffer.

Recommendation 11

Extension of Jurisdiction of Police Complaints Authority: . . . that the secretary of state be requested to review the jurisdiction of the PCA in cases of deaths in custody to include special constables, civilian gaolers and civilians employed in the escort and transport of detained persons between police stations and magistrates' courts.

MPS Response: This is not a matter for the MPS.

CPCG Reply: Disappointment was expressed at the response because it failed to indicate whether the MPS would favour the extension of the PCA's jurisdiction, particularly to include special constables. A fuller response was called for.

10 Dec Minute: The deputy commissioner confirmed that the MPS would support any debate on the extension of jurisdiction of the Police Complaints Authority, to include Special Constabulary and possibly civil staff. Commander Quinn [commander of Complaints Investigation Bureau] undertook to bring this matter to the ACPO sub-committee for debate.

Recommendation 12

Appointment of a Liaison Officer: . . . that an officer of at least the rank of inspector should be appointed immediately to act as liaison officer with the family of the deceased person.

MPS Response: It is good policing practice to do this and it already takes place. We agree that it is important to establish a point of liaison between the police and the families of people who have died in police custody. However, we believe it is more important that the person doing the work is properly trained and possesses the right qualities and skills rather than being an officer of a particular rank.

CPCG Response: While the spirit of the response was accepted members felt that, on balance, rank was more important in such circumstances than a police officer's individual qualities. The need was for a clear message to go to the family and those concerned that a death in custody was a matter of the highest importance.

10 Dec Minute: The deputy commissioner agreed for a divisional officer of at least the rank of inspector to act as local nominee for CIB to ensure appropriate family liaison.

Recommendation 13

Fact Sheet: . . . that the Metropolitan Police Service produce a fact sheet for the families of persons who die in custody with details of procedure, investigatory process and explanation of terms. The sheet should also explain the importance of appointing a solicitor immediately, the selection of an independent pathologist, and where other assistance and counselling might be obtained.

MPS Response: We fully support this recommendation and will produce a suitable fact sheet. It is essential that people receive accurate information when they find themselves in difficult situations. This applies equally to police officers whose involvement in such situations is very stressful. This is a point which was made in the report and we will endeavour to ensure that members of the public and police officers receive as much information as possible about the processes following a death in custody.

Comment: No draft of a fact sheet has been passed to the CPCG.

Recommendation 14

Disclosure of Investigation Evidence at Coroner's Court: . . . that encouragement be given to the Coroner's Society to provide advice to its members requiring the disclosure of evidence arising from investigation of the death to the family of the deceased.

MPS Response: This is not a matter for the MPS.

CPCG Reply: The response was considered unacceptable and gratuitous. The issue of disclosure is most certainly a matter for the MPS and the Group was mindful of the commissioner's decision at the recent inquest into the death of Brian Douglas.

The MPS is asked to reconsider its response.

10 Dec Minute: The deputy commissioner informed the CPCG that police officers giving evidence at coroner's court did not have access to the files. The deputy commissioner said the MPS followed legal advice that police were not obliged to disclose reports or documents to family or other parties. But police objections went deeper than this. The coroner's court was not a court of trial but was there to determine the cause of death. While the coroner was free to decide how much documentation to release, the danger of releasing too much information could turn it into a court of trial or could be detrimental to any future criminal or disciplinary proceedings.

The CPCG expressed concern over this, particularly that police did not disclose all information to the family. Mr Franklin remarked on the unfortunate and misleading phrasing used on behalf of the commissioner by counsel when before the coroner when declining requests for disclosure. The deputy commissioner agreed and said this would be reviewed. Mr Long informed them that a working group would be set up to look into the wider issues surrounding disclosure. The deputy commissioner endorsed the need for debate and would nominate a member of the solicitors' branch once the group had been established. He said any changes made would have to involve the Home Office and Lord Chancellor's Department. The MPS would willingly participate but this was a national issue.

Comment: The issue of disclosure remains a primary concern for the CPCG. Progress has been made toward the establishment of the working group and potential members invited to serve. Discussions continue about the Terms of Reference and resources.

Recommendation 15

Arrangements for Appeals for Witnesses: . . . that in all early contacts with the media following a death in custody in addition to investigating officers making direct appeals for witnesses to come forward, members of the public should, if in doubt, be encouraged to seek the advice of a solicitor or, in strictest confidence, speak to a leader of a relevant community organization, to a priest or religious leader, or to a person of similar position who would be able to assist.

MPS Response: We recognise the value in cases where a potential witness would otherwise choose not to come to the police, of that witness approaching a relevant third party to act as an intermediary. However, we would stress how vital it is for any intermediary to encourage the individual to accompany them to the police. In many cases we cannot solve crimes without witnesses.

Recommendation 16

The Role of Lay Visitors: . . . that a visit by lay visitors to the police station should take place at the earliest opportunity, in order to speak with other detainees and reassure them if the death occurred while they were also in custody. The lay visitors may, if necessary, issue a statement and seek to calm public concerns about other persons who might be in custody. Above all, a visit by independent people in the aftermath of a death is considered to be essential.

MPS Response: It is good policing practice to make lay visitors aware of situations when there has been a death in custody. However, it is a matter for the lay visitor in consultation with the other prisoners as to whether they take up an invitation to visit the police station on such an occasion.

CPCG Reply: Clarification of the response was requested. Prior to a visit a lay visitor is unable to consult with a detained person.

10 Dec Minute: The deputy commissioner agreed the MPS original response did not clarify its position and confirmed the recommendation on the role of lay visitors. The matter was being pursued by CO20 [Branch of the MPS].

Recommendation 17

Training for Consultative Group Members: . . . that the London Police Community Consultative Group Forum in conjunction with CO20 Branch of the MPS be invited to prepare a training pack for the assistance of CPCG members. Within the training pack it should be recognised that although death might occur while a person is in the care or custody of police in one division, the deceased might be from elsewhere and that the ensuing tension might be more deeply felt in the 'home' area.

MPS Response: The Metropolitan Police are open to this recommendation. If the London Police Community Consultative Group Forum choose to accept the invitation, assistant commissioner Skitt who has the portfolio responsibility for partnership, will be the point of contact.

10 Dec Minute: Mr Long confirmed that agreement had been reached at a previous exploratory discussion with assistant commissioner Skitt for the issue of a Good Practice Guide for PCCG members. The proposal had been agreed subsequently by the London Police Consultative Group Forum and a working group was to be formed in the new year with representatives from the five MPS Areas. The topics covered within the guide would include deaths in custody and community tension.

Comment: A Study Group comprising MPS officers and PCCG Chairs is currently working on a Good Practice Guide for PCCG members. At an appropriate moment the Lambeth CPCG is to be invited to assist with a number of matters, including deaths in custody.

Recommendation 18

Police Liaison with Campaign Groups: . . . that the Metropolitan Police Service encourage divisional commanders to develop relationships with campaign organizers and ensure they are kept informed of developments in the investigation. Divisional police should also be understanding of local feelings and ensure due tolerance in the policing of demonstrations, marches and vigils.

MPS Response: This is an aspect of good policing which is largely common practice across the MPS. In fact the example of officers from Vauxhall liaising with members of the Brian Douglas campaign was given in the report as being 'a model of potential good practice'.

CPCG Reply: The Group did not view this as a response but a comment. What is the MPS response?

10 Dec Minute: The deputy commissioner confirmed that it was MPS policy to liaise with campaign groups.

Recommendation 19

Improved Media Training: . . . that police officers be given training in communicating news of a sensitive nature, such as a death in custody, together with guidance on the preparation of a text, including advice on the need to address issues concerning the death within their broader context.

MPS Response: We take note of this recommendation. Some training is already given to police officers.

CPCG Reply: The Group was unsure of the MPS response. Does the MPS accept or reject the recommendation?

10 Dec Minute: The deputy commissioner accepted that there was a need for more media training and that facts should be released to the press as early as possible.

Recommendations 20 and 21

(20) 'Suspension' of Police Officer(s) from Duty: . . . that a senior officer be authorised to consider immediate removal of officer(s) from duty following a death in custody. However, unless warranted, rather than this being full suspension from membership of the force we believe it should take the form of automatic relief from duty and be subject to periodic review (for example, subject to circumstances, not less than every seven days and not more than every 28 days).

(21) Criteria for 'Relieve and Review': . . . that the *Metropolitan Police Service Instruction Manual* be amended to reflect the ACPO paper, but additionally include 'community concern' as a factor to consider. Thus, the three points of consideration for making a decision to relieve from duty would be:

- welfare of the officer(s) concerned
- possibility of criminal or disciplinary proceedings
- level of community and family concern.

The periodic review would then look to see if the situation with regard to any of the three aspects had changed in such a way as to allow full reinstatement of the officer(s) concerned. If at any time within the review period it became apparent that full suspension of the officer(s) was appropriate then that course of action should be adopted immediately.

MPS Response: (including 20) Present procedures enable an assistant commissioner, or their designated deputy, to suspend an officer if they assess that he/she may have committed a criminal or (serious) disciplinary offence. There is no provision within the Police Disciplinary Regulations for blanket suspensions to take place in such cases. There are cases (e.g. a police marksman shooting a bank robber who is threatening life) where police action is justifiable and would not necessarily justify suspension. The deputy commissioner has already agreed with the staff associations a process of removal to non-operational duties of those officers most closely involved. To achieve the conclusions the report seeks, however, would need an amendment to Regulation 27 of the Police (Discipline) Regulations 1985. For this, an approach to the Home Office will be necessary.

CPCG Reply: The Group took some time considering this response. It felt that the wording was not clear and required amplification and clarification. In view of the detail in the report the Group believed the MPS should indicate whether it supported the principle and whether the commissioner would convey the MPS views to the home secretary. However and contrary to the tone of the MPS response, on the advice of assistant commissioner Paul Manning the Working Group understood that it had found a way forward that could be achieved administratively and without the need for primary legislation.

10 Dec Minute: Mr Long said the recommendations for suspension of police officers from duty and the criteria for 'relieve and review' were made with the feelings of the public in mind. Previous incidents had been inflamed because the public felt no action was being taken toward police officers involved. The Working Group of which assistant commissioner Manning was a member, believed it had found a way through what was accepted as a difficult subject without the need for an amendment to primary legislation. It also understood that the Police Federation did not object to the principle of 'relief and review'. The CPCG members of the Working Group had agreed to the recommendations in the spirit of compromise and at considerable risk to their integrity.

The deputy commissioner said that action had been agreed with the Police Federation for officers closely involved to be removed from operational duties. He said suspension of an officer was viewed as a disciplinary action and under current regulations officers could only be suspended if they were suspected of a criminal or disciplinary offence.

The CPCG recognised the MPS point of view but said that as they were under pressure from the public to press this issue forward, it was important for them to see action taken. The deputy commissioner welcomed a debate on this issue and said it should be national, with the Home Office and ACPO involved. The deputy commissioner agreed to revisit the issue with the MPS Police Federation to see if local action was feasible and to take part in any debate with ACPO and the Home Office. Mr Long would take the issue forward with the Home Office.

Comment: As has been noted before, the previous home secretary showed no interest in the report or its recommendations. The present home secretary has indicated that he is willing to look at the issue.

Recommendation 22

Consultation with Community Representatives: . . . that the mechanism for consultation by local divisional commanders following a death in custody include liaison with appropriate representatives of the community who might include, for example and subject to circumstance, members of Parliament, local councillors, the chairperson and members of the local Police-Community Consultative Group, or representatives of a Racial Equality Council, religious groups, youth organizations, campaign groups, or similar.

MPS Response: This is another aspect of good policing which is already common practice within the Metropolitan Police Service and a recommendation which we wholly accept.

Nicholas Long is Chair of the Lambeth Community-Police Consultative Group and was formerly a lay visitor to police stations in Lambeth. During 1996 he chaired a working group that examined deaths in police custody in the Metropolitan Police Service area and produced the influential report *Lessons from Tragedy.*

Supplement to *Lessons From Tragedies:* **Extract from recorded deaths in police custody or otherwise during 1996 in the Commissioner's Annual Reports* for 1995/96 & 1996/97** * With kind permission of the Commissioner

'Lambeth Index' No.	Death certified Date	Time	Police Division	Age	Sex	Ethnic origin	1. Cause of death 2. Inquest verdict
214	4 Jan 1996	18.05	Streatham	72	M	White	1. He art attack 2. No inquest
215	19 Jan 1996	06.50	Islington	39	M	White	1. Epilepsy 2. Natural causes
216	20 Jan 1996	17.30	Ealing	38	M	White	1. Brain haemorrhage; Alcoholic poisoning; Cirrhosis of the liver; Bronchial pneumonia. 2. Accidental death.
217	5 Feb 1996	21.09	Chiswick	73	M	White	1.Acute alcohol poisoning; Hypertensive heart disease 2. Accidental death
218	16 Mar 1996	06.23	Ilford	30	M	Black	1. Acute exhaustive mania 2. Awaits
219	21 Apr 1996	14.20	Barnet	47	M	White	1. Asphyxia during restraint 2. Awaits
220	30 Apr 1996	20.38	Peckham	37	M	Black	1. Ventricular fibrilation due to: (a) Stress & exertion caused by restraint in the presence of underlying pulmonary hypertension (b) Chronic cocaine abuse 2. Accidental death
221	9 May 1996	23.27	Richmond	38	M	White	1. Mixed drug poisoning 2. Accidental death
222	21 Jun 1996	16.15	Stoke Newington	61	M	Black	1. Amitriptyline poisoning 2. Misadventure
223	12 Aug 1996	19.20	Twicken-ham	42	M	White	1. Acute Cardiac failure 2. Accidental death
224	13 Aug 1996	03.55	Leyton	nk	M	White	1. Acute Coronary Thrombosis 2. Awaits
225	23 Aug 1996	15.20	Brixton	30	F	Black	1(a). Multi-organ failure 1(b). Abdominal lacerations 2. Accidental death
226	28 Aug 1996	09.00	South Norwood	60	M	White	1. Coronary Thrombosis 2. Awaits
227	23 Sep 1996	05.07	Hammer-smith	27	M	White	1. Multiple gunshot wounds 2. Awaits
228	6 Oct 1996	00.10	Dagenham	70	M	White	1. Natural causes 2. No Inquest
229	7 Oct 1996	06.40	Marylebone	36	M	Black	1. Inhalation of vomit 2. Accidental death

230	27 Oct 1996	04.55	Peckham	64	M	White	1. Dilated cardiomyopathy and alcoholic liver disease 2. Natural cause s
231	3 Nov 1996	23.32	Hampstead	57	M	White	1. Acute pneumonia; chronic liver disease 2. Inquest
232	11 Nov 1996	01.00	Streatham	53	M	Black	1. Acute pneumonia and renal failure; hypertensive intra-cerebral haemorrhage + diabetes mellitus 2. Awaits
233	10 Dec 1996	13.45	Harrow Road	35	F	White	1. Awaits 2. Awaits

Table 1

Extract from record of deaths in police custody recorded in the Metropolitan Police Commissioner's Annual Reports 1 January 1990 - 31 December 1996

Deaths in police custody or otherwise by cause of death (1990-1996)

Year	1990	1991	1992	1993	1994	1995	1996	Total	%
Number of deaths in custody	12	13	10	12	11	9	16	83	100.0
Accidental death	5	7	-	1	1	2	6	22	26.5
Natural causes	1	2	4	3	2	2	2	16	19.25
Misadventure	1	2	4	4	1	3	1	16	19.25
Inquest pending	-	-	-	-	-	-	7	7	8.5
Open Verdict	1	1	1	1	2	1	-	7	8.5
No inquest held	1	-	-	2	2	-	-	5	6.0
Suicide	2	-	-	-	1	1	-	4	4.5
Adjourned under s.16 Coroners Act 1988	-	1	1	1	-	-	-	3	3.5
Unlawful killing	-	-	-	-	2	-	-	2	2.5
Other verdict	1	-	-	-	-	-	-	1	1.5

Table 2

Deaths in police custody by ethnic origin (1990-1996)

Year	1990	1991	1992	1993	1994	1995	1996	Total	%
Number of deaths in custody	12	13	10	12	11	9	16	83	100.0
White	8	9	8	9	6	7	11	58	70.0
Black	-	2	1	2	3	2	5	15	18.0
Asian	1	2	1	1	2	-	-	7	8.5
Unknown	3	-	-	-	-	-	-	3	3.5

Table 3

Deaths in police custody by category* (1990-1996)

Year	1990	1991	1992	1993	1994	1995	1996	Total	%
Number of deaths in custody	12	13	10	12	11	9	16	83	100.0
Alcohol-related	8	10	6	10	4	7	5	50	60.0
Following arrest (other circumstances)	1	-	2	2	3	2	11	21	25.5
Mental health/place of safety	1	1	2	-	3	-	-	7	8.5
Suicide while in custody	2	-	-	-	1	-	-	3	3.5
During attempt to escape from police	-	2	-	-	-	-	-	2	2.5

In addition, there were three deaths of prisoners while in police custody at magistrates' courts (one each in 1990, 1991 and 1992). The prisoner escort function was taken over by Securicor Custodial Services Limited from June 1994. These three deaths have been excluded for the purposes of straightforward comparison.

* Categories devised by author. All percentages are approximate

Table 4

Deaths in police custody by cause of death (1990-1996)

'Lambeth Index' No.	Death certified Date	Time	Police Division	Age	Ethnic origin	Sex	1. Cause of death / 2. Inquest verdict
111	27 Feb 1990	10.10	Marylebone	67	unknown	M	1. Asphyxia 2. Accidental death
113	1 Apr 1990	12.40	Kentish Town	23	White	M	1. Hanging 2. Suicide aggravated by lack of care
114	23 Apr 1990	22.55	Leman Street	42	White	M	1. Alcohol poisoning 2. Accidental death
115	14 May 1990	09.55	Bexleyheath	26	White	M	1. Ischaemia (heart disease) 2. Accidental death
118	27 Jun 1990	23.30	Brixton	55	unknown	M	1. Severe head injuries 2. Open
119	28 Jun 1990	09.30	Brixton	50	White	F	1. Paracetamol and propoxyphene poisoning 2. Accidental death
121	5 Jul 1990	16.45	Rochester Row	45	White	M	1. i) head injuries ii) bronchial pneumonia 2. Accidental death
125	5 Nov 1990	05.15	Harrow Road	52	White	M	1. Lobar pneumonia 2. Natural causes
126	17 Nov 1990	06.00	Greenwich	50	Asian	M	1. Alcohol liver disease 2. No inquest
128	27 Nov 1990	12.10	Vine Street	40	White	M	1. Alcohol poisoning 2. Misadventure
129	24 Dec 1990	01.52	Hammer-smith	67	White	M	1. Laceration of the heart and multiple injuries 2. Murder

130	28 Dec 1990	01.10	Holloway	23	unknown	M	1. Hanging 2. Suicide resulting from lack of care
131	8 Jan 1991	07.18	Wandsworth	38	Black	M	1. Acute pancreatitis 2. Natural causes
133	27 Feb 1991	08.15	Limehouse	34	White	F	1. (a) Acute cardio-respiratory failure (b) inhalation of vomitus (c) drugs and alcohol 2. Accidental death
134	6 Mar 1991	20.00	Leman Street	59	White	M	1. Haemorrhaging to the brain 2. Accidental death
135	29 Mar 1991	16.30	Lewisham	60 approx	Black	M	1. Acute alcohol poisoning 2. Accidental death
138	9 May 1991	23.30	Waltham-stow	50 approx	Asian	M	1. Haemorrhaging in the cranium 2. Accidental death
139	2 Jun 1991	04.07	Paddington Green	32	White	M	1. (a) Inhalation of blood into lungs (b) fracture of mandible 2. Adjourned under s.16 Coroners Act 1988
141	17 Jun 1991	05.40	Notting Hill	55 approx	White	M	1.Brain haemorrhage due to fractured skull 2. Open
142	22 Jul 1991	01.10	Kings Cross	23	White	M	1. Rupture of spleen, aorta and kidneys 2. Accidental death
143	29 Jul 1991	13.00	Wimbledon	26	White	M	1. Multiple injuries 2. Accidental death
148	9 Nov 1991	13.55	Willesden Green	57	White	M	1. Natural causes 2. Natural causes
149	14 Nov 1991	07.35	Leman Street	52	White	M	1. Alcohol and diazepam poisoning 2. Misadventure
151	18 Dec 1991	02.30	Southall	72	Asian	M	1. Suppurative bronchial pneumonia, due to hypothermia 2. Misadventure
152	21 Dec 1991	14.20	Plumstead	43	White	M	1. Subdural haematoma 2. Accidental death
155	9 Jan 1992	15.10	Limehouse	40	White	M	1. Traumatic head injury 2. Misadventure
156	15 Mar 1992	11.53	City Road	46	White	M	1. (a) Coronary occlusion (b) Coronary athersclerosis 2. Natural causes
157	16 Apr 1992	21.10	Tooting	65	White	M	1. Hypothermia and starvation 2. Natural causes
158	13 May 1992	09.15	Hampstead	50	White	M	1. Cerebral vascular accident 2. Natural causes
160	20 Jun 1992	21.52	Paddington Green	27	Black	M	1. Cardio-respiratory failure induced by haloperidol administered during the course of a struggle 2. Therapeutic misadventure
162	26 Jul 1992	02.45	Bexleyheath	28	White	M	1. Suspension by ligature 2. Open
163	29 Aug 1992	16.00	Hammer-smith	36	White	M	1. Subdural Haematoma 2. Open and adjourned pending outcome of trial

166	9 Nov 1992	02.30	Rochester Row	38	White	M	1. Pneumonia 2. Misadventure
168	19 Dec 1992	19.40	Norbury	43	Asian	M	1. Asphyxia due to inhalation of blood and stomach contents 2. Misadventure
169	31 Dec 1992	19.55	Gipsy Hill	56	White	M	1. Bilateral pneumonia cerebral ischaemia 2. Natural causes - aggravated by self neglect
170	9 Jan 1993	21.50	Paddington Green	47	White	M	1. Respiratory obstruction by laryngeal polyp whilst intoxicated by alcohol 2. Misadventure
172	22 Feb 1993	22.15	Tooting	44	White	M	1. (a) Hyperkalaemic cardiac arrest (b) Alcohol and morphine poisoning 2. Misadventure
173	13 Mar 1993	04.25	Bow Road	35-40	White	M	1. Asphyxia due to vomit inhalation 2. Misadventure
174	25 Mar 1993	05.57	West End Central	58	White	M	1. Bronchial Pneumonia together with Adult Respiratory Distress Syndrome 2. No inquest held
178	13 May 1993	15.00	Leyton	33	Black	M	1. Brain haemorrhage and rupture of the oesophagus 2. Accidental death
179	28 May 1993	01.15	Southall	57	White	M	1. Asphyxia by vomit inhalation 2. Misadventure
180	4 Jun 1993	01.35	Battersea	55 approx	White	M	1. Alcoholic cardiomyopathy and fatty degeneration of the liver 2. Natural causes
181	1 Aug 1993	21.00	Hornsey	40	Black	F	1. Hypoxic ischaemic brain damage 2. Adjourned under s.16 of the Coroners Act 1988
182	7 Sep 1993	04.35	Hammer-smith	50	White	M	1. Brain haemorrhage 2. Natural causes
183	28 Sep 1993	17.55	Whetstone	36	White	M	1. Suffocation 2. Open verdict
184	8 Oct 1993	22.40	Norbury	55	Asian	M	1. Natural causes 2. No inquest held
187	17 Nov 1993	20.30	Clapham	52	White	M	1. Natural causes (a) Acute cardiac failure (b) Acute serofibrinous pericarditis (c) Alcoholic liver disease 2. Natural causes
189	9 Feb 1994	16.30	Whetstone	20	White	M	1. Fractured skull 2. Accidental death
190	23 Mar 1994	10.30	Notting Hill	44	Black	M	1. Myocardial infarction - Natural causes 2. No inquest held
191	4 Apr 1994	01.35	Walworth	37	White	M	1. Postural Asphyxia 2. Unlawful killing
192	1 May 1994	03.00	Hackney	26	Black	M	1. Drugs overdose 2. Misadventure

194	13 Aug 1994	04.45	Ealing	26	White	M	1. Pulmonary oedema 2. No inquest held
195	16 Aug 1994	02.20	Plaistow	31	White	M	1. Hanging 2. Suicide
196	26 Sep 1994	21.55	Hounslow	38	Asian	M	1. Liver failure & Gastro-oesophagel haemorrhage 2. Natural causes
197	12 Oct 1994	05.00	Kentish Town	39	White	M	1. Congestive cardiac failure 2. Natural causes
199	11 Dec 1994	00.45	Southall	39	Asian	M	1. Alcohol poisoning 2. Open
200	16 Dec 1994	00.52	Stoke Newington	34	Black	M	1. Asphyxiation 2. Unlawful killing
201	16 Dec 1994	05.16	Hampstead	24	White	M	1. Multiple injuries 2. Open
202	29 Jan 1995	03.45	Islington	58	White	M	1. Heart attack 2. Natural causes
203	5 Feb 1995	01.47	Wandsworth	50	White	M	1. Aspiration of stomach contents 2. Misadventure
206	1 May 1995	15.50	Vauxhall	35	White	M	1. Liver and Coronary failure 2. Natural causes
207	8 May 1995	03.20	Vauxhall	33	Black	M	1. Fractured skull 2. Misadventure
208	27 May 1995	02.20	Orpington	48	White	M	1. Postural Asphyxiation; Cerebral Contusion; Alcoholic Intoxication 2. Accidental death
209	3 Aug 1995	09.30	Sutton	35	White	M	1. Hypoxic Brain injury; Cardiac Arrest; Chloromethiazole Toxicity 2. Suicide
210	19 Aug 1995	07.00	Acton	31	White	M	1. Prothiaden poisoning 2. Open verdict
212	5 Dec 1995	03.46	Brixton	25	Black	M	1. Hypertensive Heart Disease 2. Accidental death
213	13 Dec 1995	01.35	South Norwood	38	White	M	1. Alcoholic poisoning 2. Misadventure
215	19 Jan 1996	06.50	Islington	39	White	M	1. Epilepsy 2. Natural causes
216	20 Jan 1996	17.30	Ealing	38	White	M	1. Brain haemorrhage; Alcoholic poisoning; Cirrhosis of the liver; Bronchial pneumonia 2. Accidental death
217	5 Feb 1996	21.09	Chiswick	73	White	M	1. Acute alcohol poisoning; Hypertensive heart disease 2. Accidental death
218	16 Mar 1996	06.23	Ilford	30	Black	M	1. Acute exhaustive mania 2. Awaits
219	21 Apr 1996	14.20	Barnet	47	White	M	1. Asphyxia during restraint 2. Awaits
220	30 Apr 1996	20.38	Peckham	37	Black	M	1. Ventricular fibrilation due to: (a) Stress & exertion caused by restraint in the presence of underlying pulmonary hypertension (b) Chronic cocaine abuse 2. Accidental death

221	9 May 1996	23.27	Richmond	38	White	M	1. Mixed drug poisoning 2. Accidental death
222	21 Jun 1996	16.15	Stoke Newington	61	Black	M	1. Amitriptyline poisoning 2. Misadventure
223	12 Aug 1996	19.20	Twickenham	42	White	M	1. Acute Cardiac failure 2. Accidental death
224	13 Aug 1996	03.55	Leyton	nk	White	M	1. Acute Coronary Thrombosis 2. Awaits
226	28 Aug 1996	09.00	South Norwood	60	White	M	1. Coronary Thrombosis 2. Awaits
227	23 Sep 1996	05.07	Hammer-smith	27	White	M	1. Multiple gunshot wounds 2. Awaits
229	7 Oct 1996	06.40	Marylebone	36	Black	M	1. Inhalation of vomit 2. Accidental death
230	27 Oct 1996	04.55	Peckham	64	White	M	1. Dilated cardiomyopathy and alcoholic liver disease 2. Natural causes
232	11 Nov 1996	01.00	Streatham	53	Black	M	1. Acute pneumonia and renal failure; hypertensive intra-cerebral haemorrhage + diabetes mellitus 2. Awaits
233	10 Dec 1996	13.45	Harrow Road	35	White	F	1. Awaits 2. Awaits

NOTE 1: (163) No official notification has been received by the MPS. The result of the trial is believed to be manslaughter. The circumstances of the death relate to an arrest for being drunk and incapable. He was taken to Hammersmith police station. Due to slow recovery, the FME was called to examine him. He was subsequently taken to hospital where an (unspecified) injury was discovered.

CHAPTER 10

Self Harm and Suicide by Detained Persons: A Study

Alan Ingram, Graham Johnson and Ian Heyes

Deaths in police custody, especially those as a result of deliberate self harm (DSH), commonly referred to as suicide, have raised concern over recent years. In the early 1990s, HM Prison Service established their Suicide Awareness Support Unit to address the issue and the Police Complaints Authority in their Annual Reports for 1993 and 1995, expressed concerns about the number of deaths in police custody.

In 1995 the Lancashire Constabulary addressed the issue by introducing a 'suicide guide' aimed primarily at police custody staff outlining factors which could help identify those people who may be at risk of causing DSH. The 'guide' was based heavily on the extensive work already completed by HM Prison Service Suicide Awareness Support Unit.

Following acceptance of the work within the Lancashire Constabulary, and interest shown by other police forces including the then Royal Hong Kong Police, the authors identified that deaths from self harm and acts of DSH were not unique to Lancashire but were common across all forces. There was also an acceptance that the data upon which the original guide was produced related heavily to the situation in prisons. Although some of the factors and indicators were the same, operating procedures, staff levels and most importantly the limited time that most detained people spend in police custody (99 per cent under 24 hours), means that many of the factors, indicators and care programmes used by the prison service are not relevant within the police environment. Additionally, the authors were unable to identify reliable data in relation to the number of incidents of DSH which occur within police custody suites, as the information is not collected.

A research project, approved and funded by the Home Office under the Police Research Award Scheme, saw the issue self harm and suicide by people detained in police custody in England and Wales fully researched for the first time. The research examined all cases of death from DSH in police custody in England and Wales between 1990 and 1994; and a six month survey of incidents of non-fatal DSH which occurred in police custody in Lancashire, and included an examination, where appropriate of the deceased person's previous prison history.

Information about a detained person's previous DSH history is the best indicator that police custody staff can use to identify someone who may be at risk. To reduce the occurrence of such incidents, it is important that information is accurately recorded and circulated to all those with responsibility for detained persons. Having obtained that historical information it is imperative that positive action is taken by custody staff. The research highlighted that in at least 14 cases out of the 52 examined, deaths *may* have been prevented *if* information held by the Prison Service relating to DSH or suicidal tendencies had been made available to the police. The report concluded that:

- incidents occur soon after detention
- information about a detained person's DSH history is imperative
- positive action must be taken following a DSH incident
- the safety of the detained person must be maintained
- police force policies need to reflect concern of the issues outlined in the report
- information held by HM Prison Service about an individual's suicidal or DSH history should be available to the police service.

The research culminated in a report in which a total of 19 recommendations have been made, the majority of which are relevant to all police forces, and the production of a more relevant suicide awareness booklet. The report, available from the Home Office Police Research Group, gives an overview of recurring problems and identifies the common features of all police custody deaths from DSH over the five year period (Ingram *et al* 1997). The revised Suicide Awareness Booklet has been produced primarily with police custody staff in mind and will be widely circulated throughout the service. Its purpose is to raise awareness and assist the identification of those detained persons who may be 'at risk' of committing acts of DSH and provides advice and guidance for custody staff. It is presented in the form of outline points to remember and consists of:

- a mnemonic 'WHY NOT CHECK' which briefly outlines to custody staff the important factors they should consider or look for when dealing with detained persons to try to identify those who may be 'at risk'
- guidance on, and an indication of the importance of, accurately recording and circulating information
- a 'general information' section including examples of verbal and non-verbal clues given by detained persons

- a broad template on 'Who, How, When and Where' incidents occur
- some of the barriers to identification or prevention; and
- what steps custody staff should take if they think an incident may occur or what actions should be taken if an incident has occurred.

The booklet ends with a reminder to staff that vigilance must be maintained at all times and that *they* are responsible for the care of people detained in custody.

Further information can be obtained from the Home Office Police Research Group or from the authors.

Alan Ingram has served in the Lancashire Constabulary for 24 years. He is presently a geographical inspector with responsibility for the towns of Thornton-Cleveleys and Poulton. He received a Police Research Award in 1996 to examine self-harm and suicide by detained people and is currently undertaking research into deaths in police custody.

Graham Johnson has served in the Lancashire Constabulary for 27 years and has wide policing experience. He is now posted to Research and Development, with responsibility for Police Research Group Liaison. He received a Police Research Award in 1996 to examine self-harm and suicide by detained people and is currently undertaking research on behalf of the Police Research Group into deaths in police custody.

Ian Heyes is a principal prison officer with over 21 years service. He is presently at HMP Garth and has responsibility for operational matters. He received a Police Research Award in 1996 to examine self-harm and suicide by detained people.

PART THREE

Voices of Prisoners, Families and Support Groups

CHAPTER 11

The Right to Life and the European Convention On Human Rights

John Wadham (with the assistance of Richard Wald)

> In keeping with the importance of this provision [the Right to Life] in a democratic society, the court must, in making its assessment, subject deprivations of life to the most careful scrutiny, particularly where deliberate lethal force is used, taking into consideration not only the actions of the agents of the state who actually administer the force but also all the surrounding circumstances including such matters as the planning and control of the actions under examination. (European Court of Human Rights, *McCann v. United Kingdom* [1996] 21 EHRR 97).

This contribution analyses the right to life contained in the European Convention On Human Rights and begins to consider how this might impact on deaths in custody once the Convention is incorporated into domestic law. The law of the Convention is still in a state of flux on the Right to Life and space does not permit a detailed account of the law.

Liberty (the National Council for Civil Liberties) has been campaigning for civil liberties and human rights for over 60 years. Liberty undertakes research, provides advice and assistance and lobbies for rights. Liberty has a number of cases pending with the European Commission and the Court of Human Rights. Some of these cases involve the Right to Life. Relatives, their solicitors and barristers and anyone else involved in such cases can obtain expert advice directly from Liberty's legal department.

The European Convention On Human Rights in context
The Convention is an international human rights treaty. It is not, at present, directly part of the law of the United Kingdom. Even now, however, it does have some status in our law and is used in the courts to assist the judges to decide cases when our law is incomplete or unclear. It is likely to be relied upon more and more in the next few years even before it has been formally incorporated. At present if the courts do not or cannot consider breaches of the Convention the individual has a right to make an application to the European Commission of Human Rights in Strasbourg. If such an application is successful then the case will be referred to the European Court of

Human Rights. If the Court finds a breach it can order the government to pay costs and compensation and if laws or procedures in the United Kingdom are at fault these have to be changed. Unfortunately, proceedings in Strasbourg can take five years to complete.

Incorporation of the Convention into United Kingdom domestic law
The government announced in the Queen's Speech in May 1997 that it intends to incorporate the provisions of the European Convention On Human Rights directly into United Kingdom law. This will make the Convention binding on our judges and will have a very significant impact. Thus coroner's courts, civil courts dealing with allegations of negligence or assault and the High Court when considering the lawfulness of coroners' decisions will have to take it into account. It is likely that a Bill to incorporate the Convention will be published in the autumn, will obtain Royal Assent by the end of 1998 and become law in 1999. In the meantime it is likely that judges will take more and more notice of its provisions.

The rights in the Convention are contained in its first 14 articles. The rights include freedom from torture, and from inhuman and degrading treatment; freedom from arbitrary detention; the right to a fair trial; the right to privacy, freedom of expression and assembly; and freedom from discrimination.

Article 2: The Right to Life
In this contribution I will be concerned particularly with article 2, The Right to Life. Article 2 states:

(1) Everyone's right to life shall be protected by law. No one shall be deprived of his life intentionally save in the execution of a sentence of a court following his conviction of a crime for which the penalty is provided by law.
(2) Deprivation of life shall not be regarded as inflicted in contravention of this article when it results from the use of force which is no more than absolutely necessary —
   (a) in defence of any person from unlawful violence;
   (b) in order to effect a lawful arrest or to prevent the escape of a person lawfully detained;
   (c) in action lawfully taken for the purpose of quelling a riot or insurrection.

The Right to Life as a fundamental right
Article 2 deals with the first right guaranteed in the Convention, and obviously the most basic human right of all. Recognition of article two's fundamental nature lies in the fact that its provisions cannot be

derogated from in peacetime under article 15. Article 15 allows any government not to comply with specific rights in specific circumstances. However, article 2 is regarded as so fundamental that this exemption does not apply to it.

Article 2 places the state under both a positive obligation to take adequate measures to protect the Right to Life as well as a negative obligation not to take life other than in certain defined circumstances. A test of 'proportionality' sets the standard for the state's obligation to protect the right to life, and articles 2(1) and 2(2) refer to specific exceptions to the obligation not to interfere with the Right to Life. These are in circumstances of legal implementation of the death penalty, defence of a person, effecting a lawful arrest or preventing the escape of a detained person or quelling a riot or insurrection.

In applying the test of proportionality the Court in Strasbourg has decided that all the surrounding circumstances must be considered: whether the deprivation of life was 'absolutely necessary' or the particular use of force 'strictly proportionate' to the achievement of the state's legitimate ends. In particular, the court will have regard to the planning and control of actions under examination.

The Convention does not sanction the use of deadly force in the protection of property or in effecting a citizen's arrest. According to the Convention the state has an obligation to take reasonable steps to prevent the taking of life by providing police and security forces, although case law indicates that the threshold for such a violation is high, as this obligation is frequently weighed against public policy considerations.

The duty to enforce the law to protect life requires the proper investigation of all suspicious deaths (including deaths in custody) and the prosecution of public and private offenders. Such a duty is not absolute and is subject of course to the normal discretion that has to be left to the prosecutor in deciding whether or not to proceed in any particular case. This duty includes the investigation of all the circumstances which might have contributed to the death.

Practical implications of article 2 jurisprudence in UK domestic law
The case of *McCann v. United Kingdom* [1996] 21 EHRR 97 concerned the shooting by the SAS of three members of the IRA in Gibraltar. The implications of the case however are much more far reaching than the circumstances of those deaths and provide the beginnings of guidance on what article 2 means in reality.

In *McCann*, the only article 2 case to reach the court so far, the court elucidated certain principles which have substantial application to instances of deaths in custody. Broadly, the court considered that the taking of adequate measures to protect life engages the responsibility of the state at two levels: first, in the formulation of measures designed to secure the protection of life, including an effective procedure for investigating the circumstances of any loss of life; and second, in the implementation of those measures. The following principles can be drawn from the judgment in *McCann* and associated jurisprudence:

1. Training

The Court will consider both training and adherence to proper procedures of soldiers, police or prison officers in their use of force and therefore, by extension in the preservation of life generally. Any such rules must reflect both the national domestic standard and that of the Convention.

Any breach of article 2 under this head derives not merely from a consideration of the actions of the state personnel who may be in contact with the person before death but of the operation as a whole. In *McCann*, faulty planning and training in advance of the incident rendered the use of lethal force at the moment of confrontation inevitable and therefore violated article 2. The court attributed the soldiers' failure to use proper care at the moment of engagement to a lack of appropriate care in the control and organization of the arrest operation as a whole. There is therefore a broad duty on those state bodies with responsibility for preserving life to provide training and ensure proper planning. The absence of adequate measures to preserve life will create a potential violation of article 2.

Issues for consideration could include whether the training of police and prison officers to recognise and deal with life threatening situations is adequate; whether training in safe ways of restraining violent prisoners is adequate; and lastly whether the quality of medical assistance, especially to deal with emergencies, is good enough.

2. Procedures to safeguard life

In *McCann* the court stated:

> The court's general approach to the interpretation of article 2 must be guided by the fact that the object and purpose of the Convention as an instrument for the protection of individual human beings requires that its provisions be interpreted and applied so as to make its safeguard practical and effective.

Any institution that is required to detain people will at one level be responsible for their care. This will of course be more so where those people cannot come and go as they please and where their access to medical and other aid is dependent on the institution itself. Convention law creates some particularly important responsibilities on the state. Once a person is ill and unable to help themselves that responsibility is increased substantially.

Given such responsibilities there is a duty to create systems that preserve life. There will also be an even greater duty to improve systems that have failed to protect life in the past. Recommendations of inquiries and inquests will be crucial in determining whether lessons from the past have been ignored.

Issues for consideration must include the adequacies of any such systems and the effectiveness of their implementation.

3. Official investigation required

The right to life provisions must be read in conjunction with the state's general duty under article 1 of the Convention to 'secure to everyone within their jurisdiction the rights and freedoms defined in [the] Convention.' These two provisions combined with article 13 (the right to an effective remedy for breaches of other Convention rights) require an 'effective' official investigation after any death but particularly a death where the state might be culpable.

General considerations as to the nature of such an investigation are set out in *McCann*. In assessing the adequacy of inquest proceedings the court will have regard to their length, the number of witnesses involved, the quality and effectiveness of lawyers for the relatives, the availability of legal aid, and the opportunities for cross-examination of key witnesses, including any military and police personnel involved. The court will subject a defendant state to 'extensive, independent, and highly public scrutiny' in determining the quality of inquest proceedings. The inquest proceedings in *McCann* lasted 19 days and involved 79 witnesses. Although no legal aid was available the relatives were represented by very competent lawyers.

Issues for consideration include the difficulties for relatives given the absence of legal aid, the absence of a duty on the authorities to disclose material and other procedural hurdles in the inquest system. Consideration would also need to be given to the adequacy of investigation by the police of the police and the supervision by the Police Complaints Authority. In some cases the culpability of the state will be decided by actions for assault or negligence in the civil courts where legal aid, disclosure and the usual rules of fairness ordinarily apply.

Many of those who die in police custody or in prison do not have relatives who are financially dependent on them. This can result in the absence of any real claim for compensation in the civil courts and, what is often important, the impossibility of obtaining legal aid. This raises questions about the effectiveness of the investigations systems.

This analysis of the need for proper scrutiny under article 2 is reinforced by the provisions in article 13 of the Convention. Article 13 creates a right to an effective remedy for any case where there is an arguable violation of another right in the Convention (including, of course, article 2).

4. The adequacy of the law

The law that applies in England and Wales allows the use of lethal force where such force 'is reasonably justifiable'. The reasonableness of the use of force has to be decided on the basis of the facts which the user of the force honestly believed to exist—a subjective test. On the basis of that test the determination of whether the force used was reasonable must be objectively assessed—whether the force used was disproportionate to the apparent threat that it was intended to prevent. The test in article 2 is different and imposes a higher standard. The standard from the Convention is whether the use of the force was 'absolutely necessary'.

Where a death may have arisen as a result of omissions or negligence the issue for the Convention will concern the positive obligation on the state. One area currently subject to challenge concerns the responsibility of the police to protect potential victims of crime. The domestic law does not currently allow claims for negligence against the police if the police have failed to protect victims unless there are very special circumstances. This rule of law may not comply with the positive obligation of the state to protect life.

5. Discrimination

There is no 'self-standing' discrimination provision in the Convention but it is important to consider the effect of article 14 on the right to life. Article 14 states:

> The enjoyment of the rights and freedoms set forth in this convention shall be secured without discrimination on any ground such as sex, race, colour, language, religion, political or other opinion, national or social origin, association with a national minority, property, birth or other status.

Thus, if it were the case that black people or people from ethnic minorities were disproportionately represented amongst those who die in custody this might breach article 14. The Convention requires public authorities to ensure that the rights in the Convention, including the Right to Life are protected for all and that all groups are treated fairly. A breach of article 14 combined with article 2 can either be established by an application to the Commission in Strasbourg or, once the Convention has been incorporated into domestic law, by taking a case in the courts in this country.

John Wadham is a solicitor and Director of Liberty (the National Council for Civil Liberties). He has acted for applicants in a substantial number of cases before the European Commission and European Court of Human Rights. He is editor of the civil liberties section of the *Penguin Guide to the Law* and the cases reports for the *European Human Rights Law Review*. He has also contributed to many other publications and written a large number of articles on human rights and civil liberties.

Richard Wald is a legal assistant at Liberty.

CHAPTER 12

Recognising Responsibilities to Families

Paul Edwards and Audrey Edwards

Introduction

We welcome this opportunity to talk to you today because we wish to ensure that some good emerges from the tragedy of our son, Christopher's, death. We hope the right lessons will be learned and implemented by the agencies involved so that we can help to ensure that what happened to our son does not happen again.

An inquiry has been conducted into Christopher's death. It was jointly commissioned by the North Essex Health Authority, the Home Office and Essex County Council. It has cost £750,000 and has lasted about two years. We have not seen the inquiry report which will be published within the next few weeks[1] and we have been given no information by the inquiry about what happened. Essentially, this chapter contains our personal impressions of events. Everything we say today is based on our own direct experience or on official statements by other people directly involved which we have read and which are now held in safekeeping.

Christopher's story

We had a loving, devoted son who was a graduate with outstanding academic results with honours in economics and Japanese. He was a linguist who also spoke Russian, German and French, and was learning Spanish at the time of his death. He was also an excellent tournament chess player. He became ill in 1990 and saw two psychiatrists who said he was on the verge of a severe mental illness. Christopher was never violent, on the contrary he was always gentle and loving but with an inner torment. Unfortunately like many in his condition, he did not perceive himself as being ill and on the third occasion he was asked to see a psychiatrist he refused. Thereafter we had to support him ourselves with help from the community but nothing from the official health or social services other than the renewal of an original prescription for the stabilizing medication Stelazine.

On two occasions in four years his mental illness led him to behave inappropriately in public which brought him in contact with the criminal justice system. The first occasion was almost exactly six years ago today and only a short distance from where we are. He was pestering the local vicar for instant confirmation into the Church of

England and on one occasion this very tolerant and supportive vicar was away and the young curate called the local police. Christopher was arrested and then appeared before the local Uxbridge magistrates. Before going into court where we assumed he would plead guilty he had a private meeting with the court probation officer. To our astonishment and perhaps because of that conversation he pleaded not guilty, the police indicated they would not pursue the matter and the case was dismissed. We did not query this at the time but in retrospect it appears as a missed opportunity for Christopher to be required to receive medical attention.

Christopher's next and fatal encounter with the criminal justice system came three and a half years later on 27 November 1994 when, out of a sense of social isolation, he approached a young woman who was accompanied by two young men. They understandably objected, there was some disturbance and the police were called. The police rang us and we told them and the duty social worker of Christopher's mental history and that Stelazine had been prescribed for him. He was, however, deemed fit to go to court.

While held overnight in police custody his mental health deteriorated dramatically and he was very obviously mentally ill when he attended Colchester magistrates' court the next morning.

He behaved bizarrely in the court holding cells and would not instruct the duty solicitor who said he could not get through to him. The court recognised he was very obviously mentally ill and transferred the hearing to the more experienced bench of magistrates on duty that day. His appearance in court was very brief but interrupted as he tried to climb out of the witness box and he had to be taken down and brought back in handcuffs. The duty solicitor took details of his medical background from us and my husband was asked in court whether he could provide more medical information while he was in the court building. A group of young people were visiting the court that morning and as I waited outside the court I overhead one of them say to a friend 'There's a madman in there making all that noise; he's really mad'. The outcome was that he was remanded to Chelmsford prison for three days, as we understood it for psychiatric assessment, during which time we were told by the court clerk and the duty solicitor we had to find him a hospital bed with the help of a probation officer.

The understanding we had gained at the court that he would be placed in the prison hospital was reinforced when my husband spoke to the prison probation officer before Christopher arrived. After being told of Christopher's history she stated his behaviour clearly revealed mental illness rather than criminal intent and she would pass this onto the prison staff who would see him on arrival. Independently of this a senior prison officer, acting on information he received from the court before Christopher arrived at the prison, contacted the court to see if the warrant could be changed so that Christopher could be sent for hospital reports. His request was refused by the court. He also contacted the prison health centre expressing his concern.

On arrival at the prison Christopher behaved bizarrely and was placed in a holding cell before being processed individually and then taken to a cell on his own, as a prison officer said 'For his own protection'.

The killer's story

The killer, also a graduate, was two years older than Christopher. He had a history over several years of severe mental illness including lengthy periods in mental hospitals and was known to be violent. His neighbours expected him to kill someone—probably his mother who was one of the people he had assaulted.

He was in a multi-disciplinary care programme and five weeks before the killing a case conference was held at which everyone concerned with him was present, about 12 people. I quote a few of the remarks from the report of that conference.

(1) *GP stated*: Most intimidating patient ever had to visit; he could actually murder someone.
(2) *Police inspector*: One day we will be asked why the situation had been allowed to go on for so long. A lot of talking waiting for something to happen.
(3) *Secure unit representative*: Only a matter of time before he commits a serious injury on somebody; the staff are fearful; he goes for the more vulnerable people.
(4) *Psychiatrist*: People who go after him to give him Depot are frightened of him; there must be grounds for locking him up.

Five weeks later he was arrested on two charges of criminal assault and one of criminal damage. The police knew he was violent, deranged, dangerous and unfit to appear in court so they took him to the mental hospital where he was well known. The psychiatrist there said he 'was play acting.' In view of what happened within 48 hours this psychiatrist was either mistaken or, as we now suspect, he was trying to ensure the mental health services did not have to accept such a disruptive person back as their responsibility and preferred that he be put in prison. While in police custody he assaulted a police officer for which he was also charged, and on the morning of our son's death before he was taken to court his behaviour in the police station was such that the police had to strike him with a baton after giving him due warning.

160

He was escorted into the dock at the Chelmsford magistrates' court by three policemen, signifying the seriousness of the threat he represented. Despite this, the police appear not to have completed a form CID2 which is an official means of notifying the prison that a new inmate is thought to represent an exceptional risk and/or has mental illness. They did, however, give oral messages about his behaviour to prison staff when they delivered him to Chelmsford prison and he was heavily bruised because of his involvement in the incidents for which he had been charged.

The killer arrived in the prison about 30 minutes later than our son and was not processed in the normal way. He was immediately placed in a cell on his own because, according to the same prison officer who had placed Christopher in a cell on his own for his own protection, the killer 'was not fit to be placed with any other inmate'. A short time later it seems that the same prison officer transferred the killer into the same cell as our son.

Christopher's death

There is a conflict of evidence about how the death was discovered. Prison inmates later said the cell buzzer had been sounding for some time but there was no response by prison staff; a prison officer said the buzzer was not working; a senior police officer said he tested the buzzer within two hours of the murder and it was working correctly. In any event about 1.00 a.m. six prison officers looked through the cell aperture and saw the killer standing and kicking our son who was on the floor. They appear to have decided against opening the door and dragging out the killer, which may or may not have saved our son's life; instead the prison officers went off, donned riot gear and returned some minutes later only to find our son was dead. Six trained officers against one man armed with a plastic fork!

We do not know whether such an appalling response to a human tragedy is prescribed by Prison Service regulations. It may also have been because—through informal advice from the police and possibly local knowledge—they were well aware of this young man's history over several years of mental illness and violence and therefore were reluctant to engage with him.

Our son was so severely injured by the attack that we were told we should not see his body. His left ear had been cannibalised. He was identified by his dental records.

Our experience with the police

A local policeman called at our house about 5.00 a.m. to advise us our son had been found dead in his cell but he knew no further details. He gave us a telephone number to call about eight or nine o'clock when he said we would be given more information. We were then told by the police over the phone that our son had been 'murdered' by his cellmate who was a person with a background of violence, being held on charges of criminal assault and criminal damage. Later that day we were visited by the coroner's officer (a police constable) who told us he was also the point of contact with the police though he had nothing to do with the investigations into our son's death. A few days later he visited us again to take a statement. We were seeking information about what had happened and why Christopher was in a cell with another person rather than in the prison hospital, which the coroner's officer was not able to answer so it was arranged the inspector handling the case would visit us which he did ten days after the killing.

He repeatedly tried to persuade us to accept that the two young men had met in the prison reception and formed a friendly relationship and that was the reason they had been placed in the same cell. We could not accept this because it was wholly inconsistent with Christopher's character and state of mental health at the time. It was not until months later that we discovered that—at the time this explanation was being pressed upon us by the Essex police—there were statements in existence from prison officers suggesting that this was not true and that the two had not met until the killer was transferred into Christopher's cell.

We asked that the police ensure they fully investigated all matters but they would not. They would not interview the prison probation officer to whom my husband spoke before Christopher arrived; they never answered our questions about whether the cell alarm buzzer was working and whether Christopher had been instructed in its use.

The police also failed to keep us informed of developments. We were not told when the killer (who had been taken to Rampton on the day of the murder) was brought before Retford magistrates' court. This was in spite of our asking to be kept informed as we wished to be in attendance. On enquiring of the police inspector why we had not been informed of the date we were told 'Because I did not want you to be there'. Nor did the police inform us that the case had been transferred from Retford to Chelmsford Crown Court. We learned this fact from a person unconnected with the case who rang us with that information. We were not informed of the date of the inquest hearing to release Christopher's body for burial (three and a half months after death).

The police have persistently refused to release any information to us although we were told by the Crown Prosecution Service after the trial of our son's killer that we were entitled to request the documentation. They have also refused to co-operate with the independent inquiry on matters occurring after the death, i.e. including into the evidence relevant to our allegations of their attempts to cover up their responsibility for what happened.

Our experience with the Prison Service
The Prison Service initiated no contact with us following our son's death in Chelmsford prison.

As we heard nothing from the prison, we wrote to the governor asking for information. The first response told us nothing so we pressed again and received a second brief letter stating that the two young men had struck up a friendship in reception and nothing in the behaviour of either had caused the prison staff any concern. We had also written to the home secretary and in due course we received a response on his behalf from the area manager of the Prison Service. He assured us that internal Prison Service inquiries revealed there had been no serious defects but the reports could not be released to the public.

We had also written to Derek Lewis, the then director general of the Prison Service, and in apologising for a response which referred to Christopher's death as self-inflicted he stated he would be willing to meet us.

We raised a number of matters at that meeting and left him with an *aide memoire* listing them. Our priority was to press for an independent inquiry but amongst other matters we pointed out that the internal inquiries could not have been very thorough as they had not identified that Christopher's money had not been returned to us. As a side comment, subsequent contact with other parents whose young sons have died in prison revealed this to be a typical rather than an unusual experience. Mr Lewis was most embarrassed and apologetic and sent the prison governor the next week to see us and to return the money. The governor sat facing us and a photograph of Christopher and told us that in his 30 odd years prison service he had never seen anything like it and did not wish to do so again; that staff involved had received counselling; some needed pyschiatric help; and five months later some were still on sick leave. There was no acknowledgement that the tragedy occurred because of the failure of the prison staff, or of the ghastly suffering Christopher must have endured, or of the trauma and anguish of his family. I mention this not because of the offence and distress it caused us but because of the image which it conveyed to us of a Prison Service which has an inward looking, self-absorbed culture totally insensitive to the outside world of prisoners and their families. The image, we suspect, reflects the reality.

Whilst we are very angry at the failures of the Prison Service we are not seeking vengeance but we are seeking substantial improvement. As a step in this direction we sought a meeting with the former minister for prisons; there was no response. We have also suggested separately to both the Prison Service and the Prison Governors' Association that there could be mutual benefit in a meeting between ourselves and the prison officers involved. That request has twice been referred to the prison governor (a new one: the former one having died in the meantime) but without any response since we first raised it over six months ago—another example of the impermeability of the Prison Service to external influences. It is fair to add, however, that just a week ago we had a cordial and constructive meeting with the current Director General of the Prison Service at his request.

We have made a submission to the Prison Service suggesting ways in which they could improve their relationship with the families of those who die in prison and a copy of the recommendations we made is included as an appendix to this chapter (see *Appendix I*).

I have given you a very brief history of our son's tragedy and of our subsequent contacts with two of the criminal justice agencies involved. My husband will now summarise our experience with other agencies and then draw conclusions and recommendations from our experience, which we hope may be of help to you in formulating your own contributions to this conference and in the work that you do away from this conference.

Relations with other criminal justice agencies
We had dealings with several other agencies:

Magistrates' court
Whether correct or not, our impression was that although the Colchester magistrates were well intentioned neither they nor their professional staff were fully or immediately conversant with their powers vis-à-vis mentally ill offenders nor how to deal with them. We were astonished to learn Christopher had not gone to the prison health centre and that they turned down the request from the senior prison officer, acting on advice received from court, that Christopher be remanded for hospital reports. Could it be that it was their own recognition of inadequacies in their treatment of mentally ill offenders that led to the introduction of a court diversion scheme in Colchester two or three months after Christopher's death? When the police stated publicly after the event they had no reason to suspect that the killer was in any way a special risk, we were pleased to learn the Chelmsford magistrates' court made it clear to the police, though not to the public, that they knew the alleged killer was dangerous because unusually he was guarded by three police officers in the dock.

Duty solicitor
We thought he was trying to do his best for Christopher even though Christopher had refused to appoint him to act on his behalf.

Probation service
We suspect they tried to be helpful at Christopher's first court appearance in Uxbridge but arguably they did him a disservice. They were present in court at Colchester but they played no part in the proceedings. The prison probation officer was extremely helpful and understanding on the phone but clearly had no influence on the treatment of Christopher when he arrived in prison.

Coroner
He invited us to see him and explained the functions of his office clearly. He stressed that the inquest was not a forum to investigate all relevant matters or apportion blame or responsibility. He added, however, that although it would be most unusual he was prepared to re-open the inquest after the trial in order to make a statement that an independent inquiry should be held into the circumstances of Christopher's death. In the event this was not necessary as we obtained an independent inquiry. His courtesy, kindness and consideration were much appreciated.

Crown Prosecution Service
They did not seek to involve us but appeared to be sympathetic and supportive when we met them at our request. They did not consult us in advance about the change in charge from murder to manslaughter because of diminished responsibility, nor did they advise us that the plea and directions hearing—a legalistic process some might not have attended—could become the actual trial as it did.

Board of Visitors
They were sympathetic but reluctant to accept our suggestion of a meeting with them. We doubt whether they are in any way a community voice which has real influence over what happens in prison.

Chief Inspector of Prisons
Both the present holder and his predecessor were extremely courteous and sympathetic. The current chief inspector was most supportive and interested in our experience and comments. We had a very good meeting with him. Unfortunately he has no power to investigate individual cases.

Prison Ombudsman
He too was interested and sympathetic. Unfortunately he can only investigate complaints by live prisoners, not by the families of deceased ones.

Regional police authority
The chairman was interested in our representations and followed them up quite positively. In effect he appeared to be shut out by the police who deemed the matters we raised were operational and the authority, therefore, had no power to intervene.

Police Complaints Authority
They have yet to play their major role as we have deferred our formal complaints about the police until after the inquiry report is published. It was disconcerting, however, that our initial approach to them led to a response direct from the police about whom we had complained.

Independent inquiry
I should also say a few words about the subsequent inquiry into Christopher's death although that strictly speaking is not part of the criminal justice system. The inquiry is only being held because there is a National Health Service regulation that there should be an independent inquiry into a homicide involving a person diagnosed as mentally ill. By pressure and goodwill in some areas we managed to get its frame of reference extended to some degree beyond the medical issues.

We made the naive assumption at the outset that the establishment of an independent inquiry meant all our problems would be resolved. A final decision cannot be made until the inquiry report is published but our dealings with the inquiry and with the agencies who commissioned it do not give us grounds for total confidence. We hope to be surprised.

At one stage we set down our reflections on dealing with the inquiry in a paper. We then discussed this paper with the NHS Executive, and at their request, at separate meetings with the commissioning agents and the inquiry itself. We included in our paper a list of recommendations for the future of such inquiries and that list is reproduced as an appendix to this chapter (see *Appendix II*). We hope our recommendations may also be useful to criminal justice agencies as guidance in their day-to-day activities when dealing with victims and victims' families. The recommendations are really very obvious such as:

(a) advise the family about what is planned
(b) consult on the issues they want raised
(c) keep them informed of progress on a regular basis

(d) ensure the terms of reference specify the priority to be given to the family's interests and its relationship to the inquiry
(e) ensure all proceedings are user friendly.

The most challenging recommendations are probably:

(a) all inquiries should be in public
(b) families should have their reasonable legal costs covered
(c) a member of each inquiry should be someone who has been bereaved in a tragedy of some kind.

All the recommendations are directed toward improving the humanity, courtesy and efficiency of inquiries; matters which at the outset we would have assumed did not need to be said. Our experience with the inquiry proved, however, that inquiries also need to consider how to relate properly to the families of victims.

The chairman of this conference, Sir Louis Blom-Cooper QC, has chaired similar inquiries in one of which he wrote:

It is our view that the families of victims have a most central public concern and are key representatives of the wider community whose interests inquiries such as ours are established to serve. In our view they should be given the opportunity to be present at any inquiry into homicide, whether that inquiry be held in public or in private. Such opportunity might usefully be provided by the sponsoring authority in the terms of reference it gives to the independent panel of inquiry.

We would wholly subscribe to that view but we suspect that in practice it is the exception not the norm. The commissioning agencies and the inquiry panel with whom we have been dealing certainly did not subscribe to the philosophy set out in the first sentence nor did they implement the practice recommended.

There are two further points we would like to make. First, there is a major risk that inquiries become a damage control exercise for the agencies involved rather than a no-holds barred pursuit of the truth. If that is to be avoided the members have to ensure that the value of their detailed knowledge of the institutions under examination (in which they have worked in the past) is not offset by professional group loyalty. Secondly, we expect our inquiry report will be deficient in one major respect because the inquiry yielded to police pressure not to look at matters after the point of death when, on our view of the evidence, we would argue that the primary objective of the Prison Service and the police was to cover up their responsibility for what happened. The truth must out, however, if the agencies involved are to put their houses in order and retain community respect.

Conclusions

Three years ago today we were ordinary citizens trying to help our son. In so far as we thought of the criminal justice system we would have presumed it to be a fair, socially responsible and appropriately caring structure and that prisons were there to accommodate criminals. Our experience since November 1994 has shattered those illusions. We have reached a number of conclusions and recommendations for change which we will set out below. Let us say first that we believe the primary way to overcome the deficiencies we have identified is not through more resources, more policy documents, more procedural manuals, or more operational targets to be monitored, although they all have a role to play. What is required primarily is a change in the internal culture and values of the organizations and that will only come about through leaders and managers who can model different values and inspire and drive their organizations to practise them.

Secondly, we suspect that if agencies do not reform themselves reform will be forced upon them as an unintended consequence of Care in the Community. Mental illness is said to affect one in four households in this country and it does so randomly. Because the sufferers are much less likely to be hospitalised than in the past they are much more likely to come into contact with the criminal justice system. In a conflict between the traditional values and practices of the Prison Service and the police and the expectations of one-quarter of United Kingdom households as to how their mentally ill family members should be treated we suspect the Prison Service and police are bound to lose. Our specific conclusions are as follows:

1. The criminal justice system is used by the mental health service to avoid responsibility for severely disturbed and disruptive people with mental illness as is made clear by our son's tragedy and the fact that research results show 63 per cent of remand prisoners are diagnosed as mentally ill.

2. While there are good and dedicated people working within the police and prison services the prevailing institutional culture, in our experience, is one of disdain verging on contempt for offenders, particularly the mentally ill and this extends to their families.

3. Sending the mentally ill to prison leads to gross waste of public funds; there are capital savings to be made and several years in prison or special hospital involves more public expense than a pre-emptive spell of several weeks or months in secure mental health facilities.

4. There is a basic flaw in the criminal justice system in that it only recognises murder as an offence against good order within society; not as a violation of the individual by a denial of the Right to Life or a crime against the family, the basic building blocks of society. For the sake of the person who has been killed there should be recognition that a life has been taken and fulfilment of human potential denied. It is not good enough that the law considers it is just too bad—a person's life has been taken—unless there are dependents. We emphasise we are not talking about more money for victims' families, but our point is illustrated by the fact that even the upgraded Criminal Compensation Tariff equates death with loss of smell or taste and only makes payment if there is a family to receive it. So far as the impact on the family is concerned we believe the Islamic concept of formally involving the victim's family in the legal process has much to commend it because it explicitly recognises the injury done to them.

5. Criminal justice agencies could improve the quality of their performance substantially if they sought to involve prisoners and their families in the planning, delivery and monitoring of the criminal justice system.

6. There is a structural failure in the system for audit of unnatural deaths in prison. The Prison Service cannot be relied on to audit itself.

7. The voice of the community should be given more effective means of influencing the activities of the criminal justice agencies.

8. Criminal justice agencies should rid themselves of their present unquestioning assumption that when a crisis occurs self protection of the institution takes priority over service to the community, integrity in investigation and the truth.

Recommendations

1. Criminal justice agencies should unite in pressing their political masters for an end to sending mentally ill people to prison. It makes the mental condition of those affected worse; it makes prisons overcrowded and more difficult to manage for sane offenders who should be there.

2. The powers to require compulsory hospitalisation and medication of the mentally ill and the readiness of mental health professionals to exercise those powers should both be strengthened.

3. A proportion of the billions of pounds currently allocated for new prisons should be diverted to the provision of secure mental health facilities so that mentally ill people can be held in more appropriate facilities than prisons. The closure of psychiatric beds should also be halted.

4. The Prison Service must upgrade staffing and training to improve substantially its capacity to receive and retain the mentally ill for as long as it is required to do so. Other agencies such as the courts and the police should also improve their skills in this area.

5. Changes should be made to the law so that it explicitly recognises murder as not just an offence against social order but also a denial of the individual's right to life and a crime against the family.

6. All agencies dealing with offenders should be required to commit themselves to an effective policy of consultation and information sharing with prisoners, victims, families and other people involved. In social housing, which was my profession, consumer involvement through tenant participation is both best professional practice and a requirement of government policy. The principle of involving those directly affected by the actions of publicly funded agencies needs to be extended into the criminal justice system.

7. Agencies should accept from the outset that they will almost invariably have some responsibility for any tragedy; and they should be prepared to acknowledge and apologise for any failure to carry out a duty of care. Much of the stress we and people in the police and Prison Service have experienced over the past nearly three years could have been avoided if at the outset there had been a frank and open acknowledgement of the possibility of mistake or wrongdoing, an apology and a commitment to working together.

8. Meeting the legitimate interests of victims and victims' families will vary from family to family but agencies should adopt a code of practice which includes:
   (a) recognition of the indescribable grief and trauma of the family
   (b) taking the initiative in going out to the family; establishing contact quickly, nominating the contact person who will keep in touch in accordance with an agreed timetable
   (c) providing an initial explanation of the agency's role; what it expects from the family; what it can offer the family
   (d) providing answers to questions even if the answer *is* 'no'; if some matters may not be disclosed, explaining why
   (e) returning personal goods of victim immediately
   (f) being 100 per cent truthful – the truth, the whole truth and nothing but the truth
   (g) putting the interests of the family before the self-protective interests of the institution
   (h) explaining what appeal processes are available
   (i) ensuring that the family does not encounter financial hardship arising directly from the death, e.g. removal of the body back to home town or funeral expenses, either by direct support or referral to another agency which can help
   (j) giving names and addresses of relevant voluntary agencies
   (k) not consciously or unconsciously acting in a way which intimidates families, such as emphasing status or insisting on formality of processes with which the agency is familiar but which can be strange and threatening to the family.

9. There must be an open public inquiry into all cases of unnatural death in police or prison custody. A Prison Service which in two internal inquiries found no major defects in our son's case is manifestly incapable of auditing itself. Inquests have limited scope and are not effective where there are trials and trials may, as in our case, only focus on one aspect and

not on what happened or why. Trials may also, as in our case, occur as sudden transformations of plea and directions hearings.

10. The number of actual and attempted unnatural deaths in a prison or police cell must be included in measures of performance. Good management and service cultures must be backed up by effective sanctions. The former director general of prisons lost his job because a few prisoners escaped from prison through the wire even though they were recaptured. What sanctions have ever been exercised to stop 70-80 prisoners a year escaping custody through death? Unnatural deaths in prisons and police cells would be substantially reduced if their occurrence immediately led to: (a) revocation of a private prison management contract; (b) removal from office of a prison governor or other person in charge; (c) substantial financial penalties which might well be paid to criminal justice charities. My business experience is there is nothing so compelling as a blunt statement from insurers or a director of finance that the company cannot afford another similar incident. If financial penalties are paid to active reform organizations such as the Howard League, the Prison Reform Trust or Prison Watch then the positive impact will be doubled.

11. Strengthen the powers of the Prison Service Ombudsman; the Chief Inspector of Prisons; Boards of Prison Visitors; and Regional Police Authorities so they are more effective as community representatives with an impact on the criminal justice agencies involved.

12. Where there is an independent inquiry the membership, rules and procedures should explicitly recognise the legitimate interest of families and take account of the specific recommendations set out in this list.

13. Agencies must tell families what lessons have been learned and of changes made by agencies. A family is entitled to know and to be comforted by the fact that some good has come from tragedy.

14. The greatest need is not for increased resources or changes in administrative arrrangements but for changes in internal cultures and management. A properly motivated and managed service will find the way to provide a high standard of service despite resource constraints and administrative barriers.

Advice to families

It would be presumptuous for us to attempt to prescribe what other families should do when such a tragedy occurs. It is a devastating trauma which goes to the core of family life and each family will need to react differently because of its different history, structure, resources and other responsibilities. What we can do is to identify what we did which was helpful and where we found support:

1. The greatest comfort comes from the extended family; fellow church members; local community; and from people who write from out of the blue having seen a press report. Each of these can provide substantial and very moving support.

2. Contact your local MP and enlist his or her support in dealing with agencies of government.

3. Contact as many relevant voluntary organizations for help as you can identify.

4. Follow your intuitions; have confidence in your own capacity to climb mountains; seek to work with others but do not lose control of your own agenda; do not be intimidated by people in high public office with impressive titles — as a member of the community you are their employer.

5. Always be reasoned, determined and persistent in dealing with the agencies who are involved. Accept their assurances but do not rely on them until they are fulfilled. Remember the agencies are likely to be driven by an internal agenda of self-protection.

6. Respond to approaches from the local and national media who in our experience have been very helpful. Try and keep the emphasis on the facts of what happened and why, rather than the emotional aspects of how you feel about it.

7. If you can — make contact with other people who have been through the same experience. Each one of us is different and will react differently but we found we could learn from the process.

8. If you can — try and make public your experience and the lessons you have learned from it so that it may help to avoid the recurrence of similar tragedies. That is why we are here today.

Paul Edwards had 20 years as Chief Executive with the Australian Housing Corporation (1975 to 1977), the South Australian Housing Corporation (1975 to 1977) and, in the United Kingdom, the Colne Housing Society (1991 to 1996).

Audrey Edwards was a court reporter before becoming an assistant to a producer of documentaries. She was active in various committees attached to the Anglican Diocese of South Australia. She is a voluntary member of a hospital support group.

ENDNOTE

1 The inquiry report had still not been published at the time this volume went to press in January 1998, almost six months later.

Appendix I to *Chapter 12*

Recommendations to the Prison Service on How to Relate to the Bereaved Family of the Victim of An Unnatural Death in Prison. Submitted to the Prison Service in October 1996

The Need for a Change in Prison Culture

Before making specific recommendations we would make the point that prison governors or officers carrying out a series of recommended procedures relating to a bereaved family are not likely to carry much conviction with the family if their actions do not arise from a genuine feeling of concern Our strong impression is that prison staff are typically very inwardly focused and appear to have contempt for mentally ill prisoners (possibly all prisoners). These characteristics severely limit their capacity to relate to bereaved families. If the internal culture and management attitudes within the Prison Service are such that they destroy the humanity of the staff then these will have to be changed to a more outward looking culture fostering a sense of responsibility for care as well as security, if unnatural deaths are to be avoided or handled properly when they do occur. We understand that in the recent case of *Burt v. The Home Office* the courts upheld the proposition that prisons have a duty of care to their inmates.

Recommended procedures on an unnatural death in prison

1. Prison training programmes for staff at all levels should promote acceptance that staff have a duty of care towards inmates and their families and this should inform their approach to all aspects of their duties if an unnatural death is considered possible or actually occurs.

2. The Prison Service should take the initiative to contact the next of kin as soon as possible after an unnatural death, possibly by phone in the first instance, and offer an immediate visit by the prison governor. Some families may resist seeing prison governors in which case a prison chaplain or member of a Board of Visitors might be an acceptable alternative. The visit if arranged (or if no visit a letter) should comprise:

   (a) advice on release of the body;
   (b) assurances of full investigation and when and what kind of report the Prison Service will be able to give to the bereaved family;
   (c) offer to pay funeral expenses (at least in cases of suicide);

(d) timetable for action established;

(e) advice given when a more comprehensive report can be given, e.g. the coroner's inquest;

(f) assurances given about return of personal effects of the victim;

(g) offer of regular follow up contacts with a named person with contact arrangements;

(h) list of names and addresses of relevant voluntary agencies should be provided, e.g. Prison Reform Trust; Howard League; INQUEST; Prison Watch; Zito Trust; Victim Support. Prison Service Ombudsman;

(i) offer to arrange visit to site of death at any convenient time, maybe years later.

3. Even though there may be severe trauma among some prison staff this should not be mentioned to the victim's relatives whose trauma is much greater. Whatever support services are available to prison staff should be offered to the bereaved family.

4. A Prison Service representative should, if possible, arrange to attend regularly or periodically meetings of Prison Watch to get direct feedback from bereaved families.

5. It should be made clear that in assessment of efficiency of prison working, account will be taken of the number of unnatural deaths in prison. If this does not form a most important component of such assessments it will appear to both prison staff and families that such deaths are not a matter of great consequence. Suitable fines could be imposed on privately managed prisons for each such death and automatic demotion for governing staff in publicly managed prisons.

6. The person appointed to investigate unnatural deaths in prisons should be the Chief Inspector of Prisons or his nominee.

7. The Terms of Reference of the Prison Service Ombudsman should be revised to make quite clear he is entitled to receive and investigate representations by next of kin of a prisoner who suffers an unnatural death.

Appendix II to *Chapter 12*

Recommendations for the Conduct of Inquiries into Homicides Involving a Person Who Has Been Diagnosed as Mentally Ill

The following recommendations are intended to improve inquiry processes particularly from the point of view of the victim's family:

(a) families of victims should be told as soon as possible that an inquiry will be held even though its formal initiation will need to be deferred until completion of legal action;

(b) inquiries should be required to prepare and make available to interested parties a strategic plan and timetable for the conduct of the Inquiry;

(c) the victim's family should be:

i) consulted on the terms of reference, inquiry membership, secretarial arrangements and any changes thereto;

ii) given every opportunity to identify the questions they want raised and the information they believe should be made available to the inquiry; and informed whether their representations have been accepted and if not, why not;

iii) given a full explanation of procedures and what they can expect to encounter at the evidence giving stage;

iv) kept informed of progress on a regular basis, which could be as part of a general briefing for all 'stakeholders' in the inquiry;

v) informed in advance on a confidential basis of findings and recommendations so that they are not embarrassed by public disclosure;

(d) all commissioning agents should specify in their terms of reference:

i) that the interests of the victim and the victim's family are a high priority not to be subordinated to the interests of others, and

ii) the relationship they wish to be established between the inquiry and the family of the victim.

(e) whenever possible inquiries should be held in public as are coroners' inquests for which they are a substitute, but even if held in private bereaved family members should be entitled to attend hearings as observers and receive transcripts, subject to:

i) undertakings as to confidentiality;

ii) undertakings to waive rights to legal action on basis of information disclosed in private hearings but not included in the final published report;

(f) every attempt should be made to include in inquiry panels a person who has direct experience of bereavement in a similar tragedy (not necessarily homicide by mentally ill people, e.g. the Marchioness, Clapham Rail or Manchester Airport disasters);

(g) the secretariat, counsel and professional adviser to inquiries should be persons whose location and normal professional or business activities are such that they have not had and would not be expected to have past, present or future contact with witnesses;

(h) it should be mandatory that an independent barrister from another region be appointed to assess the information gathered by the Secretariat and lead the questioning of witnesses in accordance with the wishes of the inquiry panel;

(i) all members of inquiries should be of equal status, with the chairman only as first among equals, and act on a collegiate basis in reaching collective decisions on all matters relating to inquiry processes as well as findings;

(j) all members should attend all hearings with the sole exception of interviews with the perpetrator of the homicide if medical requirements dictate a restriction on those involved;

(k) inquiries should be required to minimise the formality and legalisation of inquiry hearings, and give those appearing transcripts of their evidence with the right to correct errors;

(l) inquiries should have powers to require the production of papers and the attendance of witnesses;

(m) there should be no disparity between the legal resources available to the agencies involved and the victim's family, who should be offered independent legal support in preparing statements and submissions to the inquiry and in any appearances before it;

(n) inquiries should be required by their terms of reference to search out for and publicly identify individual or agency failures in professional competence; commitment to care; or communication, and the responsibility assigned where it is due. Likewise excellent performance should be identified and praised as an incentive to good performance and to establish a case law of best practice;

(o) inquiries' terms of reference should require them to assess and comment on the management responses of the agencies involved after the event both for the light they cast on the event and as a guide to the way in which recommendations should be framed if they are to be properly implemented;

(p) inquiry recommendations should be specific and action-oriented, identifying who is required to do what and by when. There should be an automatic follow up review 12 months later leading to a summary public statement setting out what has been done and what remains to be done

(q) commissioning agencies shall be obliged to distribute copies of the final report to:
  i) all similar institutions (e.g. local hospitals, police stations) within their jurisdiction requiring them to report within three months on any action required within that institution;
  ii) all similar authorities (e.g. health authorities, chief constables, departments of social services) who should be encouraged by their central agency (e.g. NHS Executive, Home Office) to have an internal assessment carried out to see if it is appropriate for any action to be taken;
  iii) all relevant central agencies of government;
  iv) all national and local media (and respond to questions at a media conference)
  v) the family of the victim and the family of the perpetrator of offences
  vi) witnesses
  vii) others as requested.

(r) There should be a central panel (including a victim of a previous tragedy) to monitor the terms of reference, membership, business plans, secretariat arrangements, procedural guidelines of all inquiries, together with the proposed distribution of the report by the commissioning agents.

CHAPTER 13

Black Deaths in Custody: A Human Rights Perspective

Lee Jasper

The 1990 Trust is a national charity concentrating on issues affecting African, Caribbean and Asian communities nationwide. It produces research papers, briefing papers, and it also promotes the need for African/Caribbean/Asian unity in the fight against discrimination and racism. It looks at the need for networking amongst black community organizations in the UK and Europe wide.

I am here today to talk about black deaths, controversial black deaths, particularly of young black men at the hands of the police at point of arrest. I want to talk about it from a human rights perspective. I do so because the government is planning to incorporate the European Convention On Human Rights into domestic legislation and therefore the black community sees this as an opportunity to be able to pursue some of the issues of concern in a human rights format, and certainly the European Convention On Human Rights, if I can just remind you, provides for freedom from arbitrary arrest and detention. There are lots more but the ones for our attention today are the freedom from capital punishment, torture, inhumane and degrading treatment or punishment; and the Right to Life. This is encapsulated within the UN Conventions and also there are a number of other international conventions, such as the International Convention on Civil and Political Rights and the International Convention On Economic and Social Cultural Rights, along with the International Convention On the Elimination of Racial Discrimination.

To get the technical bits out the way: the government is looking at the European Convention On Human Rights with a view to incorporation. We still think that will offer greater opportunities for the pursuit of justice in relation to these matters but we are also pressing the government to incorporate the International Convention On The Elimination of Racial Discrimination, which is a much more detailed document relating to a variety of areas of social life—an international convention that has been signed by the UK but is not incorporated into British law, and we will be talking to the home secretary and others in relation to those matters in order to strengthen black communities' rights in relation to a whole range of matters, but principally for today's purposes, the right to be subject to arrest without the kind of unfair discrimination and violence that is often associated with such arrests—and to be free from the subsequent tragedies that can and indeed have, occurred.

And from within a black community, I do not think there is complete understanding within the wider community about the anguish and turmoil and level of concern that black communities have around black deaths in custody in terms of arrests. We can look at a long list of young black people who have subsequently died at the point of arrest and we can see some essential characteristics that indicate that the attempt by the families of victims in attaining justice is severely restricted. Legal aid, issues of disclosure, issues of legal aid at the coroner's inquest, and in relation to information put out about the deceased person. We have very many cases where people are arrested and Scotland Yard's press department has already issued a press release stressing a person's criminal background, trying to develop a context in which a violent arrest and a subsequent death can be explained by a person's criminal antecedents. And often those facts are wrong. If you look at the deaths of people like Brian Douglas particularly, I mention Brian Douglas and Wayne Douglas (no relation) because I think those deaths, although they have occurred, have offered a way forward in relation to the matters at hand. But if you look at those types of deaths, where you have interactions with the police on the street, where a violent arrest takes place, it tends to be young black men who are the subject of this violence. And this violence is in my view, and in the view of the black community, related to the nature of institutionalised racism within the police force. And I do know that the commissioner and others have said that they do not believe that the Metropolitan Police, or indeed police forces nationally, have imbued within their structures institutionalised racism. The explanation offered for what they see as a few bad apples—and a few rare instances—is precisely that we have a few rotten apples in the barrel. And if you look at the overall statistics in relation to policing then they give you a clue to the level of institutionalised racism that has existed and gives rise to the higher level of interaction of young black people with police officers on the street.

So, for instance, in the year 1994/5, we have the figure of around 189,000 stops and searches on the streets of the capital; 120,000 of them are black young people. Although young black people in the capital make up around 20 per cent—seven per cent of the total London population; and if you look at the arrest rates in relation to those groups that are stopped, both white and black, they are comparable for around ten per cent. White people stand a ten per cent chance of being arrested at the point of a 'stop and search' and so do those from black

175

communities. And for black communities, what that means is that there are thousands of members of the black community who are being stopped and searched on the street in the capital, who are obviously going about their law-abiding business and the over-representation of black people in the 'stop and search' figures—year in, year out—points to a level of institutionalised racism within the force. I have said on many occasions that if it's a few bad apples in the force, who are stopping the 120,000 black people—year in, year out—roughly, then they must be working all the overtime that God sends them and 365 days a year. You cannot explain such a macro impact upon the black community in terms of these figures other than talking about levels of institutionalised racism. How do I arrive at that—other than the figures? Well I believe that racism exists within the police force to a significant extent, that officers are minded to use overwhelming force when they meet black individuals. And the rationale for that overwhelming force is the view that they have about the inherent criminality—and if you like super-criminality—of the black individual. And when they approach an incident where black people are involved, their adrenalin is running, they're imagining the worst kinds of consequences, of being involved in that kind of arrest, their motivation is one which pushes them to say—we need to be very careful, we need to make sure everything is handled correctly and as a consequence they apply overwhelming and, in some cases, deadly force—where that is not necessary or where it would not be applied in other circumstances. And I have said to officers—and having spoken to over 1000, probably 1,500 officers, in the course of my training—and they testify in open sessions with myself, and other trainers, that the fact is that they *do* approach black people in a different way to that in which they approach white people. There is a qualitive difference between the policing that black people and white people receive. And that qualitive difference is exemplified in the contact between them when racism becomes a significant factor. If you can imagine being a young person on the streets and you're part of that 120,000 who are constantly being stopped and you're approached by an officer for the umpteenth time and you display a little attitude. I have known people be arrested for 'failing the attitude test', not paying due deference to the badge of the Queen and the Metropolitan Police, and police nationally. But in that context and in that crucible right there on the street—that is where it is played out and that is where, as we have said, in very many cases, and in cases that are being very well described in very many inquest courts—particularly those of Wayne Douglas and Brian Douglas—but there are lots of others as well.

But when you hear in the inquest courts what has actually happened, when you hear officers describe 'kicking a man in the head' while he's already on the ground, I have to hasten to add, 'kicking that man in the head as hard as he possibly could', when you hear the incredulous explanations of: 'I hit Brian Douglas on the shoulder with a baton, and it slid up to his head' . . . and Brian Douglas died as a result of a massive blow to the top of his head. Then you can see, I think you can see, the black community thinks you can see—we don't believe that the rest of the wider community attaches the same significance to these events. We don't think that necessarily white people will believe that police officers are applying deadly forces to black members of the community out there on the streets. But I think that the figures show that that is more likely: 'stop and search' figures, 'deaths in custody' figures, which are all outlined in INQUEST's excellent Annual Report— look at the figures and explain to me how it is we have such a disproportionate number of young black people in there. And there's two ways of going about it. At Lambeth, we took our issues to Lambeth Police Consultative Group on the deaths of Wayne Douglas and Brian Douglas and we found that we could work together to try and get a working party—we developed the report from tragedies, which sought to put our concerns in, we met with people and listed what we felt were the areas needed for action. And you will (in a workshop later) see the fruits of those labours and how we have been able to use a tragedy to still come together, accept the points of concern and develop a way forward and a response that is based on the reality of the black experience in terms of its contact with the police. And that provides a way forward. But equally there is another way forward, there is the way forward postulated by Sir Herman Ousley, who says 'Why employ in terms of racism, in discrimination and employment?' We can either work together in order to address this issue or I can drag people to court kicking and screaming all the way and get penalties imposed. And I tell you this, in terms of deaths in custody, such is the level of concern in the black community, that if and when, and it looks likely we are going to incorporate the European Convention On Human Rights into domestic law, these issues will be at the very forefront of an agenda for a Human Rights Commission. So the onus is both on campaigners from our side, and professionals on your side, to begin to look very seriously around these particular issues and develop ways forward, agendas and strategies that can actually meet the levels of concern, because otherwise we are going to find ourselves in British courts with authorities facing human rights abuse charges from black organizations, such as the organization chaired by myself. We have the capability, we have the resources, we have the expertise and we certainly have the commitment and the will so to do. So it is almost a plea to say 'Well look, let us now get our heads round the table, and begin to look at ways in which we can reduce the likelihood of a deeply abominable event such as a death in custody and a violent arrest that a member of the black community has to suffer'. We would hope that we could get to the table and begin to negotiate—that's why we're backing a commission, as called for by INQUEST, on deaths in custody, so that we can begin to work together in an atmosphere out of the heat of the campaign (because I chair a campaign organization—many of you are professionals and academics, etc—I am not that type of animal at all, I am a black activist, a political activist that pushes issues of concern on to as many agendas as I possibly can. So I have to deal out the raw edge on the coalface, if you like, in relation to these issues), but I am still wanting to have that dialogue. I am not driven by revolutionary political aims, as can often be the case. I think our work with Lambeth Police Consultative Group following the recent tragedies and on other work can testify to the desire on our part to find equitable and just outcomes to a lot of the problems that we face. Make no mistake, with the European Convention On Human Rights coming in, it will afford greater opportunity for litigation at that level in relation to very many matters that are under discussion today. And I have to say I am happy to be able to speak here today.

If we look at the United Nations pronouncement in relation to deaths in custody, we can look at what the International Convention Committee on the Elimination of Racial Discrimination said in 1996. It said:

> It is noted with serious concern that among the victims of deaths in custody are a disproportionate number of members of minority groups, that police brutality appears to affect members of minority groups disproportionately, that allegations of police brutality and harassment are reported, not vigorously investigated and perpetrators, once guilt is established, are not appropriately punished.

Well that sums up, I think, our position in relation to what we feel around deaths in custody, and you must again begin to have some empathy with and understanding about the position of a black community who are subject to institutionalised and racist forms of policing. So that when a death in custody occurs in that context then the reaction is ever more acute, and when we have the assistance of groups such as INQUEST, where we are lucky enough to get unlawful killing judgments where the jury is actually convinced that that person was unlawfully killed, then the black community has to suffer the enigmony of knowing nobody else will be held to account. We can't rely on the Police Complaints Authority to pursue our complaints in regard to this matter and only once an officer has been charged with murder or attempted murder, or whatever it was, in Leeds, in relation to these matters. And time and time again we have the example of young black people coming into contact with the police, being subject to a violent arrest, either at that point, dying, or at some point at the police station subsequently dying, and I'm not going to go into details but the role of forensic medical examiners in my view is appalling. The amount of times that we hear people being described as malingerers, fit for detention, when it is quite clear to anybody with an ounce of medical knowledge that those people are in a very serious condition. But I shan't go into that because it will be gone into later in workshops. Where you have unlawful killing verdicts, where you have the incidents where black people are dying in custody and at the end point there is no justice to be had. There is no justice to be had. We can't say to the people who've got unlawful killing verdicts, well we've had a result there haven't we? Because, quite frankly, we haven't had a result. And it points to the need for a complete reform of the inquest system, because it is incapable at the moment of delivering the kind of justice that is demanded by black communities. And Martin Luther King once said, that if the voice of the unheard is not listened to, then it will be heard in very many other ways—and this country has got a history of civil disturbances based on catalyst events that happened in terms of policing, that then are taken up and have resonance in the black community and lead to further confrontation with the police. Black communities wish to avoid those scenarios. When those things happen in our areas, our community life is set back, our community development is set back, our economic development is set back, so we are wanting to avoid those scenarios, and the best way now that we can work towards ensuring that some of these civil disturbances do not take place in the future, is by tackling the key concerns of the black community and these are 'stop and search' and deaths in custody.

We have got to reach some point where we can deliver equitable outcomes in relation to these matters: with the same standards being applied to evidence in relation to police officers as to those from every other profession in the land. I can see no rationale for police officers being in any way different, and subject to different sorts of criteria. I also think, and it will be a fact, that when the European Convention On Human Rights is brought in the Race Relations Act 1976 will have to be amended. The European Convention will apply to all aspects of government institutions so there will be no exceptions as there are currently with the Race Relations Act. There will be no exceptions and therefore the potential for litigation within the Human Rights arena in relation to these matters becomes large. And we want to establish working dialogue with institutions and organizations, seeking to find answers to what are deeply worrying problems in relation to the disproportionate level of black deaths in custody. But if people think we can reform the inquest system without reforming the police themselves in relation to these matters then that it is going to be a forward strategy. Until institutionalised racism and racist officers within the police are sacked and where racism within the police force is challenged, not on the level of having a wonderfully detailed equal opportunities policy dreamt up at the high offices of Scotland Yard, worthy as that may be, but unless an equal opportunity policy is a policy that is actually owned by the people who are expecting to implement it then it will never be implemented and it will always be undermined and discarded. That's the lesson of black people for local authorities, that's the lesson for large institutions who try to implement equal opportunities without the consensus of their work force. In point of fact with equal opportunities with the Metropolitan Police there is an unholy consensus by officers who see the equal opportunities policies as interfering with their work and therefore not worth putting in the effort to implement or uphold them—and they think that it does not in any way affect the quality of their job. And the black community on the street sees no evidence of equal opportunities anyway and so you have the alliance of the two: officers who think the policy is misguided and unhelpful; and you have the view of the black community who say 'Well you've got the policy but we never see it being implemented in the day-to-day performance of police officers on the street'.

Time and time again we're talking about deaths in custody. We have countless examples of over-reaction, over-use of force in relation to black communities. I was in a position of predicting as soon as the CS gas was introduced, I went on record in the press saying that the first person to die of a result of the introduction of CS gas will be a black man, and it gives me no pleasure at all in being confirmed—in being absolutely right in relation to that. I also said it in relation to the introduction of police batons, and we were absolutely right and the reason we were right is because we readily understand within black organizations the mind-set and the level of institutionalised racism within the force. That predicates and motivates the kind of violent arrests that we see taking place day in and day out.

These are uncomfortable issues and I'm sure the conference has been a lot more comfortable up to this point, but if we are, on my side, going to avoid the kind of scenarios we saw played out in Brixton, which was a minor squall, in 1995 after the death of Wayne Douglas, that was a very minor incident. The incidents of 1981 and 1986 dwarf that in comparison, and if we are to avoid, and I want to avoid, and no doubt you want to avoid, those occurrences happening again, we must tackle those instances that can be viewed as catalysts for that type of activity. And the main catalyst right now that will probably ignite a situation of major civil unrest in the metropolitan area, London or otherwise, will be a death in custody. While we have a system that at the end point, after you've pursued justice and you have your unlawful killing verdict, that the officers remain in post, that there are no disciplinary procedures taken against anybody, that there is no cause for concern, it is business as usual, then the conditions that are likely to give rise to the types of civil disturbances and the deaths in custody that will act as a catalyst to those events will always be ever more likely.

Lee Jasper is Director of the 1990 Trust, a policy development organization providing information and promoting networking within the black community in the United Kingdom. He is also a co-ordinator of the Operation Black Vote campaign. As one of the founding members of the National Black Caucus, and Chair of the National Black Alliance and Vice-Chair of the National Assembly Against Racism, he has become a frequent commentator on black issues. Lee Jasper writes regularly for several publications. He has also played an active role in a large number of high-profile miscarriage of justice cases. This chapter is a transcript of his presentation to the conference.

CHAPTER 14

Deaths In Custody What Lessons: An Overview of the Nigerian Situation

Uju Agomoh

There has been a lot of attention on the issue of deaths in custody. Many of these works (which are predominantly western literature) have focused on suicides in prison or police custody. Evidence shows that deaths in custody in western prisons can be attributed mainly to self-inflicted deaths. In Nigeria the situation is different.

This paper will examine the trend and the causes of deaths in Nigerian prisons. It will also attempt to draw out possible cross-cultural lessons that will aid a better understanding and management of the problem of prison deaths.

The trend

One of the most alarming indicators of the harshness of Nigerian prisons is the high mortality rate (Africa Watch, 1991: p. 2). Nigeria has a high number of deaths in prison custody but unfortunately records of these deaths are rarely kept and when available they are usually incomplete (Odinkalu and Ehonwa 1991). However, we will rely to some extent on what is officially available just to have a glimpse of the problem. *Table 1* shows the number of officially recorded deaths in Nigerian prisons and ways in which death occurred from 1980 to 1988.

Table 1: Number of Deaths in Nigerian Prisons By Method in Which the Deaths Occurred

Method of death	1980	1982	1983	1984	1985	1986	1988
'Natural deaths'	115	146	205	381	501	620	1615
By firing squad	4	NA	NA	232	257	233	207
By hanging	4	11	6	123	46	42	51
TOTAL	123	160	212	740	804	896	1875

Computation derived from: Nigerian Prisons Service (1980-86), Federal Office of Statistics (1981, 1985-87). Totals do not necessarily reflect all entries in the table. In some cases figures are missing/unavailable.

Nigeria still practices the death penalty and deaths which occurred through this are classified under the category of death by 'firing squad' and by 'hanging' as shown above. Execution by firing squad is mainly used for armed robbery convicts under military decrees, triable by special military tribunals, while hanging is mainly used for criminal homicide triable in ordinary courts. Our concern in this paper is those deaths classified under 'natural deaths'. How natural are these deaths? (We will come to this later). See *Chart 1* in the *Appendix* to this chapter for the graphical representation of the number of deaths in Nigerian prisons indicating the methods of deaths as contained in *Table 1*.

Table 2: Percentage of Deaths by Extra-Judicial Means and the Average Monthly and Daily Rates

	1980	1982	1983	1984	1985	1986	1988
%of Extra-Judicial Deaths	93%	91%	97%	52%	62%	69%	86%
Average monthly Deaths	9.6	12.2	17.1	31.8	41.8	51.7	134.6
Average daily Deaths	0.3	0.4	0.6	1.0	1.4	4.3	4.3

See the *Appendix, Chart 2* for the graphical representation of the above data

As mentioned earlier, these records are far from being representative. For instance as reported in Odinkalu and Ehonwa (1991), in Ikoyi Prison, Lagos between January and June 1988 there were 54 deaths—a period of just six months and for one prison out of a total of 1,353 prisons and 232 lock ups in the country. The same prison recorded 78 deaths between January and September 1989. In Warri prison, between January 1989 and April 1990 there were 90 deaths. At the maximum security prison, Kirikiri Lagos (the highest security prison in the country) there were 49 recorded deaths from January to December 1989. Roughly speaking, there were about 217[1] deaths recorded in just three prisons for a period of one year. Warri prison's average daily population (ADP) as at April 1990 was 1,200. Thus with 90 deaths, about 7.5 per cent of the Warri prison's total population died in custody. Also, between the three prisons—Warri (90), Ikoyi (78) and Maximum Security Prison (49)—we have an average of 72.3 deaths. Using this rough estimate, one can speculate that given a total of 135 prisons (and excluding the 232 lock ups) we will have about 9,760.5 prison deaths for the whole country. This represents about 18.1 per cent of the total prison population for that year which was 53,896.[2] With this high number of deaths annually, there is a serious problem.

While one may argue that the above figure is mere speculation and unlikely to represent the true picture, there is still cause to be worried. Even a more modest analysis using the official records of 'natural deaths' as shown in *Table 1*, still presents a bad picture. In this analysis, the yearly average rate of increase for the years 1984, 1985 and 1986 was put at 26.95. With this rate, the mathematical projection gives the figure of deaths for 1995 as 5,318.459 if the socio-economic conditions and prison conditions remain the same (Obot 1990).

Table 3: Calculated and Projected Number of Annual Prison Deaths Using the 1995 Figure and the Yearly Average Rate of Increase (of 26.95) As Given by Obot (1990)

Year	1995	1996	1997	1998	1999	2000
No. of deaths	5,318.5	6,751.8	8,571.4	10,881.4	13,813.9	17,536

These figures, as frightening as they seem, tend to be supported by eye witness accounts from prisoners and ex-prisoners. For instance, this is what one ex-prisoner had to say:

> At least in a day about ten people will die. When your friend die(s), you start fearing too that you will die. (Idowu Sanusi, male 30 years, ex-prisoner of Ikoyi Prison)

In a national survey of 56 prisons and lock-ups, it was reported that in many of the prisons there are as many as two or more deaths weekly (Odinkalu and Ehonwa 1991).

In this present study, we examined the records of deaths in 1988 as reported from January to September in the medium security prison Kirikiri, Lagos. It was found that for the nine months duration, there were a total of 89 recorded deaths. Below is the monthly distribution of the deaths

Table 4: Distribution of Deaths by Month of the Year (Kirikiri Prison, Lagos)

MONTH	NUMBER
January	6
February	2
March	1
April	8
May	11
June	18
July	25
August	15
October[3]	3

From *Table 4* above, we can say that the monthly death rate ranges from 1 to 25. There was no month without a death. In fact, this shows an average monthly death of 9.9. A further analysis of the data indicates that the number of deaths tends to be higher during the raining season (May to August). This is a period characterised by rain falls, increased farming activities and high cost of feeding. See *Appendix* to this chapter, *Chart 3* for more details.

We wanted to find out if there was any observable pattern with respect to the date/period of the month when the deaths occur. The result of this can be seen in *Charts 4* and *5* contained in the *Appendix*. In summary, we saw that there were fluctuations with respect to the days of the months when the deaths occurred. On a closer look, it seems that with each outbreak of deaths (i.e. record of high number of deaths), the death rate reduces. This was clearly the trend observed when the deaths were grouped according to five day intervals. From this evidence, it is possible that with each outbreak of deaths, the authorities tend to show more care or they improve the prison conditions which consequently results in fewer deaths. These fewer deaths tend to be short lived—as that period is followed by another outbreak shortly afterwards.

Characteristics of the victims
In trying to understand the pattern and reason(s) for these deaths in Nigerian prisons, there was a need for us to examine the characteristics that were predominant with the victims. A very obvious one is that the majority of the cases are remand prisoners. For instance, in the survey of 56 prisons and lock ups reported by Odinkalu and Ehonwa (1991), where the category of prisoners were identified (i.e. Agbor, Oko, Auchi, Ikoyi and Warri prisons), we have remand prisoners representing 83.9 per cent of all the deaths. In fact, there were cases where all the deaths recorded in a particular prison were remand prisoners, especially 'awaiting trial persons' (ATPs). The record for Ikoyi Prison Lagos between 1 January 1988 and 22 April 1988 showed that all the 54 deaths were ATPs.

In our present study, we also observed that a disproportionate number of the recorded deaths occur amongst the ATPs. Of the 89 deaths, only two were convicted prisoners, thus ATPs account for about 97. 8 per cent of the deaths recorded in the prison during the period. See *Chart 6* in the *Appendix* to this chapter for distribution of death by category of prisoners.

One may argue that this high number of ATPs accounting for the majority of the deaths can be explained by the fact that they constitute the bulk of the prison population. Studies have shown that more than 67.4 per cent of the total prison population for the whole country and

185

about 80 per cent of that of Lagos state are all ATPs (Agomoh 1996). It is however doubtful if the high population of remand prisoners in Nigeria can explain why the bulk (and in some cases all) of the recorded deaths are ATPs or remand prisoners There is a high possibility that the nature of remand and the conditions of their imprisonment are contributing factors to the high number of deaths recorded amongst them.

With respect to the nature of remand, it has been argued that suspense and anxiety relating to the trial are possible explanations for high number of deaths amongst prisoners on remand or awaiting trial (Gover 1880 as cited by Liebling 1992; Dooley 1990b; Liebling 1994). In fact in the study by Gover, it was observed that 34 per cent of the suicides in prison occurred amongst prisoners on remand or awaiting trial. In Dooley's analysis, 47.5 per cent of the suicide deaths were on remand and 27.5 per cent of those whose deaths were recorded as consciously self-inflicted (CSI) were also on remand. In Liebling's analysis, 52 per cent of the young offenders that committed suicide were also on remand.

The percentage of deaths recorded amongst remand prisoners in Nigeria seem very high and, in fact, double or triple the rates reported by Gover and Dooley respectively. What is it about remand prisoners in Nigeria that places them in such a vulnerable position and increases their rate of deaths in custody?

In an earlier comparative study of the problems of remand prisoners in Nigeria and England and Wales, it was found that despite the fact that Nigeria's legal and penal systems were transplanted from England, the country experiences a lot of problems with its remand population (Agomoh 1994). With a prison remand population three times higher than that of England/Wales and higher than any other European country, Nigerian remand prisoners are faced with numerous problems ranging from overcrowding, lack of clothing, lack of beds/blankets, poor feeding, poor medical facilities, prolonged incarceration, lack of contact with their families, lack of legal representation, to inability to meet their bail conditions, etc.

Remand prisoners in Nigeria are treated as second class citizens in prison even by fellow prisoners—and they bear the worst of the harsh conditions and poor standard of living in prisons (Odinkalu and Ehonwa 1991). This is how they put it:

> The case of awaiting of trial persons brings out both the brutality and the perversity of the Nigerian prison system. They stay longer in prison than most convicts and [they] suffer worse conditions of imprisonment than the average convict . . . All these make their life in prison more hellish than that of the average convict (p. 63).

On the question of prolonged incarceration, additional evidence exists. It has been reported that 59.8 per cent of remand prisoners spend more than five years remanded in custody (Nigerian Institute of Advance Legal Studies 1990). A further breakdown of this figure shows that 50.8 per cent spend between six and ten years, 5.7 per cent between 11 and 15 years while 3.3 per cent of them stay remanded in custody for over 15 years.

It may be difficult for one to understand the true nature of the relationship between remand prisoners or remand in prison and deaths in custody. Is it the fact of the anxiety and stress of being on remand or the conditions that remand prisoners experience by virtue of their being on remand, or a combination of both that is responsible for their high number of deaths in custody?

The nature of their crimes, the phase of imprisonment, the stage of custody, the type of sentence, age, and marital status are factors that have been mentioned in the western literature as being associated with suicides in prison (Gover 1880 as cited by Liebling 1992; Topp 1979; Dooley 1990a; Dooley 1990b; Liebling 1994). Other studies such as that on Aboriginal deaths in custody in Australia have examined the role of factors such as employment and educational status in relation to deaths in custody (including deaths by natural causes, hanging, injuries and use of alcohol and/or other drugs) (McDonald 1996). Can these factors possibly explain the kind of deaths recorded in Nigerian prisons? We do not have any available records of these factors in the lists of prison deaths to assess their validity in the Nigerian situation. However, in a survey of the socio-demographic and psycho-neurotic characteristics of ATPs in Nigeria, it was found that 97.8 per cent of the samples were male; 76.7 per cent were aged 20 to 39 years, 44.5 per cent reported the use of one or more addictive/psychoactive drugs and 48.9 per cent were married (Agomoh 1991b). The study also found that 67.7 per cent were charged with property and property-related offences, 34.4 per cent had a previous history of crime, while 54.4 per cent stated that they were innocent of the offences with which they were charged. This same study also reported a lot of social and psychological stresses and responsibilities amongst remand prisoners. For instance, 46.7 per cent had at least one child, 84.5 per cent had at least one parent alive and 78.8 per cent had at least one parent who was aged 50 years or more. This has to be viewed against the background of the extended family system and the social expectations which demand that an individual should take care of his/her aged parents. These responsibilities cannot be met while in prison and thus may add to the stress experienced by prisoners. Other possible vulnerability factors observed in the survey included poor socio-economic characteristics of remand prisoners. 87.8 per cent had minimal or no education and about 60 per cent had no employment or were 'ungainfully employed'. These factors explain why many of them could not afford the money or social contact to 'buy' food, medical treatment, bedding, clothing and other facilities as has been reported elsewhere:

> Deprived of visits from friends and relatives, as most of them (the awaiting trial prisoners) are, they have little or no money to procure bedding, clothing and other things which make life bearable in the prisons (Odinkalu and Ehonwa 1991, p. 66).

Even for some friends and families that visit, with the long period of awaiting trial, these visits drop dramatically (Africa Watch 1991).

From the foregoing, it thus seems that the conditions of remand prisoners in Nigerian prisons put them in a disadvantaged position which makes it more likely for them to be exposed to the factors that cause death. Therefore, it can rightly be concluded that being on remand is *the vulnerability factor* with respect to deaths in prison custody.

Causes of deaths in Nigerian prisons
As mentioned in an earlier study, there is no official record or evidence of death due to suicide or deliberate self-harm amongst Nigerian prisoners (Agomoh 1994). This should not be seen as implying that there are no cases of suicide in Nigerian prisons. There may be some cases of this but certainly these cases are rare. For instance, there was a case of one prisoner who jumped into a water well in the medium security prison Kirikiri, Lagos but was rescued. On investigation, it was found that this was the only experience of attempted suicide known to the prison—at least in the past 15 years.

From the official statistics as seen in *Table 1*, all the deaths that occur in prison (with the exception of those carried out in the execution of death sentences) are explained as deaths through 'natural causes'. This is highly questionable. In fact, there have been reports indicating that these deaths are far from being natural. Factors such as prison congestion, lack of adequate medical treatment, lack of or inadequate medical facilities, malnutrition, poor sanitation and torture have been reported as major causes of deaths in Nigerian prisons (Alemika 1993; Odinkalu and Ehonwa 1991; Ehonwa 1993; Agomoh 1995). We will examine briefly some of the evidence.

One of the respondents (a 26-year-old ex-prisoner of medium security prison Kirikiri, Lagos) in a study of the incidence of physical and psychological torture amongst prisoners reported that:

It is terrible inside the prison yard. There is no food, no water, and there are lots of mosquitoes. In fact, one of the inmates beside me died and for two days we did not know. We thought he was sleeping. It was when flies started perching on his eyes and ears that we knew he was dead. He had even started to smell. (Agomoh 1995, p. 4)

As frightening as the above evidence is, it is not an isolated case. There are several cases corrobrating this one. Even the Nigerian prison authorities have acknowledged that the high rates of deaths are caused by:

. . . Prison congestion, very poor standards of sanitation, malnutrition arising from poor feeding, and lack of drugs for sick prisoners. (Annual Prison Report 1984)

The prison authorities attribute this scenario to 'poor funding of the prisons arising from the present economic situation in the country' *(Prison Service Annual Report, 1984, 1986)*. However, independent observers have traced some of these causes to elaborate systems of theft and corruption, created in an attempt to ease the harsh lives of guards (Odinkalu and Ehonwa 1991). They reported instances of stealing prisoners' meagre supplies including food, bedding and drugs—thus worsening the already bad situation faced by the prisoners.

In the Agomoh study mentioned above (1995), it was observed that 71 per cent of the study sample (ex-prisoners) reported that while in custody they experienced lack of food or water, 63 per cent said they had experienced ill health without access to medical care, 100 per cent said they had been close to death and those that reported the unnatural death of a friend was also 100 per cent. This evidence shows the magnitude of the problem and explains to a great extent why there are so many deaths in Nigerian prisons.

There have also been instances of disease epidemics in prisons. For instance, it was reported that about 2,000 prisoners died in 1989 on account of an outbreak of scabies in Nigeria (Odinkalu and Ehonwa 1991). One ex-prisoner stated that the most common diseases in prison were kwashiorkor (malnutrition), tuberculosis, rheumatism, high fever, (body) pain, skin diseases. He further explained that:

TB (tuberculosis) is a famous (common) disease inside (the prison), when it catches (infects) some people, before five to seven days (they) die. People have leprosy, some people have ulcer, and when doctor recommends pepperless (non-peppery foods), they (the prison staff) don't normally give it. (Idown Sanusi, male ex-prisoner from Ikoyi Prison Lagos as reported in Odinkalu and Ehonwa 1991, p. 84)

The same study also reported gross inadequacy of medical facilities and staff in Nigerian prisons. For instance, out of 37 prisons visited, there were only three ambulances. Thus in times of emergencies, it is only these three prisons that are provided with the facility to respond. With the exception of Kaduna prison (which had three doctors), the highest number of doctors allocated to each of these prisons is one, but 11 out of the 37 prisons had no doctors. This falls short of the requirement of the UN Standard Minimum Rule for the Treatment of Prisoners which states that:

> At every institution there shall be available the services of at least a general practitioner. (Rule 21 (1))

With respect to medical beds: 15 prisons had no beds; eleven prisons had between one and three beds; five prisons had between four and six beds; four prisons had between eight and ten beds; while only two prisons had 35 and more beds. These are Port Harcourt prison (which had 35 beds) and Yola prison (which had 50 beds). See *Table 5* for a summary of the facilities observed in relation to the inmate population.

Table 5: Medical Facilities Observed in the 37 Prisons Visited

No. of prisons visited	Total inmate pop. of the prisons visited	No. of Doctor	No. of Nurses	No. of Beds	No. of Ambulance
37	26,281	27	69	165	3
Inmate ratio to facilities		1: 973	1: 381	1: 159	1: 8,760

With the above deficiencies of medical facilities, one wonders how much attention will be given to sick prisoners. There have also been instances of death due to food poisoning in Nigerian prisons. For instance, one of the ex-prisoner's testimonies reported in the above study commented that:

> While (he) was there (in prison), there were three deaths recorded in the 'welcome room'. One was as a result of cyanide acid from taking dry garri. The other was as a result of alleged poisoning administered on the victim by a prison warder in connivance with another inmate. (p. 89)

Beyond the issues of poor feeding, food poisoning, lack of medical treatment, and poor sanitation resulting in disease epidemics, there are cases of deaths caused by torture and intentional killing of prisoners by prison staff. The case of Daniel Ukpabi was one of such cases. He was reported to have been tortured to death by officers in Port Harcourt prison:

> He was singled out the next day and batoned (battered) so severely that he died the same day in cell 10 'B' Block where he's (was) dumped alone to avoid getting help from other inmates that would (have) assisted him at least to clean his battered body flooded with ground pepper . . . (Odinkalu and Ehonwa, 1991: p. 91)

In the earlier work mentioned above (Agomoh 1995), 90 per cent of the sample reported that they had personally experienced physical torture in custody and 100 per cent of them said that they had heard of physical torture while in custody. Thus, only ten per cent of the sample reported that they were never tortured physically.

The justification often given for this torture is usually linked to discipline and issues of control. However it is important to note that this is contrary to the UN Standard Minimum Rule for the Treatment of Prisoners which states that:

> Corporal punishment, punishment by placing in a dark cell, and all cruel, inhuman or degrading punishments shall be completely prohibited as punishments for disciplinary offences. (Rule 31)

Though we are focusing on deaths in prison custody, it should be mentioned that there are several incidences of torture in police custody which have eventually led to death. Ifowodo (1994) writing on this reported the testimony of Justine Jonny Eshiet, a 26-year-old driver:

> He was tied hands and legs and hung by a rope from the roof of the 'statement room'. In that position, he was flogged with metal wires by three police on different parts of the body, especially the shins of both legs, simultaneously. Two other policemen used pliers to pull at his fingernails. This treatment was interrupted only to ask whether he was ready to confess in writing . . . the torture continued, until he became unconscious, by then bleeding profusely. (pp 13-17)

This led to the death of the man and the post-mortem examination diagnosed the cause of his death as 'cardiorespiratory failure due to multiple soft tissue injury, and bilateral confluent bronchopneumonia'.

From the foregoing, it can be seen that unlike the case of deaths of Aboriginal and Torres Straits Islander people of Australia as reported by

McDonald (1996), deaths in Nigerian prisons are caused by both deliberate violence and brutality by prison staff and as a result of system failures and the failure of officers to exercise their duty of care to people in custody. With the above trend, characteristics of victims and reported causes of deaths in Nigerian prisons, one wonders what processes should be put in place to reduce this problem.

Lessons: Issues and intervention

The above evidence indicates that there are cross-country and cross-cultural lessons to be learned with respect to the type, rates and causes of deaths in prisons in both developed and developing countries. Using Nigeria as the case study, it is obvious that factors such as poor feeding, inadequate medical facilities, ill-health and torture are factors that account for a majority of the deaths in custody. Similar trends have also been observed in some other African countries. For instance, in 1995, Kenya's home affairs minister disclosed that about 583 prisoners died in Nairobi remand prison between May 1989 and June 1994 (thus an average of 9.6 prisoners died per month within the 62 months). The reasons given for these deaths by the minister were malaria, diarrhoea, tuberculosis and other lung diseases (Hunter and Odinkalu, 1997). The authors also reported that the incidence of mass starvation in Zairian prisons in recent times were only prevented by the intervention of humanitarian and religious organizations.

In Western countries, for instance the UK, we see a different trend. The bulk of the deaths in custody are linked to suicides or deliberate self-harm.

One therefore needs to ask, what is it about the Nigerian situation that makes suicides in prison a rare occurrence? How can the country learn from the experiences of other countries (especially the western countries) to provide a better standard of living for its prisoners and thus reduce the high incidence of deaths in custody? For the first question, answers can be found in the nature of African culture. Practices such as communal life, superstition, belief in life after death, the extended family system and the low level of individualism are possible explanations. Another possible explanation may lie in the fact that the prisoners are kept in dormitory-like accommodation as against single cells. This in addition to the fact that there is a high incidence of overcrowding which makes it difficult for any prisoner to be alone at any given time (except those in isolation cells), reduces the situational circumstances that are likely to facilitate successful suicides.

On the second question, there is a need for the Nigerian criminal justice system to reduce its prison population, especially those on remand. When this is done, it will make the prisons more manageable and less resources will be spent to achieve a better standard of living for the prisoners. Ways of achieving these have been enumerated elsewhere (see Agomoh 1996).

It is important to have an inquest on all deaths recorded in Nigerian prisons and police cells. To ensure unbiased evidence, the inquest must be carried out by independent people and when a trial/jury is constituted, the judgment should be impartial.

At present the situation does not present a good picture. It has been reported that no single instance is known in which:

> A judicial authority inquired into the cause of the death of any prison inmate, as required by Principle 34 of the Body of Principles for the Protection of All Persons Under Any Form of Detention or Imprisonment. Nor do we know of any in which an autopsy was conducted by a physician to ascertain the cause of death and his report made available to the public. (Africa Watch, April 1994, p. 3)

In the UK, all deaths in prisons are reported to the local coroner, and all inquests into prison deaths are held before a jury (Dooley, 1990b). There should not be any reason why this practice cannot be instituted in Nigeria. This will help keep track of all deaths in custody and unravel the reasons behind their occurrence, thereby ensuring that any person responsible for these deaths is brought to book.

It is important to mention that unlike suicide, deaths in custody due to an act or omission of another person (even if the person is a prison officer) is a culpable homicide.

As a rule, there should be comprehensive records of all deaths in prison. These records should contain information such as the age of the victim, the phase of his/her imprisonment, time of death, previous medical/mental state, treatment given etc. This is the only way proper research can be carried out on the subject. These researches will hopefully lead to findings which will aid the reduction or prevention of these deaths.

Another thing that will help encourage proper record keeping and inquests will be to prohibit the burying of any dead prisoner by the prison authority. Most often, prisoners are usually asked to bury the dead when the death occurs. As a rule, all dead prisoners should be deposited at the mortuary and the responsibility for burial should be passed to their families. In the absence of this, the state should take the responsibility. We believe that this arrangement will make it mandatory for families to be informed of the death of a family member in prison as soon as it occurs and for a proper post-mortem to be carried out. This will also put a form of check on the behaviour of prison officers, when they realise that other agencies will be involved in assessing the true cause of death of the victims.

Responses from the voluntary sector

What is needed to reform the Nigerian prisons and put in place structures that will help reduce the number of deaths in custody is the WILL. Such will may be difficult to find in the prevailing political climate. This is why a shift is necessary. The voluntary sector has a lot to do. Responses so far by the voluntary sector include the following:

- provision of basic necessities—food, drugs, clothing, soap, chewing sticks, disinfectants etc. Many of these donations are from religious groups. There have been reports that some of these drugs get stolen by some warders. There are instances of good warders, who will genuinely distribute these items to prisoners. Another way of ensuring that the items get to the prisoners is for the donating organizations to physically distribute the items to the prisoners. Many of the religious groups do this. They usually carry in cooked foods and distribute these by themselves to sick prisoners. Some of these religious groups often provide legal and medical assistance by bringing in their own lawyers and doctors/nurses.
- decongestion of the prison population and promotion of alternatives to incarceration. As was mentioned earlier, the problem of the high remand population in prison is one very significant contributing factor to the increase in deaths in Nigerian prisons. Assistance towards this can be divided into two: legal aid and facilitation of initiatives to promote alternatives to custody even at the remand stage. With respect to the first, there are a lot of organizations providing one form of legal aid or another. There is still need for more work in this area. More specialisation, co-ordination, networking, and quality legal representation is what is required to improve the effectiveness of these initiatives.
- our organization Prisoners Rehabilitation and Welfare Action (PRAWA)[4] is working towards the promotion of alternatives to incarceration. We have in February this year launched the handbook on good practice which contains practical and simple strategies for decongesting the remand population. The book is entitled *Decongesting The Nigerian Prisons and Police Cells: A Handbook of Practical Strategies for The Remand Population*. In following this up, we have tried to sustain the debate on the state of the Nigerian remand population. This we have done through

194

several media campaigns—using both the print media and audio-visuals.

- on training, PRAWA believes that many of the prison staff need a re-education based on the Standard Minimum Rule for the Treatment of Prisoners. They also need to have imparted adequate skills to carry out their duties in a just, humane and effective manner. To date, PRAWA has trained 86 prison staff drawn from several prisons in the country. This is just the tip of the iceberg. With a staff population of more than 22,000, there is still much to be done. There is also the need for more attention to focus on the issue of torture.
- research and documentation: as seen from the list of references made on the state of Nigerian prisons in this paper, there has been considerable work on this topic. This is commendable but more needs to be done. We need to have a clearer picture of the pattern, characteristics of victims and causes of deaths in Nigerian prisons.

Conclusion

Bernheim (1994) concluding his paper on 'Suicides and Prison Conditions' stated that:

> From the statistics and information gathered it is now no longer possible to question the fact that the high suicide rate in certain prisons or categories of prisons is directly and without any doubt related to inhuman prison conditions. (p. 108)

This statement is very true of the Nigerian situation. The high number of deaths in Nigerian prisons which are often passed as 'natural deaths' are directly linked to the terrible conditions in the Nigerian prisons. What we see is how gross human rights abuses and poor prison standards are linked to deaths in prison. This raises very serious moral and philosophical questions. What justification can there possibly be for these numerous deaths by prisoners awaiting trial who even the Nigerian law recognises should be presumed innocent until it is proved otherwise (Section 33(5) of the 1979 Constitution of the Federal Republic of Nigeria and Section 35(5) of the 1989 Constitution). Furthermore, the Nigerian Constitution guarantees the Right to Life:

> Every person has a right to life and shall not be deprived intentionally of his life, save in execution of the sentence of a court in respect of a criminal offence of which he has been found guilty in Nigeria. (Section 30(1) of the 1979 Constitution)

Though the appropriateness of the above provision is still questionable (especially in arguing against the issue of the death penalty) it is however clear that intentional killing of prisoners or the creation of conditions that will lead to their death is legally unacceptable for remand prisoners. Even for sentenced prisoners, the Right to Life can only be taken away when a death sentence has been passed after due trial and conviction in a court of law.

This paper has shown that deaths in Nigerian prisons are rarely as a result of suicides or deliberate self harm, rather they are deaths that are directly linked to factors such as food, medical facilities/treatment, diseases, torture and other related factors. These deaths are man made and can be easily prevented. The respect of basic fundamental rights of prisoners and the observance of the provisions of the UN Standard Minimum Rules for the Treatment of Prisoners is all that is needed to reduce deaths in Nigerian prisons.

What we observe is not usually abrupt death like in suicides or accidents, rather a process of dying. A gradual death and, no doubt, this will be even more painful to the victims.

Uju Agomoh is Founder/Director of Prisoners' Rehabilitation and Welfare Action (PRAWA), a charity based in Lagos, Nigeria which is committed to the provision of support services for prisoners, ex-prisoners and their families, as well as to change within the Nigerian criminal justice system. She is also the West African regional co-ordinator of the Africa Network Against Torture (ANAT). Ms Agomoh lectures in criminology and the sociology of law at Lagos State University.

ENDNOTES

1 The inclusion of four months (i.e. January to April 1990) for the data on Warri Prison can be adjusted by the three months (i.e. October to December) excluded from the figure for Ikoyi Prison in 1989.

2 Nigeria prison population for the year 1989 as given by the *Annual Abstract of Statistics* (1995 edition), *Table 88*, p. 137.

3 Data was available for only to the the third day of the month.

4 PRAWA is a non-governmental organization (charity) established in December 1994. Its main objective is to facilitate the improvement of the Nigerian criminal justice and penal syste and to provide support services for prisoners, ex-prisoners and their families.

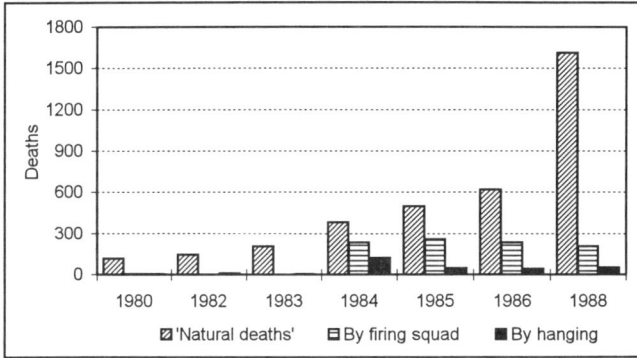

Chart 1: Number of Deaths Resulting from the Major Causes of Prisoners' Deaths

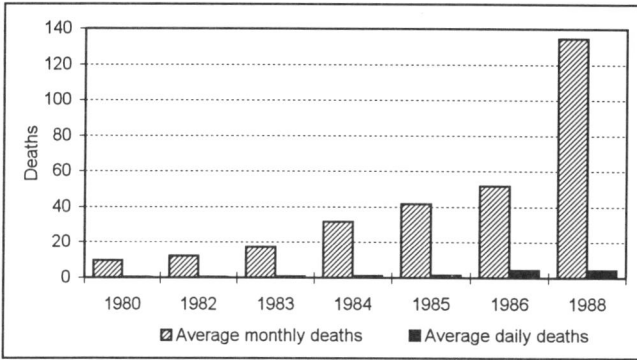

Chart 2: Average Monthly and Average Daily Deaths

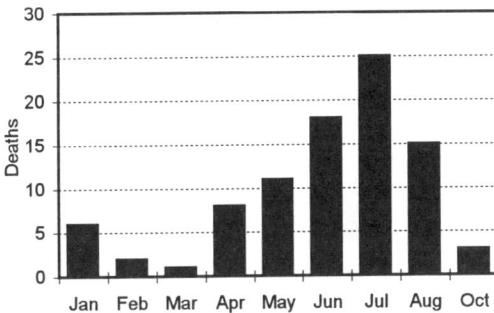

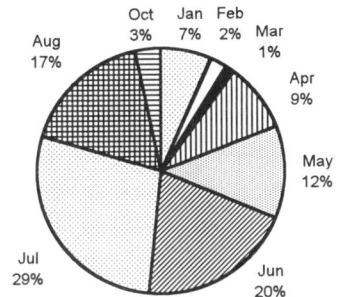

Chart 3 (a) and (b): Frequency of Deaths for a Period of Nine Months

197

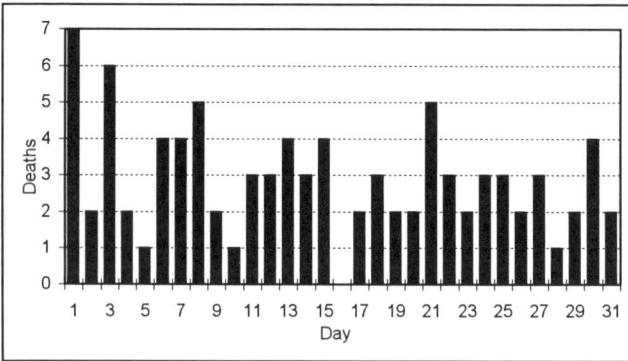

Chart 4: Daily Distribution of Deaths

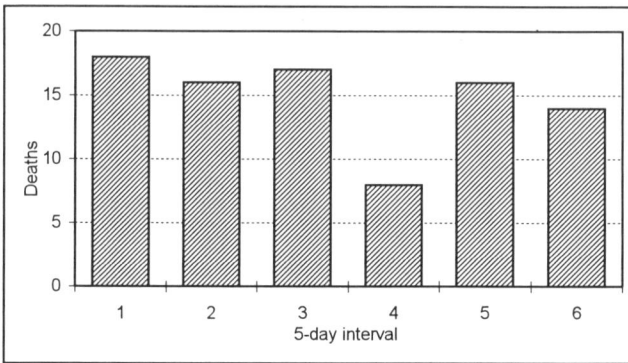

Chart 5: Number of Deaths During Every Five Day Interval

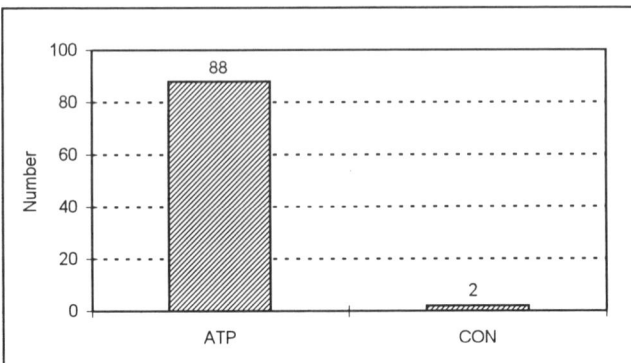

Chart 6: Number of Awaiting Trial and Convicted Prisoners Deaths

PART FOUR

Prevention of Deaths in Custody

CHAPTER 15

Prevention of Suicides in the Dutch Criminal Justice System

Eric Blaauw, Frans Schilder and Stef van de Lande

Introduction

In many countries, suicides in the criminal justice system are a matter of concern. Although every such unnatural death is one too many, it is not actually the *number* of suicides that causes such concern. Suicides in prisons, remand centres and police stations occur in much smaller numbers than for instance traffic accidents or homicides in the community. Instead, it is the suicide *rates* that give reasons for concern. Several publications and previous international conferences of the Institute for the Study and Treatment of Delinquency (ISTD) have shown that suicide rates in custody are higher than are those in the general population. European and Australian prison system suicide rates are between three and eleven times the rate in the community (Liebling, 1992 p. 24) and the suicide rate in the United States of America criminal justice system is at least three times the national average (Tuskan and Thase 1983).

Suicide rates are higher among unsentenced prisoners than among sentenced prisoners and higher in jails or remand centres than in prisons. In the USA, the suicide rate in jails is approximately six times the suicide rate in prisons (see Hayes 1989, 1995). In England and Wales, the percentage of remand prisoners in the suicide group was found to be more than four times the percentage of remand prisoners in the total detainee population (Dooley 1990). In Scotland, Canada, Norway, and surely many other countries, unsentenced prisoners also account for higher proportions of the suicide groups than of the general population (cf Backett 1987; Hammerlin and Bodal 1988; Scott-Denoon 1984). The few existing studies on police custody suicides invariably show that police custody suicide rates are even higher than prison system suicide rates. An Australian study showed that the self inflicted death ratio was higher in police custody than in prison (McDonald and Thomson 1993). The suicide rate in the United States of America criminal justice system increases from approximately nine times the rate in the community to approximately 16 times the rate in the community when police lock ups are included in the equation (Hayes 1983). In South Carolina, the suicide rate in police department lock ups was even found to be 250 times the rate in the state's general population (Memory 1984). The conclusion that can be drawn from these findings is that suicides occur more often in the early stages of confinement than in the later stages.

In the past years, both the number of Dutch police custody suicides and Dutch prison system suicides have fluctuated. Overall, in the past decade an average number of two detainees committed suicide whilst locked up in a Dutch police station and an average number of six to seven detainees committed suicide whilst imprisoned in the Dutch prison system. In the years 1995 and 1996, the figure rose to 14 and 16 prison system suicides respectively. The vast majority of these deaths occurred among the unsentenced population (Kerkhof and Bernasco 1990). The numbers of suicides are small when one considers that the Dutch criminal justice system consists of about 2,000 police cells and 12,000 prison system cells and that there are about 160,000 police lock ups and 32,000 imprisonments each year. Conversely, the Dutch numbers of suicides are high when one converts these numbers into rates per average daily population of 100,000 persons, and when one subsequently compares these rates to the rate in a Dutch male population with the same age distribution (Blaauw, Kerkhof and Vermunt 1997). The Dutch police custody suicide rate is twice as high as that in the Dutch prison system, whose suicide rate is about eight times as high as that in a Dutch male population (respectively, 210, 105 and 13 per 100,000). Based on these rates, one has to conclude that suicides in the Dutch criminal justice system give reason for concern.

Suicides are not the only problem in Dutch police stations. Deaths due to intoxication are an area of concern also. On average, two police custody detainees die from alcohol or drugs poisoning each year. As was also the case with the suicide fatality number, the small poisoning fatality number represents a high poisoning fatality rate. The rate of fatal intoxications in police custody is 200 per average daily population of 100,000, which is 50 times as high as that in the Dutch prison system and also 50 times as high as that in the Dutch general population. The Dutch situation is not unique in this respect because deaths due to poisoning are also a problem in police custody in Canada, Denmark, Australia, England and Wales, and probably many other countries (cf Giles and Sandrin 1992; Johnson 1982; Segest 1987; Thomson and McDonald 1993). All in all, the Dutch criminal justice system is not different from any other when it comes to unnatural deaths.

Explanations for different suicide rates
Several factors may contribute to the excess of suicides in the early stages of confinement. One possible explanation is that average daily population rates are not advantageous, especially not for police stations. Average daily population rates allow for the possibility that the rate is

overstated because the person-year is shared by several people whose risk of suicide may be greater in the early days of custody, and the possibility that the maximum rate of 100 per cent is breached again because the person-year is shared by several people (O'Mahony 1994). Clearly, police stations have a shorter duration of stay than do remand centres, and remand centres have a shorter duration of stay than do prisons. In The Netherlands, a person-year in Dutch police stations consists of 182.5 detainees and can thus sustain up to 182.5 suicides. A man-year in the Dutch prison system consists of 3.5 detainees and can thus sustain up to 3.5 suicides. With equal numbers of person-years, police stations thus have a larger population at risk than do remand centres.

Another possible explanation for the excess of suicides in the early stages of confinement is that police stations have to deal with proportionally more people at risk than do remand centres. The police bring in mentally ill people and suicidal people for reasons of assistance only. They also arrest many mentally ill people and suicidal people for fairly trivial offences. Several of these people are then admitted elsewhere due to treatment considerations dominating over legal considerations or due to the absence of legal considerations. It is also likely that some of the acutely suicidal people commit suicide in the early stages of confinement and thus never reach a remand centre or a prison. Clearly, the higher rate of fatal poisonings in police stations as compared to remand centres and the community can be accounted for by this explanation. The proportion of intoxicated people in police stations is usually higher than that in the community because the police arrest a lot of people for reasons such as driving under the influence of alcohol, public drunkenness, and drug-trafficking. The number of intoxicated people is also proportionally higher in police stations than that in remand centres because people stay a couple of days in a police station before being transferred to a remand centre. By the time such a transfer takes place, hazardous intoxications have already resulted in death or have already been dealt with.

A third possible explanation for the higher suicide rate in police stations as compared to remand centres or prisons is that detainees experience disproportionate amounts of stress especially in the early stages of confinement. Most symptom levels are at their peak immediately after incarceration and tend to decrease with time spent in jail or prison (cf Gibbs 1987; Paulus and Dzindolet 1993; Zamble and Porporino 1988). Moreover, police custody detainees suffer more from depressive and psychosomatic symptoms than do remand centre detainees (Blaauw, Kerkhof and Vermunt, in press). These effects are probably predominantly due to the abruptness of the life changing event, the high levels of uncertainty, and the many deprivations in especially the early stages of confinement. Clearly, the transition from liberty to incarceration is usually more sudden for police custody detainees than for remand centre or prison detainees because the former experience a transition from freedom to incarceration whilst the latter experience a transition from one lock up situation to another lock up situation. In addition, levels of uncertainty are usually higher in the initial phases of the legal process. Furthermore, police station cell-blocks are usually less comfortable and more depriving than are those in penal institutions. For instance, remand centres generally provide detainees with work, exercise, telephone time, visiting hours, books, movies and television whilst police stations generally do not (cf Blaauw, Vermunt and Kerkhof 1997; Kleinjan and Smidt 1994).

A fourth possible explanation for the suicide rates being respectively lower through the sequential stages of confinement is that preventive measures are better and/or more extensive in the later stages of confinement. Although there is no empirical evidence about which measures, or combinations of measures, are successful for the reduction of imminent suicide risk, there are several measures that can be used to reduce acute suicide risk. Obviously, an important first preventive measure is to identify those with heightened suicide risk. An important second preventive measure is to provide psychological support for suicidal detainees. According to Kerkhof and Diekstra (1995, p. 113):

> the most powerful preventive strategy for acute suicide risk is to offer a close personal contact with an understanding and caring person who is willing to stay and to be available to share the emotional turmoil and despair.

A third preventive measure is to observe suicidal detainees closely. Close monitoring increases the chances that suicidal persons are caught in the act, and increases the chances that there is sufficient time to still save them after the act. A fourth preventive measure is to disarm suicidal detainees of the instruments that can be used to commit suicide. Such measures includes the removal of potentially hazardous materials, like belts, shoestrings and ropes, and the construction of cell-blocks that are supposed to minimise the possibilities for committing suicide. A fifth preventive measure is to transfer suicidal detainees to institutions that are better equipped to deal with suicidal behaviour, such as general hospitals or psychiatric institutions. Generally, procedures for suicide prevention must be clear for all employees in contact with detainees. Preventive measures must also be applied consistently. A suicide prevention protocol is beneficial, if not necessary. Training programmes for the people involved with detainees serve the same purpose. Assuming that the most effective suicide prevention programme consists of a multitude of strategies (see Felthous 1994), it is possible that the police have adopted a smaller number of preventive measures than have remand centres or that some of their preventive measures are of poorer quality.

In what follows, we discuss these possibilities in greater detail, specifically which preventive measures are taken by Dutch police stations and which by Dutch remand centres, or houses of detention as we call them. Information about the preventive measures in Dutch police stations predominantly stems from a study that Blaauw, Vermunt and Kerkhof (1997) conducted on detention circumstances in 60 Dutch police stations. That about preventive measures in houses of detention predominantly stems from the personal experiences of the second and third author of this chapter, and many conversations with psychologists working in Dutch penal institutions whom we regularly met in a post-doctoral course about suicide prevention in penal facilities.

Suicide prevention in police stations
There are many differences between Dutch police stations. Basically, all that can vary between police stations actually does vary. Some police stations are large, whereas others are small. Some police stations have the custodial task assigned to specialist personnel, whereas others have the custodial task assigned to regular police officers on duty. Some cell-blocks are old and have few facilities, whereas others are modern and fully equipped. Some police stations provide detainees with good quality facilities, whereas others provide them with poor quality facilities. Some police stations treat all detainees alike, whereas others treat specific groups of detainees in accordance with their special needs. Large police stations generally provide detainees with better housing, interaction, and differential treatment than do small police stations (Blaauw, Vermunt and Kerkhof 1997). Police stations with specialised custodial divisions generally provide detainees with better detention circumstances than do police stations without specialised custodial divisions.

Some measures for the prevention of suicides also vary between police stations. Other measures, however, do not vary between police stations. Screening for suicide risk is similar in all Dutch police stations. Protocols and training procedures are also not much different between police stations. However, monitoring procedures, provision of psychological support, disarmament of suicidal instruments, and procedures for the transfer of suicidal detainees to other institutions differ between police stations. As a matter of fact, such procedures also vary within police stations, depending on which officers are on duty. These variations within police stations probably reflect the great authority to make decisions given to individual officers. Therefore, our discussion of preventive measures in Dutch police stations only gives a description of the customary measures in those stations. As a result, one has to keep in mind that at the collective level (police stations) as well as on an individual level (police officers) there is considerable variation.

Screening for suicide risk

There are some characteristics that are common among Dutch police custody suicide victims (see Blaauw, Kerkhof and Vermunt 1997). Generally, Dutch police custody suicide victims are young, isolated (single, separated or divorced, widowed), unemployed, repeat offenders who have been arrested for either property offences or major offences. In addition, they are typically substance dependent, former psychiatric patients who abused substances shortly before their arrest. Furthermore, many suicide victims at some time during their incarceration threaten to kill themselves and are known to have a history of previous suicidal behaviour. Some of these characteristics do not have discriminative power in the Dutch police custody population because the regular detainees have the same characteristics as do the suicide victims, but there are also some characteristics that distinguish suicide victims from detainees who are not suicidal. Unemployment is somewhat more common among the regular police custody population than among the suicide cases. Histories of any psychiatric treatment and of in-patient psychiatric treatment are slightly more prevalent among the suicide cases than among the regular detainees. The prevalence rates of substance abuse and substance dependence are substantially higher among the suicide victims than among the regular police custody detainees. Suicide victims more often seem to display suicidal ideation and suicidal communication, and more often seem to have a history of previous suicide attempts. Therefore, looking out for suicidal remarks, questioning detainees about suicidal intent, and screening all new detainees about whether they are unemployed, histories of psychiatric treatment, substance abuse, substance dependence, and a history of previous suicide attempts will definitely provide some information about the presence of suicide risk. Screening for suicide risk and being alert to suicidal communication will unavoidably lead to many detainees being wrongfully detected as suicidal because assessment of imminent suicide risk is complex, especially when one deals with a population that is characterised by those characteristics that predispose for suicide. This is not a good reason, however, for not screening detainees on the presence of suicide risk.

Screening new detainees for the presence of suicide risk is not standard procedure in police stations in The Netherlands. As a matter of fact, none of the 60 police stations that were visited in an earlier study (see Blaauw, Vermunt and Kerkhof 1997) were found to screen new detainees for suicide risk, let alone ask newcomers about suicidal intent. Inadequate equipment is not the reason for this omission. Approximately 80 per cent of Dutch police stations make use of computer-software programmes, for the registration of new detainees, that includes a question about the suicidality of the new detainee. The reason for the absence of screening may be that Dutch police organizations do not always know which characteristics are associated with suicide risk. The findings of the study on police custody suicides became available only recently. It is also not standard procedure in the Dutch police stations to call in psychiatrists for the assessment of detainees who are considered suicidal or who may be suicidal. Police employees have the possibility of notifying psychiatrists or psychologists of regional centres for outpatient mental health care in relation to detainees who may be suicidal, but they do not always make use of it. In doing so, police employees take a risk because assessment of imminent suicide risk often requires knowledge of diagnostic criteria of psychiatric disorders which are usually associated with suicide risk, like schizophrenia, major depression, and borderline personality disorder. All in all, the quality of screening procedures in Dutch police stations is not good, making improvements possible and desirable.

Monitoring procedures

There is some debate about how often regular and irregular detainees should be monitored. Frequent monitoring increases the chance of swift reactions in emergencies and lets detainees know that police officers care about the well-being of detainees. On the other hand, frequent monitoring can only be maintained with sufficient numbers of employees and it may cause detainees discomfort due to invasion of their privacy. Nevertheless, it seems worthwhile to monitor suicidal persons very frequently, for instance once every five minutes, and to monitor them at irregular intervals so that they do not know when they are being monitored. In the United States of America, the National Commission on Correctional Health Care issued strict monitoring guidelines. According to these guidelines, detainees who have recently attempted suicide should be checked every five to ten minutes while asleep and continually while awake. Detainees who are considered a high risk of suicide should be checked every ten minutes while asleep and every five minutes while awake. Detainees who have been assessed as being a moderate risk of suicide should be checked every 30 minutes

207

while asleep and every ten minutes while awake. Level four detainees, who might be at risk of becoming seriously depressed, should be checked every 30 minutes while asleep and while awake. In The Netherlands, there are no specific guidelines for suicide prevention, but an interpretation of Dutch ministerial guidelines for the treatment of police custody detainees suggest that suicidal detainees should be monitored at least once every 15 minutes.

From our studies it became clear that Dutch police stations predominantly rely on monitoring procedures for dealing with suicide risk. The Dutch police typically check irregular detainees approximately once every 15 minutes or once every half hour, although some police stations check irregular detainees only once every hour or once every two hours. The police usually do not, in their monitoring procedures, make a distinction between suicidal schizophrenic detainees, suicidal detainees who have a borderline personality disorder, or suicidal detainees who are suffering from alcohol dependence/intoxication, major depression, or other psychiatric disorders. All suicidal detainees are usually treated alike and monitored with about the same frequency. The fact that suicides have occupied in the past years are proof of the flaws of those monitoring procedures. Eleven suicide victims had not had contact with a police officer in over half an hour. Six suicide victims had not had contact with a police officer in over two hours. Clearly, such a long duration of time is sufficient to commit suicide.

Dutch police stations do not have a 'buddy' suicide watch system for the continuous monitoring of suicidal detainees (see Rowan 1994). The one-person-per-cell policy, the Dutch Code of Criminal Conduct, and the necessary voluntary participation of several detainees (due to ethical reasons and the fairly short duration of stay) stand in the way of such a measure. Instead, the police often rely on camera-cells (There are about 80 camera-cells in police stations in the Netherlands). The Dutch Code of Conduct for police officials specifically states that this measure is allowed when detainees are suicidal, however only after approval of the Crown counsel. Of course, placement in a camera-cell is not a guarantee of continuous monitoring, so that such a measure is not always sufficient to prevent suicide. Also, one of the suicide victims was able to commit suicide despite the presence of a camera in his cell. One must conclude from these findings that, although Dutch police stations rely heavily on monitoring procedures, such procedures are not of the best quality, which again makes improvements possible and desirable.

Disarmament of suicidal instruments
In The Netherlands, there is some discussion about whether police custody detainees should be allowed to have potentially hazardous

materials available in their cells. When a suicide has occurred in a Dutch police station, one often hears the question 'Why was his belt not removed?' or 'Why did he still have his shoelaces available?' These questions are quite legitimate because the policy of the Dutch police is to remove objects that can be used to cut or hang oneself. A survey revealed that less than five per cent of Dutch police stations allow detainees to keep their belts, shoelaces, or jewellery (Blaauw, Kerkhof and Vermunt 1993). More than a quarter of police stations also remove detainees' spectacles, shoes, handkerchiefs, and bras. Some police stations do not even allow detainees to keep their contact lenses. Moreover, when detainees are considered to be suicidal, even their clothes are sometimes removed. Another policy of the Dutch police is to remove all objects from cells that can be used to attach a hangman's rope. This policy is partially led by a Ministerial decree which asserts that the interior of all cells should be such that suicides are avoided as much as possible. Dutch cells typically consist of nothing else than a bunk that is attached to the floor, a concrete chair and a concrete table which are attached to a wall, a steel toilet that is attached to the floor or a wall, and a steel door. Sometimes cells also consist of a water fountain that is made of steel and attached to a wall. All in all, Dutch police stations greatly value the disarmament of suicidal instruments and do a great job in this respect.

There is reason to believe that the removal of potentially lethal objects and the placement of detainees in 'suicide-proof' cells are not always effective preventive measures. In some suicide cases in Dutch police stations, victims did not have belts or ropes, but were very creative in finding other materials that could be used to commit suicide, such as clothes or even handkerchiefs. Furthermore, some of the suicides took place in cells that were considered to be suicide-proof. Here too detainees were very creative. Eight people had no trouble in finding an object to attach the rope to due to constructional shortcomings in the cell-block. Thus, the restriction of easy access to lethal methods may be an important step in the prevention of suicide, but surely is not always an effective measure. Once more, improvements are possible and desirable.

Provision of psychological support
Providing psychological support to suicidal detainees is not an easy task. Many skills are needed to identify the suicidal person's expression of feelings of rage, anger, aggression, resentment, inferiority, remorse, and sadness to influence the suicidal person's psychological state and his or her reasons for wanting to die, a discussion of those reasons, and an investigation of which problem-solving strategies have not been

tried yet. A complicating factor in police stations is that the vast majority of detainees are depressed and many threaten to kill themselves, simply because they are faced with a very threatening situation. As a consequence, many police officers, but also many (mental) health care professionals, have a tendency to view suicidal behaviour in cell-blocks as acts of manipulation instead of actual suicidal behaviour (cf Kerkhof and Bernasco 1990). One Dutch suicide victim demonstrated the wrongfulness of this tendency. This person continuously threatened to kill himself, but was not taken seriously. A day after his arrest, he showed a police officer that he had cut himself with a plastic knife. The general practitioner who treated his wounds stated that he believed that it was an act of manipulation. The next day, the detainee showed that he had cut himself once more. Again, a general practitioner declared that it was probably an act of manipulation. Police officers searched the detainee's cell for the presence of sharp objects, and found a pile of pills that had been gathered in the previous days. Although the police officers did not consider the detainee to be suicidal, they locked him up in a cell without any furniture. One day later the detainee showed a police officer that he had swallowed some buttons from off of his mattress and some pieces of 'Seven-Up' cans. Once more, police officers considered this behaviour to be manipulative. After the detainee had hung himself in the shower, the 'Rijksrecherche' concluded that the death was probably the result of manipulation which had got out of hand. This case demonstrates that, although lock ups appear to be inextricably associated with high levels of depression and many suicidal acts, this does not indicate that depression and suicidal behaviour should not be paid attention to. The presence of a *reason* for depression or suicidality does not constitute a reason for ignoring its presence (Fawcett 1972).

None of the Dutch police stations focus on the provision of psychological support as a preventive measure for suicide. Police employees providing custodial care are responsible for many aspects of the daily routine in police station cell-blocks. This means that they do not have much time to spend with an individual. Apart from lack of time, police employees providing custodial care usually do not have the skills to provide adequate psychological support to suicidal detainees. Police officials can contact mental health professionals from regional mental health care institutions, but these professionals do not treat detainees within cell-blocks. They give advice about whether the detainees can be held locked up at all and they assist in finding a suitable place to which the detainee can be transferred if it is decided that the police cell is deemed unsuitable. Finally, it is not feasible to allow family members, partners, or other close relatives to be constantly present in the cell-blocks, because this would disrupt the daily routine considerably and would require the availability of special rooms. All in all, police stations are not equipped to provide extensive psychological support to suicidal detainees. We have to conclude once more that improvements are possible and desirable.

Transfer of suicidal detainees to other institutions
Each police station in The Netherlands has to make its own arrangements for transferring exceptional detainees elsewhere. Dutch police stations often have contracts with regional medical health care services for the examination of ill or physically injured detainees. These health workers can also assist in finding a suitable hospital or shelter when such detainees are considered unfit for lock up. Dutch police stations usually also have contracts with regional mental health care services for the examination of mentally ill and suicidal detainees. These mental health workers also assist in finding a suitable psychiatric hospital when detainees are considered unfit for lockup and when there are no serious charges. The problem is, however, that general hospitals and psychiatric hospitals are usually reluctant to admit police custody detainees because they focus on treatment instead of safety. Consequently, it frequently occurs that police stations fail in their attempts to have unusual detainees, such as suicidal detainees, admitted elsewhere. Even (mental) health care workers cannot always solve this problem. In the period 1983 to 1993 there were two suicide victims who were brought to the police station *because* they were suicidal. Certainly, it would have been better if these individuals had been brought elsewhere.

Recently, Dutch police stations seem to have started to recognise the possibility of transferring suicidal detainees to houses of detention. It is common practice to transfer police custody detainees to a house of detention after a couple of days, but on occasion the police have requested the admittance of a suicidal detainee to a house of detention earlier because the detainee was no longer manageable. Transferring suicidal detainees is, however, not common procedure in police stations. Thus . . . improvements are both possible and desirable. In this case, however, they seem to be in progress.

Protocols and training
The fastest developing aspect of suicide prevention in police stations in The Netherlands is the development of protocols and training. Recently, the Dutch Ministry of the Interior decided to create a training programme for police employees providing custodial care as part of the package of so-called assigned training programmes. This means that the

costs of this training programme are refunded by the Dutch Ministry and that police stations are encouraged to send their personnel to it. In the past, only a few police stations sent their custodial officers to training programmes. Moreover, all the training programmes were suited to the police stations' demands, which hardly ever included training in suicide prevention. Prevention protocols are also improving at a fast rate in many police stations. In 1994, a new Police Law was issued, which included several regulations for the custodial task. This new law forced Dutch police stations to adapt their local duty prescriptions. In the process of incorporating the new regulations and procedures in the new duty prescriptions, several police stations took the opportunity to reconsider and modify their procedures for suicide prevention. Other police stations, however, still have their old duty prescriptions. We discovered from the study of detention circumstances in police stations that many of the old duty prescriptions are far from effective when it comes to suicide prevention. Many duty prescriptions do not even mention measures for suicide prevention and of those that do mention such measures several are limited to a description of monitoring procedures and the removal of potentially hazardous objects. All in all, suicide prevention protocols and training programmes are improving, but the position is still far from satisfactory.

Suicide prevention in houses of detention
Dutch houses of detention have their own procedures and protocols concerning suicide prevention. In the best cases, there are comprehensive protocols and in the worst cases no protocols for the prevention of suicides whatsoever. As a consequence, preventive measures vary between Dutch houses of detention, and in some cases also within houses of detention. The descriptions below, therefore, only provide a general description of preventive measures in houses of detention in The Netherlands. Preventive measures are not entirely different between houses of detention. All houses of detention have their Psycho-Medical Council that forms the core of all suicide prevention measures. Members of the Psycho-Medical Council communicate about detainees regularly and work together in order to establish and provide co-ordinated professional care. The Psycho-Medical Council also advises administrators and correctional officers (in The Netherlands they are called penitentiary institutional workers) about intervention procedures and internal and external transfers. The core of the Psycho-Medical Council consist of an institutional medical practitioner, a nurse, a psychiatrist, a representative of the social work profession and a psychologist. The medical practitioner, assisted by

nurses, deals with the identification and treatment of medical problems. The psychiatrist establishes the presence of mental illnesses and provides medical treatment or gives advice about which environmental conditions may be beneficial for dealing with a troubled detainee. The social worker assists with a detainee's psycho-social problems, such as divorce, financial problems, or loss of employment. Finally, the psychologist helps detainees to cope with cognitive, emotional, and behavioural problems. In some instances, other care services are represented in the Psycho-Medical Council as well. For instance, a humanist counsellor, a vicar or a pastor can join the Psycho-Medical Council when detainees are troubled by problems of an existential, religious, or life-contemplative nature. Although members of the Psycho-Medical Council have their specific orientation, there is actually quite an overlap in their activities. All have direct contact with their clients and all serve as detectors of psychological, social, medical and economic problems. All in all, the Psycho-Medical Council provides the basis of the suicide prevention measures.

The sudden rise of the suicide-rate in houses of detention in 1995 and 1996 caused a nationwide re-evaluation of the (standard) preventive measures. A conference was held in Amsterdam (November 1995) and administrators in several houses of detention instigated task forces and conducted surveys. A suicide prevention training course for correctional officers was set up by the training institute of the Dutch penitentiary system, which course has already been taught to some groups. Additionally, post-doctoral suicide prevention courses for criminal justice system psychologists were set up by the Vrije Universiteit Amsterdam and Groningen University, which courses will eventually be attended by all psychologists working in Dutch houses of detention. Furthermore, the Ministry of Justice commissioned the Department of Clinical Psychology of the Vrije Universiteit Amsterdam to conduct research with the aim of developing an accurate screening list for the identification of suicide risk. Recently, four houses of detention participated in a graduate student survey about which risk factors are considered important by correctional officers. Finally, the Ministry of Justice is assembling all existing notes and protocols with the aim of the central development of standardised guidelines for procedures and protocols. All in all, there is reason to believe that preventive measures will be more equivocal in the near future.

Screening for suicide risk

Basically, profiles of suicide victims in Dutch houses of detention seem to be fairly similar to those of Dutch police custody suicide victims (Kerkhof and Bernasco 1990). However, alcohol and substance abuse as risk factors differ from those in police stations because intoxication at the time of arrival in the facilities is rare, but the detainee can, however, suffer from withdrawal or can be confronted by problems that were formerly suppressed by the use of substances. Unfortunately, many contributing factors still remain obscure because comprehensive research on suicide risk factors has not been conducted yet in The Netherlands.

In most houses of detention it has become good practice for the booking office and admissions department to be alert to possible signs of psychiatric states like depression, psychosis and severe conduct disorders. In the admission interview at the medical department in houses of detention, nurses routinely inquire about medical and psychiatric history and about previous suicide attempts. It is also quite common among nurses, however, not to inquire about previous suicide attempts because they consider such questions to be inappropriate or too confronting.

New arrivals are usually placed in a so-called 'incoming division', to which placement they have to adjust one way or the other. In such a division they have to engage in contacts with other detainees, which may induce anxiety and stress and create feelings of shame and loss of status, perhaps especially for those detainees without prior criminal histories or those charged with sex-related offences. Therefore, correctional officers of the incoming divisions have an essential role in the identification of signs of mental or behavioural problems which might add to suicide risk. Each correctional officer of the incoming division, and any other member of staff, is usually encouraged to warn a member of the Psycho-Medical Council if he or she feels that he or she has spotted a sign of suicidal ideation. In most cases, the psychologist then makes the (first) thorough assessment of possible suicide risk.

All in all, several arrangements exist to identify detainees with heightened suicide risk. None of these arrangements are entirely standard though. Detainees are not screened on the basis of an instrument that includes all risk factors for suicide and that includes specific questions about suicidal ideation and suicidal intent. Therefore, improvements are possible and desirable.

Monitoring procedures

Different degrees of monitoring of suicidal detainees are possible during the night. Detainees with imminent suicide risk are usually monitored up to once every half hour. Detainees with less imminent suicide risk are usually monitored once every hour or once every two hours. In practice, such monitoring consists of a correctional officer opening the hatch and looking carefully for life signs. When the detainee is awake, it is customary to inquire about his or her condition. The Psycho-Medical Council, or under certain circumstances the head of duty, decides whose name shall be put on the monitoring list, the so-called night-watch list. When detainees' names are on the monitoring list, they also receive special attention during day-time. This includes checking whether they engage in the activities provided and keeping an eye on them when they do not engage in the daily activities.

Depending on diagnostics and risk level, the Psycho-Medical Council can arrange regular supervision by one or more care providers on a daily to weekly basis. Of course, for the sake of continuity, this requires good communication between the several care providers. The Psycho-Medical Council can also assign a suicidal detainee to the Special Care Division where more extensive and specialised attention is possible. The Special Care Division predominantly houses mentally ill detainees, detainees with a serious medical problem, and vulnerable detainees (including suicidal ones) of whom it is considered that they are not able to cope in a regular division. Special Care Divisions have a higher detainee/staff ratio than do ordinary divisions, and staff consist of specialised correctional officers who are carefully selected and trained to deal with these difficult categories of detainees. In addition, the Special Care Division has got its own regime with possibilities for care on an individual basis, and a short communication route to the members of the Psycho-Medical Council.

All in all, the intensity of monitoring is dependent on the imminence of the suicide risk. However, even in the best scenario the intensity of monitoring does not approach the guidelines issued by the American National Commission of Correctional Health Care, which mandated an intensity up to once every five minutes or even continual monitoring. Some houses of detention have camera-cells, which allow for the continual impersonal monitoring of suicidal detainees. Continual personal monitoring of suicidal detainees in Dutch houses of detention is not yet possible. Although spontaneous warnings concerning suicide risk are sometimes given by fellow detainees, there is no provisi on for a 'buddy-suicide watch' system (Rowan 1994) in the sense that other detainees are trained and used as a suicide watch. Improvements are thus possible.

Disarmament of suicidal instruments
The removal of suicidal means from the cell of a suicidal detainee is standard procedure in Dutch houses of detention. In most houses of detention this means that cutlery, belts, shoestrings, sharp objects and glass (including television), and other hazardous materials are removed from the cells. However, correctional officers individually assess the potential lethalness of objects. Moreover, cells are usually stacked with

detainee's personal belongings and various objects, which makes removal of objects a time-consuming task. For this reason, some special care divisions in houses of detention have so-called 'strip-cells' where curtain-rails can be removed easily and where all protrusions are limited and made of vandal-proof material.

All Dutch houses of detention have isolation cells. Such cells are typically approximately 12 square metres in size, with nothing in them but a mattress, a steel toilet and an opaque window. The toilet can be flushed only from the outside. In the isolation cell it is standard procedure to remove a detainee's clothes and provide him or her with a 'tear-resistant' shirt. Although placement in an isolation cell is a humiliating situation for many detainees, it is still common practice in houses of detention to transfer detainees with imminent suicide risk, or detainees with possible suicide risk, to the isolation block. During working hours, transfer to the isolation cell happens only after careful assessment by the psychologist or another member of the Psycho-Medical Council. After working hours and at weekends, when there is no psychologist present, transfer to the isolation cells is often decided upon without careful assessment. This option is usually chosen because the isolation cell is believed to be the place with virtually no possibilities to commit suicide. The most severe form of restraint is to buckle up a detainee onto a safety-bed, so that he or she can no longer move his or her limbs. This happens only in the extremely rare cases where people severely injure themselves, for example by endlessly biting body-parts or thumping their heads against a wall.

As was discussed earlier, the removal of objects and placement in 'suicide-proof' cells (regular cells, strip-cells, or isolation cells) may not always be effective. This was demonstrated by a suicidal detainee who showed 21 possible ways to commit suicide in a strip-cell. There are also a few ways to commit suicide in an isolation cell and, as odd as it may seem, there even is a way to commit suicide while restrained on a safety bed. Thus, again, improvements are desirable.

Provision of psychological support
Once potentially suicidal detainees are identified and diagnosed by the Psycho-Medical Council, actions are undertaken by each care provider. As was mentioned earlier, professional support can include medical treatment of physical or mental illnesses, creation of a beneficial environment, assistance with psycho-social problems (divorce, financial problems, loss of employment, etc.), help to cope with cognitive, emotional, and behavioural problems, and help with problems of an existential, religious, or life-contemplative nature. However, such contacts are usually limited to only a few minutes per professional so

that additional psychological support is provided by correctional officers. Such personnel can enter the cell, accompany the detainee for a few minutes, inquire about the detainee's mood, chat about all sorts of things, just smoke a cigarette together, or just pat the detainee on the shoulder. Correctional officers also stimulate suicidal detainees to maintain their physical health (sleeping, eating, drinking), take their medicine and engage in daily activities. However, the normal routine in houses of detention generally provides only limited possibilities to provide adequate additional psychological support to detainees with severe emotional problems. In addition, information about changes in mood states is sometimes difficult to obtain, especially because there are no dormitories or multiple cell settings where other detainees could assist in making such assessments. Detainees live in blocks of 12 to 48 detainees on a wing, with only one or two correctional officers working there in the daytime.

The Psycho-Medical Council structures the daily routine for suicidal detainees and provides correctional officers with guidelines about how to deal with the suicidal detainees. The extent of structuring and the contents of guidelines usually differs from detainee to detainee depending of the detainee's psychiatric background. At times, a minimum of support and a minimum of structuring provides the best results and in other cases a maximum of support and a maximum of structuring is required. Suicidal detainees who suffer from a crisis because of a shocking event, such as the death of a spouse or the incarceration itself, are provided with as much support as possible. Correctional officers are encouraged to provide such detainees with personal contact with empathy, respect and acceptance of suicidal feelings. Correctional officers can serve as mentors, keep in contact and design an explicit daily programme (including appointments with care-providers), thereby coaching such suicidal detainees through a difficult period. The members of the Psycho-Medical Council strive to have the problems communicated and the suicidal feelings vented. They try to explain to the detainee what is happening and help him or her to cope in a better way. During the crisis period, a detainee can be placed in the Special Care Division. Severely depressed detainees are usually also placed in the Special Care Division. Correctional officers are advised to be alert for behavioural changes. All personnel are encouraged to offer personal contact with a supportive, attentive attitude, but without getting overly warm or friendly. Furthermore, correctional officers are encouraged to stimulate severely depressed detainees to keep up the daily routine (eating, drinking, getting dressed, washing, etc.) and engage in offered activities (work, games, creative crafts, etc.). The members of the Psycho-Medical Council strive to enhance the detainee's coping potential and they appraise the detainee's view of the future.

Suicidal detainees who have a borderline personality disorder are characterised by control-deficits, impulsive and unpredictable behaviour, and mood-swings. Correctional officers are usually told to provide such detainees with a structured, friendly environment, which means that explicit instructions are given and that appointments and agreements are made. The officers are also advised to be careful in their contacts with such detainees due to the tendency borderline patients have to play people against each other. Correctional officers usually have the task of helping to solve detainees' problems, but in cases of borderline patients there are often no simple solutions to their problems. Suicidal schizophrenic detainees have even more problems that incapacitate interactions with correctional officers. As a result, correctional officers are usually instructed to only pay attention to the daily routines and not to over-stimulate or under-stimulate such detainees. They are advised not to adapt to the detainee's delusions, but to hold up reality. Furthermore, correctional officers are instructed to stimulate the detainee to take his or her medicine in accordance with the psychiatrist's prescription.

All in all, the extent to which psychological support is provided usually depends on the detainee's pathology. Some support is given by the members of the Psycho-Medical Council and some by the correctional officers. Procedures and the extent of support vary between suicidal detainees who suffer from a crisis and those who have a major depression, borderline personality disorder, or schizophrenic disorder. Procedures and the extent of support also vary between the houses of detention. In all cases the provision of psychological support is limited due to lack of personnel, making improvements possible.

Transfer of suicidal detainees to other institutions
Transfers to other institutions are generally indicated when the severity or complexity of the detainee's problems surpass the facility's ability to handle those problems. Such transfers prevent detainees from deteriorating and prevent other detainees from having to suffer from the detainee's disturbing or even threatening behaviour (and also from too much attention diverted to a single detainee). As with police stations, houses of detention can attempt to transfer troubled detainees to psychiatric hospitals. However, such attempts are hardly ever successful as psychiatric hospitals have restrictive policies for the admission of patients of penal institutions. Basically, there are four types of special institutions that do accept troubled detainees from houses of detention. Detainees can be transferred to Individual

Guidance Centres that have a total capacity of 114 places, the forensic observation and guidance centre that has a capacity of 60 places, the division of clinical psychological observation of the Penitentiary Selection Centre that has a capacity of 18 places of which a maximum of five places can be used to hold detainees in crisis, and so-called TBS-institutions that have a total capacity of 835 places. These institutions generally have smaller units than do houses of detention, which is beneficial for dealing with disturbed detainees. In addition, all these special institutions have better trained correctional officers, a higher correctional officer/detainee ratio, and staff consisting of more psychologists/psychiatrists than do houses of detention. In general, the Psycho-Medical Council advises on all transfers, but the special institutes or admission boards decide about whether or not to actually admit. In most cases, the solution is only temporary because special institutions have the policy of returning detainees to houses of detention as soon as this is possible.

Transfer to an individual guidance centre is indicated when the behavioural problems of a mentally disturbed detainee requires a regime with more possibilities for individual guidance than can be offered by special care divisions. The individual guidance centres can provide detainees with a fairly extensive individual approach. The four individual guidance centres for houses of detention operate regionally. They accept detainees with personality disorders, but especially detainees with psychiatric disorders. Suicidal detainees are accepted only when suicide is not imminent and when their suicidality exists in conjunction with a personality disorder or a psychiatric disorder.

Transfer to the division of clinical psychological observation of the Penitentiary Selection Centre (PSC) is indicated when there is a severe imminent crisis of a *psycho-social* nature of whatever origin (severe guilt over the offence, threats to be liquidated, death of a spouse, etc.) Chronically suicidal detainees or detainees with a personality disorder or psychiatric disorder are not accepted unless they are suffering from a severe imminent crisis. The PSC has the possibility of clinical psychological assessment, crisis-intervention and psychotherapy.

Transfer to the forensic observation and guidance centre is indicated when there is an acute and serious crisis of a *psychiatric* nature. Suicidal detainees suffering from a crisis or suicidal detainees with a personality disorder are not accepted, unless they also have a psychiatric disorder. This institution has a hospital status, which makes coercive medication possible and gives possibilities of clinical psychological assessment, psychiatric assessment, and crisis-intervention.

TBS is a special hospital order imposed under the Dutch Criminal Code to have mentally disturbed offenders detained for treatment in a TBS institution. The Dutch TBS system consists of six treatment institutions, one clinical observation institution, one selection institution, three forensic psychiatric hospitals, and several forensic psychiatric divisions of regular psychiatric hospitals. TBS institutions differ in their approach to treatment (analytical therapy, client-centred therapy, behavioural therapy, etc.) and some specialise in certain types of offenders (e.g. those involved in sex-related offences, intellectually disabled offenders). Transfer to one of these institutions is possible when a judge considers that an offender cannot be held responsible for the offence and that his or her behaviour poses a threat to members of the community. In addition, such a transfer is possible in cases of a detainee who, during his or her detention, becomes severely disturbed and is therefore unfit for prolonged detention. However, in the latter case, a long and difficult procedure has to be followed, which makes it difficult for houses of detention to transfer suicidal detainees to a TBS institution. As a result, houses of detention hardly ever transfer detainees to TBS institutions on grounds of suicidality.

All in all, there are several possibilities to have suicidal detainees externally transferred. However, the criteria for admission are strict and dependent on the receiving institution. As a result, such a transfer requires thorough argumentation. In some instances an attempt to transfer is doomed to fail. Apart from that, due to lack of space it can take a while before the detainee is actually transferred. Here too, improvements are possible.

Protocols and training
As was mentioned above, Dutch houses of detention have their own protocols concerning suicide prevention. In the best cases, they are comprehensive protocols containing theoretical information about suicidal behaviour (definition, causes, risk factors, risky moments) as well as information about general preventive measures (adopting a professional attitude, notification of colleagues, assessment of coping skills, creation of a good psycho-social climate) and specific preventive measures (the use of a screening list, monitoring procedures, removal of potentially harmful objects, transference to specially designed cells, notification of professionals, etc.). In the worst cases, there are no protocols for the prevention of suicides whatsoever. As was also mentioned in the introduction of this paragraph, the Dutch Ministry of Justice is currently gathering all existing notes and protocols with the aim of the central development of standardised guidelines for procedures and protocols. Therefore, there is reason to believe that in

the near future all houses of detention will have fairly comprehensive protocols for dealing with suicidal behaviour.

Until recently, there were no specific courses in The Netherlands for handling suicidal detainees. As a result, correctional officers, psychologists, psychiatrists, and other members of staff were not trained in suicide prevention measures. Recently, post-doctoral suicide prevention courses were set up for criminal justice system psychologists. These courses address such issues as backgrounds of suicidal behaviour, engaging in contacts with suicidal detainees (with or without psychiatric disorders or personality disorders), enabling the suicidal person's expression of feelings, influencing the suicidal person's psychological state and his or her reasons for wanting to die, discussing those reasons, investigating which problem-solving strategies have not been tried yet, giving instructions to personnel, and dealing with detainees and correctional officers after a suicide has been committed.

Recently, a suicide prevention training course for correctional officers was set up as well. On this course, personnel are taught that the 'golden rule' when working with suicidal detainees is to trust their own judgment and to act on their beliefs if they believe someone is in danger of suicide (see Rowan 1994). Correctional officers are also taught to learn to follow the recommendations of the Psycho-Medical Council. Furthermore, myths are discussed, such as 'When a detainee has made up his mind to commit suicide, it is unlikely that he is going to tell anyone' and 'Manipulators won't commit suicide'. Attention is also given to implementing specific prevention measures (removal of potentially hazardous objects, the use of isolation cells, etc.), dealing with mentally ill detainees, adopting good social skills and good attitudes. All in all, improvements are in progress.

In conclusion
In this chapter, we discussed the fact that criminal justice system suicides give reasons for concern. We also discussed that suicides occur more often in the early stages of confinement, especially in the stage of police custody. We gave several explanations for this phenomenon. It is difficult, if not impossible, to determine which explanation, or combination of explanations, is the best. It may be problems with the calculation, the differences in suicide vulnerability of the incoming population, or the disproportionate levels of stress in the early stages of confinement. In our opinion, as we have made clear, the excess of early custodial suicides may also be due, at least in part, to the better or more extensive preventive measures in the later stages of confinement. Assessment of suicide risk is maintained at a higher level in Dutch

houses of detention than in Dutch police stations. Suicidal detainees are generally under closer surveillance in houses of detention than they are in police stations. Houses of detention provide suicidal detainees with more and better psychological support than do police stations—and they have more possibilities of transferring suicidal detainees elsewhere. Houses of detention also have better protocols than do police stations, and their personnel are more often specially trained to deal with suicidality. Police stations predominantly rely on building suicide-proof cells and on disarmament of potentially hazardous objects. It is our belief that the Dutch police stations and the individual police officers are very motivated to prevent detainees from committing suicide. Nevertheless, it seems to be a good measure to transfer suicidal detainees from police stations to houses of detention whenever detainees have been recognised as a suicide risk. Of course, it is also desirable that preventive measures are improved in police stations. Because we have reasons to believe that the Dutch police are doing equally well if not better than the police in many other countries, it may be that even more improvements are possible in other countries.

Transferring suicidal police custody detainees to houses of detention is not the entire solution to the Dutch custodial suicide problem. As was mentioned, Dutch houses of detention have a high suicide rate as well. We showed that several measures can be improved in The Netherlands. Screening for suicide risk can be made part of the standard booking procedure. In our opinion, all detainees should be asked about suicidal behaviour in the past. After all, it takes only five minutes to ask some standard questions about such behaviour. Simple questions could be asked such as 'Have you ever tried to kill yourself or seriously harmed yourself?' The answer 'Yes' should give the warning signal that this person needs extra attention. In addition, houses of detention should receive information about the detainee's behaviour in the police station. The use of isolation cells can also be decreased. Knowing that isolation can add to the onset of psychiatric symptoms and suicidality, it is our opinion that the option of isolation should become a non-automatic response to cases of suicidality. The fact is that the suicide risk can never be eliminated while a suicidal detainee is kept alone in his or her cell.

Monitoring of suicidal detainees can also be improved in Dutch houses of detention. It may be possible to instigate a 'buddy' suicide watch system (Rowan 1994) on a small scale. It may be worthwhile to investigate the option of placing suicidal detainees in special care divisions in a large cell along with two or three trained volunteers from other divisions. Furthermore, the provision of psychological support can be improved. Currently the medical institutional practitioner is the only care provider who can be called on a 24 hour basis. It may be a good idea to also have a psychologist on stand-by 24 hours a day, seven days a week. Of course, houses of detention would also benefit from more psychologists and more correctional officers, but financial means may not allow for such improvements. Finally, protocols and training programmes can be implemented where absent, and improved where present. In this respect, it has to be mentioned that psychiatrists and medical institutional practitioners could benefit from courses on treatment with medication or from having the possibility of mandatory medicine use. Stokes (1993) showed that pharrmacotherapy currently seems to be the most effective treatment for moderate to severe depression. Especially the newer anti-depressants seem to make a real breakthrough in the treatment of depression. Because suicidal behaviour seems to be associated with serotonergic abnormalities (cf Korn, Brown, Kotter, Gordon and van Praag 1995), medication may prevent some suicides from occurring.

Despite the aforementioned possibilities of improvement, it needs to be said that the situation is relatively good in The Netherlands. The Dutch system of transferring suicidal detainees to special divisions in the institution or to other specialised institutions and of providing psychological support to (suicidal) detainees are satisfactory. Given the fact that Dutch penal institutions as well as the Dutch Ministry of Justice and researchers are currently paying much attention to, and are also working hard on, several measures for suicide prevention, the situation will hopefully be even better in the near future. We hope to be able to return then and inform you about a very effective solution to the problem of suicides in the criminal justice system, or at least the solution to the problem of suicides in the Dutch criminal justice system.

Eric Blaauw is a forensic (research) psychologist at Vrije University, Amsterdam and The Netherlands Institute for the Study of Criminality and Law Enforcement, Leiden. He is currently conducting research on assessment of suicide risk in remand centres and prisons, psychopathology in remand centres and specialised penal institutions, and decision-making regarding the placement of certain offenders.

Frans Schilder has been a forensic psychologist at the house of detention, De Schie, Rotterdam, since 1989. Prior to that he worked at an institution for juveniles. He writes many reports for the Dutch courts concerning the accountability of offenders. He is also involved in the assessment of suicide risk in remand centres and prisons.

Stef van de Lande MA, is currently employed as a psychologist in a penal institution, De Stadspoort in Amsterdam.

CHAPTER 16

Jail Suicide: Preventing Future Casualties

Lindsay M. Hayes

> When death occurs, it is shocking—inside or outside an establishment.
> When it happens inside it is even more so and whether from natural or
> other causes, friends, relatives and staff have a strong desire to know how?
> Why? Could it have been prevented? Could I have done more? Stress,
> anxiety, guilt, anger, hostility and despair are all present. I have
> experienced this myself as governor.

With those words, Ian Dunbar, Director of Inmate Administration for
the Prison Service in England, opened the second international
conference on 'Deaths in Custody' at Cambridge University in April
1994. There are many casualties following a jail suicide, most notably
the inmate but also the correctional staff responsible for their care and
supervision. Detailed below are four separate examples of casualties
from a jail suicide: three inmate deaths and an officer permanently
scarred by the experience.[1]

Case 1: Suicide of Matthew Cullen

Matthew Cullen, aged 26, was a first-year law student at the State
University's College of Law. In the early morning hours of 23
September 1994, Mr Cullen left a local pub where he had been watching
a televised college football game with his friends. A short time later his
vehicle was stopped by Johnson City police officer, Gail Burrows, and
he was charged with driving under the influence of alcohol. Mr Cullen
was initially transported to the Johnson City police department for
administration of a breathalyzer test and further questioning. The test
revealed a blood alcohol count of 0.18, almost twice the legal limit.
During questioning, Mr Cullen appeared despondent and 'in a daze'
according to officer Burrows. He expressed concern to the officer that
because it was his second arrest for drunk driving, his future in law
school was in jeopardy. How would his parents react? At one point
during the process, Mr Cullen lamented, 'It's all over for me . . . you'll
see my obituary in the paper within the next week.' Officer Burrows
replied, 'Don't say that', and attempted to downplay the significance of
the arrest. She was not overly concerned about this apparent suicide
threat, later stating that most intoxicated arrestees make similar
statements and Mr Cullen '. . . did not appear to me to be somebody
that would be suicidal.' Officer Burrows also stated that she would have

taken the threat seriously if Mr Cullen '. . . had said it more than once' and appeared depressed while making the statement.

Upon completion of the processing at the Johnson City police department, Mr Cullen was transported to the Stuart County jail by police officer Fred Williams. During the short ride, Mr Cullen continued to express concern over his arrest. According to officer Williams, the arrestee kept repeating, 'It's over for me today, they'll probably kick me out, it's over for me, this is it.'

Officer Williams arrived at the Stuart County jail at 3.45 a.m. and left Mr Cullen in the custody of Sully DeJames, the dispatcher at the facility. Built in 1890, the four-story stone and cement structure was last renovated in 1980 when new showers, toilets and sink fixtures were installed. The facility held approximately 50 inmates on three floors and had a troubled past. Over the years several investigative committees had criticised county officials for both structural deficiencies and inadequate staffing in the linear-designed jail. According to one report:

> This facility shares many of the problems found in other facilities of this type. The ability to know what is going on in inmate housing areas and to respond to inmate requests is dependent on staff making frequent security rounds. As a result, this facility is difficult to supervise effectively . . . Staff are not posted in ways that makes them immediately available to respond to emergency situations . . . The most obvious area of non-compliance is the failure to have an officer post on the second and third floors . . .

The most recent inmate suicide in the antiquated facility had occurred in 1991, and a correctional officer had been severely beaten in June 1994.

Shortly after Mr Cullen's arrival, the dispatcher alerted Robert Tracey, the lone correctional officer in the jail, that a new inmate needed to be processed. Officer Tracey escorted Mr Cullen to the booking area, converted from an old cell and located on the first floor, where he conducted a strip search. According to officer Tracey, it was a routine booking and Mr Cullen appeared 'very happy, joking, and talking about the football game on T.V.' Mr Cullen was given an orange jumpsuit, blanket and sheet. Although jail policy required that inmates who were intoxicated and/or required close supervision be housed in close proximity to jail staff on the first floor, Mr Cullen was inexplicably escorted to the third floor where officer Tracey placed him in 'Cell 12, Range 3, Left', a cell that was the farthest location from the dispatcher's office and booking area. The time was approximately 4.15 a.m.

County jail policy also required that officers conduct cell checks at 30 minute intervals and document their observations in a log book. Suicidal inmates were required to be observed at 15 minute intervals. A recent memorandum from the jail administrator reinforced this policy:

225

Word has been given to me that routine 30 minute rounds are not being made on a consistent basis. Even though it may be logged in the book that rounds are being made, I'm getting too many complaints to the contrary. This is an important function of the officers on duty, so as to prevent a lot of things from happening. Please make your physical rounds every 30 minutes, it may prevent a lot of embarrassment!

According to the log book completed by officer Tracey, cell checks were completed at 4.30 a.m., 5.00 a.m. and 6.00 a.m. At 6.15 a.m., an inmate trustee housed two cells away from Mr Cullen was allowed out of his cell in order to begin serving meals. Upon entering the cell the trustee looked to his right and observed Mr Cullen hanging from the cell bars by a pair of socks. His body was clearly visible to any observer in the corridor. The trustee called out to officer Tracey, 'You have one hanging down here.' The officer then proceeded to walk down the corridor to Mr Cullen's cell. Although trained in first aid and cardiopulmonary resuscitation (CPR), officer Tracey did not check the inmate for a pulse or breathing, later stating, 'I just visually checked him, I didn't want to touch anything, didn't want to disturb anything.' Officer Tracey then walked back to a desk, picked up his radio and called downstairs to the dispatcher. He requested backup assistance from patrol deputies and emergency medical services (EMS) because 'We have one swinging.'

Two patrol deputies arrived at the facility at 6.20 a.m. and proceeded up to Mr Cullen's cell on the third floor. Upon arrival, they presumed that Mr Cullen was dead and began taking photographs of the scene. The inmate's body remained undisturbed and hanging from the cell bars. Ten minutes later two paramedics from the county EMS arrived at the jail. Although they had no knowledge as to the nature of the emergency, they began to proceed upstairs with their equipment when they were stopped by dispatcher DeJames. As later stated by Charles Griffin, the EMS driver:

. . . All they told us was an unknown medical problem at the jail . . . We didn't know what we were coming into. When we found out that he wasn't breathing, we got all the essential materials that we needed and then we were told as we walked upstairs that we wouldn't need the equipment. It's just confusing on our part not knowing exactly what we were responding to . . . And having to stay downstairs while they were taking pictures. We weren't told they were taking pictures at the time. So we were like, 'He's not breathing and they're taking pictures?' That tells us something . . .

Denied entry into the jail for ten minutes, the paramedics were finally escorted upstairs to Mr Cullen's cell at 6.40 a.m. They checked his vital signs and it soon became obvious that the inmate had been dead for quite a while. The medical examiner later estimated that Matthew Cullen had died at approximately 5.00 a.m. It was subsequently revealed that officer Robert Tracey had not made any cell checks after 4.30 a.m., leaving Mr Cullen and other inmates (including one on suicide watch) completely unsupervised for almost two hours.

As had been predicted by Matthew Cullen earlier that morning, his obituary appeared in the local newspaper a few days later.

Case 2: Suicide of Carol Grant
Carol Grant had a very troubled past. A 34-year-old mother of two young children, she suffered from both mental illness and substance abuse. As a child, she was the victim of child abuse. As an adult, she had been convicted of child abuse and neglect, and her two children had been removed from the home and placed in state custody. In April 1989, a third child was born but tragically died a few months later of what was thought to be sudden infant death syndrome. Ms Grant became quite distraught following the child's death and told John Saunders, her ex-boyfriend and father of the deceased infant, that 'maybe it would be better if I were dead.' Cognizant of her troubled past, Mr Saunders called the police and Ms Grant was referred to the emergency room at the local hospital in Harrison, a small community of 3,600 residents. She was seen by a physician who diagnosed her as suffering from 'acute situational depression with suicidal ideation', but she was not deemed to be a present threat to herself. Ms Grant was sent home and recommended for out-patient treatment. Two weeks later on July 28 her daughter's mysterious death was changed to murder and Ms Grant was arrested and charged with the killing.

While confined at the Harrison City jail, Ms Grant was viewed as a difficult prisoner. She was unable to sleep, had a poor appetite, complained of being cold, and experienced mood swings of crying and yelling. She made frequent requests to jail staff and continually asked to call the local mental health centre. As a result, Ms Grant's request for treatment was limited to learning relaxation exercises over the telephone from a counsellor with the mental health centre, who viewed her symptoms as normal anxiety caused by her confinement. Due to her substance abuse history, mental health staff were reluctant to assess Ms Grant for psychotropic medication, and wouldn't visit her during confinement unless jail staff viewed her as self-destructive.

In early October 1989, Ms Grant was released on bond under the supervision of a third party custodian by the name of Susan Ravens. Ms Ravens, a family friend, had been instructed to monitor Ms Grant's activities 24 hours a day and report any violations, including the consumption of alcohol or drugs, to the court. Ms Raven's role as third party custodian soon became unmanageable because of her friend's propensity to ignore most of the court's orders, including abstinence from alcohol. On several occasions she tried without success to remove herself from the custodian responsibilities.

On the morning of 14 November 1989, Susan Ravens became concerned that Ms Grant might be suicidal after finding a kitchen knife in the bathroom of her home. Carol had also spoken about suicide the previous day. When confronted, Carol appeared distraught, shaking, crying, fearful of returning to jail, and 'at the end of her rope.' Ms Ravens decided to take her to the mental health centre.

Upon arrival at the centre Ms Ravens informed the psychologist, Sharon McCullough, Ph.D., that her friend had been drinking and was suicidal. Ms Grant met privately with Dr McCullough and denied any suicidal ideation, although admitted she was depressed, did not feel very strong, and remained fearful of her legal situation. Based upon Ms Grant's denial of suicidal ideation, Dr McCullough did not think that in-patient commitment was appropriate and scheduled an out-patient session with her for the following day. Although Ms Grant appeared relieved, Susan Ravens was frustrated that the mental health centre had decided not to pursue civil commitment. She then took Ms Grant to the local hospital in an effort to convince those staff that Ms Grant required in-patient emergency room treatment. They met with emergency room nurse Betty Thomas, and Ms Ravens again related that Carol was suicidal and had been drinking. Ms Grant talked with the nurse, appeared moderately intoxicated and complained of being lonely, but denied any suicidal intent or need for emergency room services.

A short while later, and outside the presence of Ms Ravens, Carol walked away from the hospital. Upon discovering that she had left, Ms Ravens called the Harrison Police Department and informed an officer that Ms Grant had left her custody and was suicidal. Ms Ravens also called assistant district attorney Claire Thompson, who had been assigned to prosecute Ms Grant in the murder case. A warrant was issued for Ms Grant's arrest. A short time later, Ms Grant walked into the yard of a residence close to the hospital and asked to use the telephone. Franny Ledger, baby-sitter at the home, described Ms Grant as distraught, crying, and having difficulty walking. Ms Grant called Mr Saunders, her ex-boyfriend, and asked for his help, but he rejected her plea and informed her that their relationship was over. Ms Grant left the residence and walked into the yard of Barry Flynn. According to Mr Flynn, Ms Grant was acting very strange and he offered to drive her to a women's shelter. While en-route, Mr Flynn flagged down a police officer who placed Ms Grant under arrest and transported her to the Harrison City jail, arriving at approximately 4.30 p.m.

There were several police personnel at the facility, as well as assistant district attorney Thompson, when Carol Grant arrived. She appeared intoxicated and according to one observer—'There was talk amongst the persons present of Grant being suicidal.' She was booked by jailer Steve Williams, who asked dispatcher Maggie Anders to thoroughly search the prisoner because, according to the dispatcher, 'I was told she could be potentially suicidal . . . I then made a special effort to look for anything that she might hurt herself with.'

Carol Grant was placed in a cell at 5.00 p.m. A short time later, jailer Williams allowed her to make two telephone calls—one to Mr Saunders and the other to Betty Thomas at the hospital. In the conversation with her ex-boyfriend, Ms Grant was overheard by several police personnel as feeling lonely and concerned about whether Mr Saunders would support and visit her in jail. In her conversation with Ms Thomas, she requested mental health treatment. Carol sounded distraught and told the nurse that 'she couldn't take it anymore.' When Ms Thomas asked to speak with Steve Williams, she was informed by the jailer that Ms Grant was simply being manipulative and could not see anyone from the mental health centre because she was scheduled to be transported to a larger jail facility later that evening. According to the jailer, 'Carol will do anything, basically, to get out of jail, and her usual technique is to request medical care for various reasons. We've taken her up to the hospital in the past, and it usually comes down to nothing. There's been no organic problems, I think the last one just said basically stress.' Ms Grant was returned to her cell and provided with a meal which she did not eat.

At 6.30 p.m. jailer Williams checked on Ms Grant and found her to be sitting in a foetal position on the floor near the cell door. She was crying. He later admitted that Ms Grant engaged in self-destructive behaviour while in the cell, that is, banging her head against the bunk rail four or five times. Despite this behavior, Williams did not consider Ms Grant to be suicidal because '. . . she'd been evaluated and found to be non-committable earlier today, which to me indicates that the person is not a suicide risk.' When her constant requests for use of the telephone or head banging became bothersome, jailer Williams simply closed the food slot window opening in her cell door. 'She was displeased', admitted the jailer. 'But closing the window usually has a calming effect on most of these people. When you break off the communication they'll quiet down in a couple of minutes, which she did.'

Jailer Williams also admitted that he wanted to expedite Ms Grant's transfer to the larger facility because 'I had enough concerns about Carol . . . I wanted to get her out of here and I wanted to get her some help.' Yet jailer Williams decided to leave the facility at 6.30 p.m. without authorizing an increase in her observation based upon either her potential for suicide or high level of intoxication. The sole responsibility for supervising Ms Grant and three other inmates in the facility was then turned over to dispatcher Jeff Morrison, who periodically observed the inmates through a closed circuit television (CCTV) monitor in his office.

According to the dispatcher, 'Officer Williams advised me that I should keep watch on her because we weren't certain how she may react to being in jail.' Despite this vague instruction, Mr Morrison did not observe Ms Grant through the CCTV monitor for over 60 minutes. Instead he left the dispatch area and went downstairs to prepare and eat his dinner.

At 7.35 p.m., dispatcher Morrison finished his dinner and proceeded to the cell area to check the inmates. Upon arrival at Ms Grant's cell, the dispatcher opened the food slot window in the door and observed her hanging from the door hinge by a pair of knee socks. He immediately called out for assistance to officer Mike Rogers, who was in the building. Morrison and Rogers entered the cell together and cut Ms Grant free from the noose. Despite the presence of CPR equipment a few feet away from the victim, these two officers treated the area as a 'crime scene' and began taking photographs of the victim's body. Incredibly, when EMS personnel arrived several minutes later to assess Ms Grant's condition, officer Rogers appeared more concerned about preserving the scene than preserving Ms Grant's life. 'I took two photographs of Grant with the heart machine connected to her', stated the officer. 'At my request the body was disturbed as little as possible. The EMS had connected the machine by making small slits in her clothes and inserting the connections from the machine through them.' Ms Grant was pronounced dead at 7.45 p.m. When reached at home and notified that an inmate had committed suicide in the jail, jailer Williams was not surprised to learn that the victim was Carol Grant.

Case 3: Suicide of John Keller

John Keller, aged 43, was arrested for public drunkenness by Ackinsburg Police Department officer Michael Lang on 23 May 1994 because he '... was drunk to a degree that he was a danger to himself and others.' According to officer Lang, the arrestee's extreme intoxication was evident: 'Keller mumbled when he spoke, was swaying back and forth, had an odour of alcohol, his eyes were bloodshot, his speech was slurred, and he had difficulty in understanding some of the directions.'

Officer Lang transported Mr Keller to the Ackinsburg Police Department where he was processed and placed in cell number 6 in the basement at approximately 6.30 p.m. Cell number 6 is the only cell in the six-cell facility that is observed via a CCTV monitor located in the dispatcher's office. While observing the CCTV monitor at approximately 7.15 p.m., dispatcher Sally Schwartz noticed that Mr Keller was tying his clothes to the bars of his cell door. She called officer Lang into her office and he made the same observation. While viewing the monitor, officer Lang also noticed that Mr Keller appeared to be yelling, although the words could not be understood because the cell did not have any audio monitoring equipment. Officer Lang then proceeded downstairs to the basement and, when he approached cell number 6, observed that Mr Keller's shirt, pants and socks were tied together and around the bars of his cell door. The inmate was sitting on his bunk. Officer Lang asked Mr Keller what he was doing, and the inmate's response was incoherent. Officer Lang made no other inquiries and asked Mr Keller for his clothes. The inmate complied and gave the officer his shirt, pants and socks. Mr Keller remained in the cell clothed only in his underwear. Officer Lang told Mr Keller to lie down and go to sleep. He placed the inmate's clothing on a table outside the cell and proceeded upstairs to the dispatcher's office. Officer Lang told dispatcher Schwartz that he had removed Mr Keller's clothes and then proceeded to an office to continue the processing of another arrestee. Officer Lang later stated that he took Mr Keller's clothing because 'I didn't want him creating a disturbance, to keep on getting the attention of the dispatcher, because he wanted our attention to keep on coming down there'.

According to dispatcher Schwartz, she observed Mr Keller via CCTV at approximately 8.30 p.m. and he appeared to be sleeping on his bunk. At approximately 9.00 p.m., the dispatcher could not observe the inmate in the monitor, but assumed that he was using the toilet which is out of the monitor's view. When dispatcher Schwartz still could not observe Mr Keller at 9.06 p.m., she called downstairs to detective Roger Travis and inquired as to whether Mr Keller had been released from custody. Detective Travis and officer Jake Jacobs, also in the office at the time, were not aware of Mr Keller's custody status. Detective Travis agreed to check on the inmate. He then proceeded to cell number 6 and upon arrival observed that Mr Keller was sitting on the floor with his back to the cell door. His underwear was tied around his neck and through the cell bars. Detective Travis ran back to his office and grabbed a pocket knife while Officer Jacobs ran upstairs to the dispatcher's office to get the keys to Mr Keller's cell. Dispatcher Schwartz was instructed to call EMS personnel. The time was now 9.13

p.m. Detective Travis ran back to the cell and cut the underwear away from the inmate's neck. Officer Jacobs arrived with the keys, opened the cell door, and caught the inmate as he fell forward. Mr Keller's body was pulled out into the hallway and his vital signs were checked. A weak pulse was detected but soon went away. CPR was not initiated by any of the police officers. EMS personnel arrived at 9.16 p.m. and initiated CPR. Mr Keller was transported to the hospital and pronounced dead upon arrival.

Case 4: Suicide on the block

When conducting a suicide prevention training seminar and explaining the importance of each correctional agency to offer critical incident stress debriefing, a process designed to mitigate the impact of a traumatic event and assist affected personnel in recovery, a correctional officer will invariably approach me at the end of the workshop and begin to explain the lack of debriefing following their experience with an inmate's suicide. Their voices are always characterised by frustration. The main part of the story of Tee's suicide in his prison cell has already been reproduced in the *Introduction* to this volume (see p. *ix*). His story continues:

> We recently had another suicide at the jail. I knew I had to be there. I knew I could help. I could try to do something, anything just so nobody had to feel the things I felt as hard as I did.
> I will make it. That's what I told myself. I will always make it. I have been through a lot in my short life. Life, death, hope, despair, celebration, and tragedy I don't believe in religion but I do believe in God. There is nothing I can say or do to change the past. I can only try to help others.

Conclusion

What does all this mean? How are these four separate events, three inmate suicides and an officer's scars from another death, related? How do we prevent future casualties? First, we must remove the obstacles to prevention, those negative attitudes that impede prevention efforts by insisting that inmate suicides cannot be prevented. Second, we must carefully examine each suicide through an administrative and/or clinical review process and ask a two-fold question: What happened in this case and what can be learned to help prevent future incidents? Finally, we must offer critical incident stress debriefing or similar intervention to any individual who is adversely affected by a traumatic event. In the end, the degree of humanity exemplified by a jail or prison system and its ability to prevent future suicides should not only be measured by the circumstances surrounding individual deaths, but by the steps taken to correct problems and relieve the stress caused by these preventable deaths.

Lindsay Hayes is the Assistant Director of the National Center on Institutions and Alternatives. He is nationally recognised as an expert in the field of gaol and prison suicide. He has been the Project Director for the only three national studies of gaol and prison suicide in the USA. In addition, Lindsay Hayes serves as a technical assistance consultant in gaol and prison suicide prevention, conducting training seminars, assessing suicide prevention programmes and serving as an expert witness in various state and local jurisdictions throughout the USA. He has also published extensively in this field.

ENDNOTES

---

[1] In order to ensure complete confidentiality, certain identifying information regarding the sucide victims and jail facilities have been changed. No other modifications have been made.

CHAPTER 17

Impact of the Custodial, Controlled Environment and Inmate/Patient Behaviour on Practices of some Health Care Providers: Recommendations for Resolution of this International Problem

Joseph R. Rowan

Falling victim to the 'Manipulation Syndrome': the greatest peril

Some health care providers with doctor's and nurse's degrees and other levels of education fall victim to the 'Manipulation Syndrome.' Based on my work in a dozen different countries, some inmate-patients the world over manipulate for secondary gains. Perhaps they hope for better housing, referral to a mental health facility where living conditions are better or for charges against them to be dropped. Whatever the reason, some health providers, after being manipulated by inmates numerous times, react negatively and seem to forget their professional training. The result is that inmate patients with legitimate health problems are handled as manipulators. This in turn sometimes leads to deaths, lifetime injuries and/or highly agitated inmates who file grievances and produce lots of paperwork and bad publicity for the facility, or, as is common in the USA, file lawsuits.

In such systems, many inmates, including non-manipulators, will repeatedly *test* the system and cause a great amount of extra work and turmoil. In the American Medical Association's prison and jail pilot standards and accreditation programme, it was found that inmate testing and manipulating of the system *decreased* as the *systems* improved.

Authoritarian environment

Even in the best, newest institutions, the environment produces anxiety, feelings of hopelessness, separation feelings and frustration in inmates. Adjustment to the authoritarian, militaristic style of day-to-day living is extremely difficult for and emotionally disturbing to many inmates. Some of these factors also have an impact on health care providers, causing them undue stress. Delays in providing health services are a common problem, influenced by having to wait for inmate patients to be brought to the clinic. Routine prison security measures prevent expeditious movement. Some prisons have resolved the problem by assigning special escort officers to the clinic, who speed up the delivery of inmate patients.

Practice in privacy abridged
While it is not difficult to practice privacy in the community, it is not always possible in detention and correctional facilities. It is somewhat common to see two inmate patients receiving services in the same room because of space problems. In some instances an officer will remain in the room with a dangerous offender because the clinic does not have a glazing panel which allows the officer to observe from outside the room.

Imbalance in staff gender in male institutions
The *myth* that it is unsafe for a female to work directly with male inmates has prevented many male institutions from hiring any female officers and nurses. A first-of-its-kind national survey of male maximum security prisons in the USA last year debunked this myth. Nationally, female officers were assaulted only 28 per cent as often as their male peers. The seven states which had twice as many female officers as the national average not only had 47 per cent fewer assaults on female officers, but assaults on male officers decreased 41 per cent, compared to the national average. In the USA several surveys of assaults on police officers showed the same results.

In 1980 the huge Texas prison system had less than 10 per cent female nurses. It now has over 90 per cent female nurses. Wardens/governors testify that female nurses, unlike some of their male peers, rarely get assaulted.

Insensitivity increases with longevity
More experience in years often guarantees better performance. The opposite, unfortunately, is true for some health care providers who fall victim to their environment and become insensitive. Inmates pick up on this and grievances are common, particularly in institutions where more than one doctor or nurse practices, which allows comparisons of practitioner attitudes and manners. Where the insensitive practitioner is the only provider, the inmates will often challenge and test the system. Lawsuits result in the USA; in other countries, coroner's juries render negative public reports when sub-standard health care is provided due to the practices of insensitive providers.

Inadequate self-understanding by practitioners lessens treatment benefit

Failure of health practitioners to *understand themselves* and what makes them do what they do is the major factor which produces 'I-me' practitioners instead of 'we-TEAM workers.' They lack *self-respect*, which, according to responses to our national research, is considered the most important trait to look for in hiring people to work in the criminal justice field.

In the USA we have developed two training packages, the 'Twenty-six Do's and Don'ts of Good Resident Management and Mental Health' and 'MAP' Training which addresses *motivation, attitudes* and *philosophy* of health care and correctional personnel.

Negative outcomes: deaths, permanent injuries/disabilities and/or pain/suffering

Numerous lawsuits in the USA have produced adverse court verdicts against custodial institutions wherein deaths, permanent injuries/disabilities occurred, or where pain/suffering resulted because the duty of care was carried out negligently or with deliberate indifference.

In one of our prison systems, 19 of 25 correctional officers reported that '. . . almost all of the health care providers treat almost all of the inmates as though they were faking or manipulating.' The health care staff did not recognise the reality of this terrible situation. When 'widening of the net' occurs—as it did in this chaotic system—deaths and permanent injuries occur because those inmates with real health problems are considered to be faking or manipulating.

Remedial/preventive measures

Unless manipulation is treated as an illness, health care providers will be in professional trouble. One experienced physician said 'We must study (diagnose) manipulation longer and deeper. It must be handled as an illness. It is much easier to diagnose a physical problem. If we slough the inmates off as trouble-makers, the problem just continues and worsens. They need some attention, and listening to them courteously, with a question or two asked about 'what' and 'why' may result in a truthful response from them. You cannot say 'We can find nothing wrong' unless you have truly diagnosed their reported problem. When no discernible problem is found and you politely tell them that, the testing or manipulation for secondary gain may stop.'

The manipulation and insensitivity syndromes can be combatted by continuing education and open discussion. Although few health care seminars in the USA ever address the subject, I know that many more are aware that some of their fellow workers fall victim to the manipulation and insensitivity syndromes because, in my eight hour training of staff (over 900 institutions since 1982), approximately two to three hours of the training pertains to this subject.

More administrators and providers should lend support for more training in self-understanding which I consider more important than skills training. Professionals are often unaware that they are becoming insensitive. It takes place gradually. Supervisors have an obligation to broach the provider about the problem, often initiated by complaints or grievances filed. If there is no professional supervisor in the scenario, the correctional administrator should discuss the complaints and grievances with the provider. If the matter is not resolved and it is considered serious enough, the local medical society may offer assistance if the correctional administrator wishes to take that step. Not renewing that provider's contract is the ultimate decision.

I am not singling out prison and other criminal justice facilities regarding this problem area. Our surveys of nearly two dozen medical, mental health and skilled nursing care facilities have shown a similar incidence of personnel succumbing to the manipulation and insensitivity syndromes.

Joe Rowan has had 55 years of experience in criminal and juvenile justice, including working as Commissioner/Director of two state detention and correctional systems and as Administrator of four national private correctional agencies. He was an elected member of the Commission on Accreditation for Corrections and the American Correctional Association, which developed the National Standards for Detention, Correctional Facilities and Field Operations. He directed the American Medical Association's Health Care in Correctional Institutions programme of standards development and accreditation and thereafter served as Vice-president of the current National Commission on Correctional Health Care.

CHAPTER 18

Deaths in the Care of the State: Issues and Lessons

Vivien Stern

It is a great honour and privilege to be asked to give the closing address at this very important conference. I want to start by thanking the ISTD for inviting me. ISTD is a unique and admirable organization. It was founded 65 years ago and stands for something very important. Even though it is non-political and does not campaign it stands for solutions based on reason, evidence and argument rather than emotion and revenge. That is very important. It also starts from the assumption that everyone wants to do things right, based on evidence and arguments and that this applies to practitioners such as prison guards or police, activists, non-governmental organizations, and also to those who have suffered by bad or abusive practices. The presentations show that these are not opposing camps, but that everyone is seeking the best answers together. That is also very important. It is an enormous pleasure to be addressing so many friends and colleagues from the United Kingdom and around the world.

I am particularly pleased to see colleagues from Eastern Europe and Central Europe. Having been born into democracy and taking it for granted it is perhaps good for us to realise how some people have had to fight for it and what a privilege it has been to be able to help them and support them. So I congratulate the ISTD on their initiative in broadening their invitation list. I also congratulate them on continuing with this topic. It is not a cheerful topic—it is sad and depressing. Indeed it is the darker side of justice.

Two life-sentence prisoners from Louisiana wrote a book about life in prison. One of the essays was about 'Dying in Prison'. They wrote:

> It's dying away from home, alone, with strangers, in the callous atmosphere of prison, being treated and cared for, more often than not, by an indifferent hand.[1]

It is sad. But it reminds us very starkly of the need for organizations such as ISTD, INQUEST, the Moscow Centre for Prison Reform, the Belarus League for Human Rights, and of the need for constant vigilance over the agencies of the state that lock up our fellow citizens in our name.

Perhaps those words sound very pompous—*lock up our fellow citizens in our name*. But in many countries the public is beginning to forget they are fellow citizens. Instead they are seeing them as the enemy. Some images that come, particularly from the USA, of prisoners in chains, guarded by armed officers, wearing orange jumpsuits and other humiliating clothes, suggest a state of war, where criminals are the enemy and prisons are not places for social education but of containment.

I wanted to start my contribution by telling you about a visit I made to Malawi, in Africa, the sixth poorest country in the world, in 1995. I was visiting the Central Prison, in a party, with the chief commissioner and others. We went through the main gate into the main yard. It was a very large area with cell blocks around it. We went first to the one called 'Hospital'. The man in charge of the hospital was a prison officer who had done one year's training at a hospital. People who are *really sick* go to the local hospital to see a qualified doctor, we were told. No doctor comes to the prison.

We went up a rickety staircase to the wards. There was a man lying on a bed suffering from what they call 'bloody diarrhoea'. He was a Zambian, in prison until 2001 (I doubt that he will live that long). We went round this room full of dying people. There were eight cases of TB, one whose knees were full of fluid, one with bloody diarrhoea. Between the beds lying on the floor was a man with a most amazing skin disease. His legs looked as if they were covered with burnt shiny black plastic. He could not move. One had malaria. They were lying on filthy foam rubber mattresses with no coverings and had over them one ragged, filthy sheet.

Then we went outside. Outside in the grassy area was a prisoner lying on the ground. Someone turned him over and we found he was ill, taking tablets for 'bloody diarrhoea'. He was told to go back and lie in his cell but then they changed their minds and ordered someone to take him to the hospital. There were no empty beds there so I wondered who would be thrown out to make room. The people who showed me round were reluctant, not because they did not want me to see it but because they felt great shame at what they had to do with so few resources. They were humiliated by it.

Brazil, unlike Malawi, is quite a rich country, in parts anyway. One Friday afternoon this February I visited the Professor Anibal Bruno Penitentiary in Recife. This was a prison built for 700 and holding 1,840. They were all pre-trial prisoners. Ten per cent of them had their own lawyer which means that the rest of them were very poor.

When we arrived we were taken into the very scruffy director's office. The prison director, as is common in Brazil, wore jeans and a T-shirt. We chatted whilst waiting for the national guard. Eventually eight well armed national guard, plus two equipped with machine guns, arrived, and we were able to begin the tour. We went into a courtyard. No-one was in it but around it were locked doors and barred windows crammed with heads trying to get a look at us. Also in this courtyard were the security cells, that is the punishment cells, which had no windows at all but a barred grating above the door. There were also heads peering out of this so presumably they were standing on each other. The rooms were basically dark dens and the windows which had no glass were covered with plastic and cardboard. We moved through the courtyard into a building with cell corridors. The cell doors were open and it was clear that some prisoners were living much better than others. The rooms were divided with makeshift string and tablecloths and other pieces of cloth hanging down. In these cubicles, some had managed to pack a fridge, a fan, a television and a radio. Others had nothing. In the corridor some makeshift cubicles had been rigged up with bits of rope and material which apparently were for the weekend conjugal visits. It gave the families a little more privacy than they would otherwise get if they had to have their conjugal visits in the cells. I noticed that there were about 20 cats. They were all extremely thin.

I arrived home on the Monday morning. I was unpacking my suitcase and listening to the World Service when I heard that there had been a very serious incident at the Professor Anibal Bruno Prison in Pernambuco the day after my visit. Some prisoners tried to escape. Thirty prisoners' visitors, relatives and friends, and others were taken hostage and it all ended with six deaths. Four prisoners were killed. One member of a prisoner's family was killed, and one military policeman.

Lets look at Russia. In 1994 the head of the Penitentiary Department of the Russian Ministry of the Interior was a man called General Kalinin. He came to an ISTD conference two years ago. In that year he told a Parliamentary committee:

> I have to confess that sometimes official reports on prisoners' deaths do not convey the real facts. In reality, prisoners die from overcrowding, lack of oxygen and poor prison conditions . . . Cases of death from lack of oxygen took place in almost all large pre-trial detention centers in Russia.[2]

And further East, in Kazakhstan, a major problem in prisons is shortage of food. Prisoners die from malnutrition. The press reported a case of cannibalism where five starving prisoners had killed and eaten a cell-mate. It is estimated that 10,000 prisoners are suffering from tuberculosis. Infection spreads rapidly because of overcrowding. It has been alleged by Amnesty International that sometimes prisoners were put into a cell of prisoners seriously ill with tuberculosis to expose them to infection as a punishment.[3]

A very different insight comes from Illinois, in the USA. A legislator there drafted legislation that would require the State Department of Corrections to: (1) count the rapes committed in prison; (2) warn incoming prisoners of the danger of being raped; (3) provide prison staff with *two* hours of training in how to prevent sexual assaults and respond more effectively when such assaults occur. This legislator had been moved to introduce this legislation by what happened to one of his constituents. The constituent was a 25 year-old who became infected with HIV as a result of repeated rapes at a correctional centre in Illinois. The legislator concluded: 'He is a thief who received an unadjudicated death sentence'.[4]

Many of you will remember what happened here in Britain in August 1991 to a young man, aged 18, called Lee Waite. He was picked up by the police in possession of a stolen car. He was sent to Feltham young offender institution, an enormous establishment for youthful criminals, probably the biggest in Western Europe. Whilst there, he fell into the hands of the bullies, those who use violence, to be found in any institution, but particularly those for young people. Two other boys stole his training shoes and his wristwatch. He was sexually assaulted with a billiard cue. On 31 August 1991 he was found hanging from a sheet from his upturned bed. They called a unit after him where people who use violence are sent and treated very toughly until they give it up. Very recently an untried prisoner, still not convicted of anything, in the care of a private security company, killed himself.[5] According to the press: 'A prisoner who died in a courthouse cell was left hanging from a light fitting for nearly ten minutes' because security company staff believed he was faking a suicide attempt and 'the magistrates decided a planned bail hearing should take place outside his cell. Lawyers began arguing the case as he lay motionless on the floor'.

And of course there is the death penalty. This may be outside the remit of this conference but it is indeed a death in custody. Last year in April there were 3,122 people on Death Row in the USA. Less than half, 1,493, were white. 1,272 were black. Black people make up 12 per cent of the USA population. These are the questions all Death Row prisoners have to answer in the final hours.

> Do you understand what will happen to you?
> Do you have any questions?
> What do you want for a last meal?
> Do you plan to make a last statement?
> What do you want us to do with your body?
> What do you want to do with your property?

241

Who do you want to have your money?
Who will witness your execution?
Do you know what we expect you to do?
Are you comfortable?
If not, what can we do?
If your stay is denied, who do you want to call?
What color clothes do you want to die in? [6]

I visited San Quentin prison in California where I met some prisoners on Death Row. One of them asked me where I was from. I replied that I was from England. 'We are always pleased to meet people from England' he said. 'People in England write to us prisoners on Death Row'. He was referring to the organization called Lifelines, set up by Jan Arriens in Cambridge, which finds people to write to Death Row prisoners, and of which we can all be very proud.

Finally let us remember that prisoners kill each other. In Venezuela in 1996 four prisoners a week were killed by other prisoners. In 1995 in Oklahoma, 12 prisoners were killed by others and in Florida the figure was seven.

All these deaths in all the parts of the world occurred when people were in the care of the state and should have been protected. And I have not included the incidents of deaths in police lock ups and police cells when people are under interrogation.

I am from Penal Reform International. Penal Reform International is an international non-governmental organization with 400 members in 80 countries. It is registered in The Netherlands and owes a great deal to the generosity and support of the Dutch Government. It has a head office in London and offices in Paris and Puerto Rico. It was established at a meeting in November 1989, on the day the Berlin Wall came down.

It has consultative status with the United Nations and the Council of Europe. It has observer status with the African Commission on Human and Peoples' Rights. The members are human rights activists, government officials, academics, lawyers and ordinary citizens. These are our objectives:

- first, to promote the development and implementation of the international human rights instruments about law enforcement.
- second, Penal Reform International works to end discrimination in penal measures. All around the world prisons are full of the poor. The few women in prison are often there because they have finally returned the violence that is imposed on them by their husbands or partners. In prisons all over the world minorities are over-represented. In England many black people are in prison. In Eastern Europe gypsies (Roma) are overrepresented. In New

Zealand Maori people fill the prisons. And in the USA of course the incarceration rate for white people overall is 187 per 100,000. For black people it is 1,433.

- third, Penal Reform International works to abolish the death penalty.
- fourth, prison is used too much in the world. So Penal Reform International works to reduce the number of people in prison. In Russia, over a million people are in prisons and labour camps. This means about 690 people out of every 100,000 of the Russian population. In the United States of America about 1.6 million people are in prison, about 615 for 100,000 of the population.
- finally PRI supports the idea of alternatives to prison that are constructive and meaningful to victims.

PRI is a human rights organization. Deaths in custody is at the heart of the human rights concern about custody. Article 10 of the International Covenant on Civil and Political Rights makes it clear that:

All persons deprived of their liberty shall be treated with humanity and with respect for the inherent dignity of the human person.

People who are detained are entitled to the same basic rights as those who are free. And the first is the right to life and the integrity of the person. Second is the state's duty of care. It is often said, and especially by people from poor countries, 'Why should prisoners get enough to eat and be given medical care when those who have not broken the law often do not have enough to eat and cannot afford any medical care for themselves or their children?'

The answer is clear. Once somebody is in prison, the state has accepted the responsibility to feed, cloth and care for that person, whatever the economic circumstances. People cannot be locked up in prison and then allowed to die from neglect.

Next year is the fiftieth Anniversary of the Universal Declaration on Human Rights. It was signed on 10 December 1948. It was a declaration that emerged for a reason. Never again, everyone said, would we let such things happen. Never again would it be possible for people to treat other human beings that way. So in 1945 the United Nations set out on its task of drawing up all the declarations and conventions on human rights that are the official framework for the whole world on how states should treat their citizens.

Those who drew up the Universal Declaration in 1948 had a clear picture in their minds of what a state can do to anyone it decides are its enemies. They had seen in reality or on film the concentration camps. They had heard and read of the mass deportations, using people as slave labour until they dropped dead from starvation or disease, putting to immediate death by gassing those who did not look strong enough to work well and be worth feeding, using some as guinea pigs for medical experiments and others to work in officers' brothels.

The nations of the world resolved that in future states who had signed up to the Universal Declaration would know that their treatment of all people had to fall within the bounds of the values enshrined in it.

Let us come back to importance. Why is this conference so important? Because we are beginning to forget. Every now and then we get very clear reminders of why these things are necessary, and, especially when people are imprisoned, how easy it is for people who are given power over others, when the pressure is on, to forget that the human beings they are guarding are human beings. The potential for ill-treatment when one group of people locks up another is always there. Even in Canada, that most liberal of countries, an incident occurred at the Federal Prison for Women, where a number of women were stripped naked by an all-male emergency response team and put into restraints. The Canadian Correctional Investigator described the exercise as degrading and dehumanising.[7] And the subsequent judicial enquiry led to the resignation of the Commissioner of Corrections.

How can deaths in custody be prevented? How can a higher value be placed on the lives of those locked up?

Some cannot be, of course. Some people are determined to kill themselves. Other deaths are tragic accidents. But very often someone or some group is or are responsible and neglected in some way to care enough.

How could we do better? This is a difficult question, but there are some answers. People must remember all the time that they are not just doing a job and become absorbed with the details of that job. They are doing something more than a job. They are dealing with fellow human beings. This is much harder to do when people have been dehumanized and degraded, by keeping them dirty, making them live in fear, making them wear ill-fitting and humiliating clothes, putting them in chains perhaps.

Then it is easier to forget they are fellow human beings. The tasks facing penal reformers in the world of 1997 are great. There are many problems, and there are serious dangers. But there are also great opportunities.

Those who drafted the 1948 Declaration would, I think, be pleased to see what is going on at this conference. They would welcome many things—the meeting together of prison staff, who really care about protecting human life, with non-governmental organizations and voluntary groups. The painstaking work many people do to save life,

244

The Samaritans working alongside prison staff in many prisons to prevent suicide, the improvements in the way British prisons deal with the families of those who have died in prison compared with 15 years ago, the many systems of monitoring police stations, prisons and mental hospitals that are now in place.

But there is still much to do. The increasing urge to lock people up, which is sweeping across the United State and infecting Western Europe, presents new dangers.

So all I can say in conclusion is that the task for penal reformers is clear. The ISTD is to be congratulated on choosing such a vitally important topic for its Annual Conference and the support and encouragement the conference has given to all those concerned with deaths in custody is very great.

Thank you for listening

Vivien Stern is Senior Research Fellow at the International Centre for Prison Studies, having previously been Director of NACRO between 1977 and 1996. She has also been Secretary-General of Penal Reform International since 1989. Vivien Stern has written extensively on the penal system, most notably *Bricks of Shame*, and has been a member of various boards and commissions. She travels frequently, both presenting papers and acting as rapporteur at international conferences and seminars.

ENDNOTES

1. Wilbert Rideau and Ron Wikberg, *Life Sentences: Rage and Survival Behind Bars*, Times Books, New York, 1992, p. 171
2. Quoted in Moscow Center for Prison Reform, *In Search of a Solution, Crime, Criminal Policy and Prison Facilities in the Former Soviet Union*, Human Rights Publishers, Moscow, 1996, p. xv
3. See Amnesty International, 'Kazakstan—Ill-treatment and the death penalty: a summary of concerns', July 1996 p. 1
4. See *Criminal Justice Newsletter*, Vol 26. No 7, 3 April 1995
5. See Howard League for Penal Reform, *Suicides in Feltham*, 1993, pp. 5-8
6. See Marie Mulvey Roberts (Compiler and Editor), *Out of the Night, Writings from Death Row*, New Clarion Press, 1994, p. 174
7. See R L Stewart, Correctional Investigator, *Special Report of the Correctional Investigator Concerning the Treatment of Inmates and Subsequent Inquiry Following Certain Incidents at the Prison for Women in April 1994 and Thereafter*, Minister of Supply and Services, Canada, 1995, p. 5.

References

Adams, Phillip, ed. 1997, *The Retreat from Tolerance: A Snapshot of Australian Society*, Sydney: ABC Books.

Agomoh (Chiemeka) U. R. (1991b), *Detention and The Criminal Justice System in Nigeria* (Unpublished M.Sc. Thesis, Department of Sociology, University of Ibadan, Nigeria).

Agomoh (Chiemeka) U. R. (1994), *Imprisonment Before Trial: A Critical Appraisal of the Problems*, (Unpublished M. Phil Thesis, Institute of Criminology, Cambridge, England).

Agomoh (Chiemeka) U. R. (1995), 'Torture and Rehabilitation of Tortured Prisoners in Nigeria: A Need for Intervention' (Paper presented at the VIII International Symposium on Torture and Rehabilitation of Torture Survivors, November 1995, Cape Town, S.A.).

Agomoh U. R. (1996), *Decongesting the Nigerian Prisons and Police Cells: A Handbook of Practical Strategies for the Remand Population*, PRAWA: Lagos.

Alemika E. (1993), 'Trends and Conditions of Imprisonment in Nigeria', *International Journal of Offender Therapy and Comparative Criminology*, 37 (2): 147-52.

Amnesty International (1996), *Kazakstan: Ill-treatment and the Death Penalty: A Summary of Concerns*, Amnesty International: London.

Annual Abstract of Statistics (1995 edition), Federal Office of Statistics: Lagos.

Alpert, Geoffrey P. (1997), *Police Pursuit: Policies and Training*, NIJ Research in Brief, Washington, DC: National Institute of Justice.

Antoniadis, N. 1988, *Suicide Risk and Prevention: A Study of Coroners' Files*, Wellington, New Zealand: N. Z. Dept of Health.

Atkinson, J M (1982), *Discovering Suicide: Studies in the Social Organization of Sudden Death*, London: MacMillan.

Australian Bureau of Statistics (Quarterly), *National Correctional Statistics, Prisons*, Melbourne: ABS National Correctional Statistics Unit.

Backett, S. (1987), Suicides in Scottish Prisons, *British Journal of Psychiatry*, 151: 218-221.

Backett, S. (1988), Suicide and Stress in Prison, in Backett, S., McNeil, J., and Yellowlees, A. (eds.), *Imprisonment Today*, London: MacMillan.

Banerjee, S., Bingley, W. and Murphy, E. (1995), *Deaths of Detained Patients: A Review of Reports to the Mental Health Act Commission*, London: Mental Health Foundation.

Banks, C., Mayhew, P. and Sapsford, R. (1975), *Absconding from Open Prisons*, Home Office Research Study No. 26, HMSO: London.

Banks, T., *The Death of Jimmy Kelly* (Unpublished and undated manuscript).

Bernheim J. (1994), 'Suicides and Prison Conditions' in Liebling A. and Ward T. (eds), *Deaths In Custody: International Perspectives*, Whiting and Birch: London.

Bettleheim, B (1960: 1987 ed.), *The Informed Heart*, Penguin: London.

Biles, David, and McDonald David (eds.) (1992), *Deaths in Custody Australia, 1980-1989: The Research Papers of the Criminology Unit of the Royal Commission into Aboriginal Deaths in Custody*, Canberra: Australian Institute of Criminology.

Blaauw, E., Kerkhof, A. and Vermunt, R. (In press), 'Psychopathology in Police Custody', *International Journal of Law and Psychiatry*.

Blaauw, E., Kerkhof, A., and Vermunt, R. (1997), 'Suicides and Other Deaths in Police Custody', *Suicide and Life-threatening Behaviour*, 27(2), 153-163.

Blaauw, E., Vermunt, R., and Kerkhof, A. (1997), 'Detention Circumstances in Police Sations: Towards Setting the Standards', *Policing and Society*, 7, 45-69.

Blom-Cooper, L., QC, Brown, M., Dolan, R. and Murphy E (1992), *Report of the Committee of Inquiry into Complaints About Ashworth Hospital*, Vols. I and II, Cm. 2028-I and II, London: HMSO.

Blom-Cooper, L., QC (1993), 'Public Inquiries' in Freeman, M. and Happle, B. (eds), *Current Legal Problems*, Oxford University Press.

Blom-Cooper, L., QC, Hally, L. and Murphy, E. (1995), *The Falling Shadow: One Patient's Mental Health Care: 1978-1993*, London: Duckworth.

Blom-Cooper, L., QC, Grounds A., Guinan P., Parker A. and Taylor M. (1996), *The Case of Jason Mitchell: Report of the Independent Panel of Inquiry*, London: Duckworth.

Bottoms, A. E. (1990) 'The Aims of Imprisonment', in Garland, D. (ed.) (1990), *Justice, Guilt and Forgiveness in the Penal System*, Occasional Paper No.18, Centre for Theology and Public Issues, University of Edinburgh: 3-37.

Bukstel, L. H. and Kilmann, P. R. (1980), 'Psychological Effects of Imprisonment on Confined Individuals', *Psychological Bulletin*, 88(2): 469-493.

Burridge, R. *et al* (1985), 'The Inquest as a Theatre for Police Tragedy', *Journal for Law and Society*, 12 25-61.

Carcach, C., and McDonald D. 1997, *National Police Custody Survey August 1995*, *Research and Public Policy*, Canberra: Australian Institute of Criminology.

CERD (1996), *Concluding Observations of the Committee on the Elimination of Racial Discrimination: United Kingdom of Great Britain and Northern Ireland*, United Nations.

Clarke, R. V. G. and Martin, D. N. (1971), *Absconding from Approved Schools*, Home Office Research Study No. 12, HMSO: London.

Clemmer, D. (1940), *The Prison Community*, Holt, Rinehart and Winston: New York

Clothier, Sir C., QC (1996), 'Ruminations on Inquiries' in Peay, J. (ed.), *Inquiries After Homicide*, London: Duckworth.

Cohen, S., and Taylor, L. (1979), *Psychological Survival*, Penguin: Harmondsworth.

Coggan, G. and Walker, M. (1982), *Frightened for My Life*, London, Fontana.

Crichton, J. H. M. (1994), 'Comments on The Blackwood Inquiry', *Psychiatric Bulletin*, 18: 234-237.

Dalton, V. (1997), *Australian Deaths in Custody and in Custody-related Police Operations 1996*, Canberra: Australian Institute of Criminology.

Dexter, P (1993), *Suicide Attempts at Highpoint Prison* (M.Sc. thesis: Birbeck College).

Dooley, E (1990a), 'Prison Suicide in England and Wales 1972-1987', *British Journal of Psychiatry*, 156: 40-45.

Dooley, E. (1990b), Non-natural Deaths in Prison, *British Journal of Criminology*, 30(2): 229-34.

247

Douglas, J. (1967), *The Social Meanings of Suicide*, London: Routledge.

Eastman, N. (1996), 'Inquiry into Homicides by Psychiatric Patients: Systematic Audit Should Replace Mandatory Inquiries', *British Medical Journal*, 313: 1069-1071.

Ehonwa O. L. (1993), *Prisoners in the Shadows, A Report on Women and Children in Five Nigerian Prisons*, CLO: Lagos.

Erikson, R. V. (1975), *Young Offenders and their Social Work*, Heath: Massachusetts.

Farran (1996), *The UK Before the European Court of Human Rights*, Blackstone.

Fawcett, J. (1972), 'Suicidal Depression and Physical Illness', *Journal of the American Medical Association*, 219, 1303-1306.

Feld, B. C. (1977), *Neutralizing Inmate Violence: Juvenile Offenders in Institutions*, Ballinger: Massachusetts.

Felthous, A. R. (1994), 'Preventing Jailhouse Suicides', *Bulletin of the American Academy of Psychiatry and Law*, 22, 477-488.

Fleming, J. (1989), *Preliminary Analysis of A.C.T. Suicides 1 January 1980 to 30 June 1988*, Canberra: Criminology Research Unit, Royal Commission into Aboriginal Deaths in Custody.

Fleming, J., McDonald, D., and Biles, D. (1992), 'Deaths in Non-Custodial Corrections, Australia and New Zealand, 1987 and 1988' in *Deaths in Custody, Australia, 1980-1989: The Research Papers of the Criminology Unit of the Royal Commission into Aboriginal Deaths in Custody*, edited by D. Biles and D. McDonald, Canberra: Australian Institute of Criminology.

Foucault, M. (1975), *I, Pierre Riviere, Having Slaughtered My Mother, My Sister and My Brother*, University of Nebraska Press.

Gallo, E. and Ruggiero, V. (1991), The Immaterial Prison: Custody as a Factory for the Manufacture of Handicaps, *International Journal of the Sociology of Law*, (19): 273-291.

Giddens, A. (1984), *The Constitution of Society*, Polity Press: Cambridge.

Gibbs, J. J. (1987), 'Symptoms of Psychopathology Among Jail Prisoners: The Effects of Exposure to the Jail Environment', *Criminal Justice and Behaviour*, 14, 288-310.

Giles, H. G., and Sandrin, S. (1992), 'Alcohol and Deaths in Police Custody', *Alcoholism: Clinical and Experimental Research*, 16, 670-672.

Grounds, A. (1997), 'Commentary on "Inquiries: Who Needs Them?"', *Psychiatric Bulletin*, 21: 134-135.

Hall, S. *et al.* (1978), *Policing the Crisis*, London, MacMillan.

Hammerlin, Y., and Bodal, K. (1988), *Suicide and Life-threatening Activities in Norwegian Prisons During the Period 1956 Through 1987*, Norway: Ministry of Justice, Prison Department.

Haney, J. (1990), *Report On Self-Injurious Behaviour in the Kingston Prison for Women* (Unpublished report to the Correctional Service of Canada: Ontario).

Harris, O'Boyle and Warbrick (1995), *Law of ECHR*, Butterworths.

Hayes, L. M. (1983), 'And Darkness Closes In . . . A National Study of Jail Suicides', *Criminal Justice and Behaviour*, 10(4), 461-484.

Hayes, L. M. (1989), 'National Study of Jail Suicides: Seven Years Later', *Psychiatric Quarterly*, 60(1), 7-29.

Hayes, L. M. (1995), 'Prison Suicide: An Overview and Guide to Prevention' (Part 2), *Crisis*, 16(1), 9-12.

Hayes, L. (1994), 'Jail Suicide Prevention in the USA: Yesterday, Today and Tomorrow', in Liebling A. and Ward T. (eds.), *Deaths In Custody: International Perspectives*, Whiting and Birch: London.

HMCIP (1993), 'Report of An Unannounced Short Inspection by H M Inspectorate of Prisons', *HM YOI and RC Feltham*, Home Office: London.

HMCIP (1990), *Report On a Review By Her Majesty's Chief Inspector of Prisons for England and Wales of Suicide and Self-Harm in Prison Service Establishments in England and Wales*, HMSO: London.

Home Office (1984), *Suicides in Prison*, Report by H. M. Chief Inspector of Prisons, HMSO: London.

Home Office (1986), *Report of the Working Group on Suicide Prevention*, HMSO: London.

Home Office (1997), *Report of the Disasters and Inquests Working Group*, London: Home Office.

Howard League for Penal Reform (1993), *Suicides in Feltham*, London: Howard League.

Hunter F. and Odinkalu A. C. (1997), 'Crime and Punishment: Prisons in Africa', *West Africa*, 10 - 16 February, 1997.

Human Rights and Equal Opportunity Commission (1997), *Bringing Them Home: Report of the National Inquiry into the Separation of Aboriginal and Torres Strait Islander Children from Their Families*, Sydney: Human Rights and Equal Opportunity Commission.

Ifowodo, O. (1994), 'Police Abuses', *Annual Report on Human Rights In Nigeria 1993*, CLO: Lagos.

Ingram, A., Johnson, G. and Heyes, I. (1997), *Self-Harm and Suicide by Detained Persons: A Study*, Lancashire Constabulary: UK.

INQUEST (1990), *Black Deaths In Police Custody*, London: INQUEST.

INQUEST (1996), *Racial Discrimination and Deaths in Custody*, Report submitted to the UN Committee on the Elimination of Racial Discrimination, London: INQUEST.

Institute of Race Relations (1991), *Deadly Silence: Black Deaths in Custody*, London Institute of Race Relations.

ISTD, *Criminal Justice Newsletter* (1995), Vol. 26. No 7, 3.

Jacobs and White (1996), *The ECHR*, Oxford: Clarendon Press.

James, J.T.L. (1990), *A Living Tradition: Penitentiary Chaplaincy*, Correctional Service of Canada, Ottawa, Canada.

Jefferson, T (1990), *The Case Against Paramilitary Policing*, Milton Keynes, Open University Press.

Johnston, E. (1991), *Royal Commission into Aboriginal Deaths in Custody: Report of the Inquiry into the Death of John Peter Pat*, Canberra: AGPS.

Johnson, R. and Toch, H. (1982), *The Pains of Imprisonment*, Sage: London.

Johnson, H.R.M. (1982), 'Deaths in Custody in England and Wales', *Forensic Sciences International*, 19, 231-236.

Kerkhof, A. J. F. M. and Bernasco, W. (1990), 'Suicidal Behaviour in Jails and Prisons in the Netherlands: Incidence, Characteristics, and Prevention', *Suicide and Life-threatening Behaviour*, 20, 123-137.

Kerkhof, A. J. F. M. and Diekstra, R. F. W. (1995), 'How to Evaluate and Deal with Acute Suicide Risk: Guidelines for Health Care Workers' in R. F. W. Diekstra, W. Gulbinat, I. Kienhorst and D. de Leo (eds.), *Preventive Strategies on Suicide* (pp. 97-128). Leiden, The Netherlands: E. J. Brill.

Kleinjan, H.R. and Smidt, R. E. de (1994), 'Deaths in Dutch Prisons' in A. Liebling and T. Ward (eds.), *Deaths in Custody: International Perspectives*, Bournemouth, England: Bourne Press.

Knapman and Powers (1985), *The Law and Practice on Coroners*, Barry Rose.

Korn, M. L., Brown, S. L., Kotler, M., Gordon, M. and van Praag, H. M. (1995), Biological Aspects of Suicide: Serotonergic Function in Suicide Attempters. In R. F. W. Diekstra, W. Gulbinat, I. Kienhorst and D. de Leo (eds.), *Preventive Strategies on Suicide* (pp. 97-128), Leiden, The Netherlands: E. J. Brill.

Laycock, G. K (1977), *Absconding From Borstals*, Home Office Research Study No. 41, HMSO: London.

Lester, David (1983), *Why People Kill Themselves: A 1980s Summary of Research Findings on Suicidal Behaviour*, 2nd ed., Springfield, Ill.: Thomas.

Liberty (1996), 'Update', *Agenda*, May.

Liebling, A. (1992), *Suicides in Prison*, Routledge: London.

Liebling, A. (1994), 'Suicides Amongst Women Prisoners', *Howard Journal*, 33(1): 1-9.

Liebling, A. (1995), 'Vulnerability and Prison Suicide', *British Journal of Criminology*, 35(2): 173-187.

Liebling, A and Krarup, H. (1993), *Suicide Attempts in Male Prisons*, Home Office: London.

Liebling A. (1994), 'Suicide and Suicide Attempts Amongst Young Prisoners: The UK Experience', in Liebling A. and Ward T. (eds.), *Deaths In Custody: International Perspectives*, Whiting and Birch: London

Liebling, A. and Ward, T. (eds.) (1994), *Deaths in Custody: An International Conference* Whiting and Birch: London

Liebling, Alison (ed.) (1996), *Deaths in Custody: Caring for People at Risk*, London: Whiting and Birch.

Lloyd, C. (1990), *Suicide in Prison: A Literature Review*, Home Office Research Study No. 115, HORPU: London.

Maguire, M. and Corbett, C. (1991), *A Study of the Police Complaints System*, London: HMSO.

Matthews and Foreman (1993), *Jervis on Coroners*, Sweet and Maxwell.

Masters, B. (1985), *Killing for Company: The Case of Dennis Nilsen*, London: Cape.

Masters, B. (1993), *The Shrine of Jeffrey Dahmer*, London: Hodder and Stoughton.

Masters, B. (1996), *'She Must Have Known': The Trial of Rosemary West*, London: Doubleday.

Mathiesen, T. (1965), *Defenses of the Weak: A Sociological Study of a Norwegian Correctional Institution*, London: Tavistock.

McConville, Mike, Sanders, Andrew, and Leng, Roger (1991), *The Case for the Prosecution: Police, Suspects and the Construction of Criminality*, London: Routledge.

McDonald, David (1996a), 'Australian Deaths in Custody: The Impact of the Royal Commission into Aboriginal Deaths in Custody' in *Deaths in Custody: Caring for People at Risk*, edited by A. Liebling, London: Whiting and Birch.

McDonald, David (1996b), 'Deaths in Police Custody' in *Australian Policing: Contemporary Issues*, edited by D. Chappell and P. Wilson, Sydney: Butterworths.

McDonald, D. and Thomson, N. J. (1993), 'Australian Deaths In Custody, 1980-1989', *The Medical Journal of Australia*, 159, 581-585.

Memory, J. M. (1984), 'Jail Suicides in South Carolina, 1978-1984' (Unpublished paper) Columbia, SC: Office of the Governor, Division of Public Safety Programs.

McGurk, B. J. and McDougal, C. (1986), *The Prevention of Bullying Among Incarcerated Delinquents*, D. P. S. Report Series II, No. 114 (Restricted circulation), London.

Mills, Heather (27 July 1997) 'Insult Added to Widow's Injury', *Observer:* 5.

More, H. (1992), *Special Topics in Policing*, Cincinnati: Anderson.

Moscow Center for Prison Reform (1996), *In Search of a Solution, Crime, Criminal Policy and Prison Facilities in the Former Soviet Union*, Human Rights Publishers, Moscow.

National Commission on Correctional Health Care (1987), *Standards for Health Services in Jails*, Chicago, IL.

Nigerian Institute of Advanced Legal Studies (1990), 'Prisons' (Paper presented at the National Seminar on Prison Reforms In Nigeria), June 1990: 22.

Nigerian Prisons Annual Report 1984, pp. 5-6.

Nigerian Prisons Annual Report (1980- 1986 editions).

Obot I. S (1990), 'Morbidity and Mortality Among Inmates In Nigerian Prisons: Causes and Solutions', (Paper presented at the National Seminar on 'Prison Reforms in Nigeria', June 1990): 20.

Odinkalu A. C. and Ehonwa 0. L (1991), *Behind the Wall: A Report on Prison Conditions in Nigeria and the Nigerian Prison System*, CLO: Lagos.

Office of the Aboriginal and Torres Strait Islander Social Justice Commissioner (1996), *Indigenous Deaths in Custody 1989-1996*, Canberra: ATSIC.

O'Mahony, P. (1994), 'Prison Suicide Rates: What Do They Mean?' in Liebling, A. and Ward, T. (eds.), *Deaths in Custody: International Perspectives*, Whiting and Birch: London, pp. 45-57.

Paulus, P. B. and Dzindolet, M. T. (1993), 'Reactions of Male and Female Inmates to Prison Confinement', *Criminal Justice and Behaviour*, 20, 149-166.

Prins, H., Backer-Holst, T., Francis, E. and Keitch, I. (1993), *Report of the Committee of Inquiry into the Death in Broadmoor Hospital of Orville Blackwood and a Review of the Deaths of Two Other Afro-Caribbean Patients: Big, Black and Dangerous?*, London: Special Hospitals Service Authority.

PCA (1994), *Annual Report for 1993*, London: HMSO.

PCA (1997), *Annual Report for 1996/7*, London: Stationery Office.

Prison Watch (1991), *Nigeria: Behind The Wall*, 24 April 1991, Africa Watch: London.

Reder, P. and Duncan, S. (1996), 'Reflections on Child Abuse Inquiries' in Peay, J. (ed.), *Inquiries After Homicide*, London: Duckworth.

Reiner, R. (1994), 'Policing and the Police' in *The Oxford Handbook of Criminology*, edited by M. Maguire, R. Morgan and R. Reiner, Oxford University Press.

Report of the Committee of Inquiry into Complaints about Ashworth Hospital, Vol. 1 (London. HMSO), 1992: 211.

Rideau, W. and Wikberg, R. (1992), *Life Sentences: Rage and Survival Behind Bars*, Times Books, New York.

Ritchie, S., QC (1985), *Report to the Secretary of State for Social Services Concerning the Death of Mr Michael Martin at Broadmoor Hospital on 6 July 1984*, London: HMSO.

Roberts, M. M. (ed.) (1994), *Out of the Night, Writings from Death Row*, New Clarion Press.

Robertson and Merrills (1993), *Human Rights in Europe*, 3rd Edition.

Rock, P. (1996), 'The Inquiry and Victims' Families' in Peay, J. (ed), *Inquiries After Homicide*, London: Duckworth.

Rose, N. and Miller, P. (1992), 'Political Power Beyond the State; Problematics of Government', *British Journal of Sociology*, 43(2) pp. 177- 205.

Rowan, J. (1994), 'Prevention of Suicides in Custody' in A. Liebling and T. Ward (eds.), *Deaths in Custody: International Perspectives* (pp. 166-174), Bournemouth: Bourne Press.

Royal Commission into Aboriginal Deaths in Custody (1991), *Royal Commission into Aboriginal Deaths in Custody: National Report*, Commissioner Elliott Johnston, Canberra: AGPS.

Ryan, M. (1983), *The Politics of Penal Reform*, London: Longman, *Chapter 3*.

Ryan, M. (1996), *Lobbying from Below; INQUEST in Defence of Civil Liberties*, UCL Press, London, *Chapter 2*.

Sapsford, R. (1978), 'Life Sentence Prisoners: Psychological Changes During Sentence' *British Journal of Criminology*, 18: 128-45

Sapsford, R. (1983), *Life Sentence Prisoners*, Open University Press: Milton Keynes.

Scraton, P. and Gordon, P. (1984), *Causes for Concern*, London: Penquin, *Chapters 2 and 3*.

Scraton, Phil and Chadwick, Kathryn (1987), *In the Arms of the Law*, London: Pluto.

Scraton, P. (ed.) (1976), *Law Order and the Authoritarian State*, Milton Keynes, Open University Press.

Scott-Denoon, K. (1984), *B.C. Corrections: A Study of Suicides 1970-1980*, British Columbia: Corrections Branch.

Segest, E. (1987), 'Police Custody: Deaths and Medical Attention', *Journal of Forensic Sciences*, 32, 1694-1703.

Sheppard, D. (1996), *Learning the Lessons* (2nd edition), London: The Zito Trust.

Sim, J (1990), *Medical Power in Prisons*, Open University Press, Milton Keynes.

Sim, J (1991), "We are Not Animals, We are Human Beings": Prisons, Protest and Politics in England and Wales 1969- 1970', *Social Justice*, Vol. 18, No. 3.

Sinclair, I (1971) *Hostels for Probationers,* Home Office Research Studies No. 6, HMSO: London.

Sparks, J. R. (1994), 'Suicides in Prison' by Alison Liebling, a review in *British Journal of Criminology* 34(1): 82-84.

Stewart, R. L. (1995), *Special Report of the Correctional Investigator Concerning the Treatment of Inmates and Subsequent Inquiry Following Certain Incidents at the Prison for Women in April 1994 and Thereafter,* Minister of Supply and Services, Canada.

Stokes, P. E. (1993), 'Fluoxetine: A Five-year Review', *Clinical Therapeutics*, 15(2), 216-243.

Thomson, Neil, and David McDonald (1993), 'Australian Deaths in Custody, 1980-1989: 1. Relative Risks of Aborigines and non-Aborigines', *Medical Journal of Australia,* 159 (November): 577-81.

Thomson, N. J., and McDonald, D. (1993), 'Australian Deaths in Custody, 1980-1989', *The Medical Journal of Australia*, 159, 577-581.

Toch, H., Adams, K. and Grant, D. (1989), *Coping: Maladaptation in Prisons,* Transaction: New Brunswick.

Toch, H (1992), *Mosaic of Despair: Human Breakdowns in Prisons* (Revised edition), Easton Publishing Services: Easton.

Topp D. O. (1979), 'Suicide in Prison', *British Journal of Psychiatry,* 134: 24-27.

Tuskan, J. J., and Thase, M. E. (1983), 'Suicides in Jails and Prisons', *Journal of Psychosocial Nursing and Mental Health,* 21(5), 29-33.

Walker, N. (1983), 'The Side-Effects of Incarceration', *British Journal of Criminology* 23: 61-71.

Walker, N. (1987), 'The Unwanted Effects of Long-Term Imprisonment' in Bottoms, A. E. and Light, R. (eds.), *Problems of Long-Term Imprisonment,* Gower: Aldershot.

Walmsley, R., Howard, L., and White, S., *The National Prison Survey 1991: Main Findings* HMSO: London.

Wansell, G. (1996), *An Evil Love: The Life of Frederick West,* London: Headline Books.

Ward, T. (1986), *Deaths and Disorder*, London, INQUEST.

Williams, M. (1997), *A Cry of Pain*, Penguin: London.

Wootten, J. H. (1990), *Royal Commission into Aboriginal Deaths in Custody: Report of the Inquiry into the Death of Mark Anthony Quayle,* Canberra: AGPS.

Wootten, J. H. (1991), *Royal Commission into Aboriginal Deaths in Custody: Report of the Inquiry into the Death of David John Gundy,* Canberra: AGPS.

Wyvill, L. (1990), *Royal Commission into Aboriginal Deaths in Custody: Report of the Inquiry into the Death of Fay Lena Yarrie,* Canberra: AGPS.

Zamble, E. and Porporino, F. J. (1988), *Coping, Behaviour and Adaptation in Prison Inmates* New York: Springer-Verlag.

Cases cited

McCann v. United Kingdom [1996] 21 EHRR 97

R v. Adomako [1995] 1 AC 171

R v. Chief Constable of the West Midlands Police, ex p. Wiley [1994] 3 WLR 433

R v. Chief Constable Thames Valley Police, ex p. PCA (1994), unreported

R v. Coroner for Humberside, ex p. Jamieson [1994] 3 WLR 82

R v. Hammersmith Coroner ex p. Peach (1980)

R v. Birmingham Coroner ex p. Home Secretary (1990) (Attwal)

R v. DPP, ex p. Jones, O'Brien and Treadaway, Queen's Bench Divisional Court (Rose, LJ and Jowitt, J), 23-30 July 1997, unreported

R v. Inner London Coroner, ex p. Douglas-Williams, High Court (Laws J), 31 July 1997, unreported

Taylor v. Anderton [1995] 2 All ER 420

Treadaway v. Chief Constable of West Midlands Police, The Times 25 October 1994, *The Independent* 23 September 1994

Quayle v. New South Wales (1995) Aust Torts Reports 62, 792

EHRLR [1995] Launch Issue: Special Case Note, *McCann and Others v. UK*

EHRLR [1996] Issue 6: Cases and Comments, pp. 661-664.

Speakers' Biographical Details

Information about the speakers whose materials are also contained in this volume are reproduced at the end of their respective chapters. The following also took part:

SIR LOUIS BLOM-COOPER QC (The Chair of the Conference) is Chair of National Victim Support. He was previously Chair of the Mental Health Act Commission and has headed many high profile public inquiries such as the Jasmine Beckford Inquiry and the Committee of Inquiry into Complaints About Ashworth Hospital. He was called to the Bar in 1952 and has written numerous books and articles on the penal system. He received a knighthood in 1992.

JANOS BOROS is head of the Department of International Relations in the Hungarian Prison Administration (HPA). He has previously been a prison psychologist and has also conducted research for the HPA. He has taught at both the ELTE and KLTE universities in Budapest and has published widely.

MERG BRAY has been a Samaritan in the Putney branch for 12 years. She has been involved with the branch's prison befriending since it began in Wandsworth Prison in 1990. Having had experience in training potential volunteers through that branch, she was actively involved in setting up and training the Listeners in Wandsworth in 1992. She joined the national Prison Support Team in 1995 as co-ordinator for the London region and attends Listener training and support as well as Suicide Awareness Team meetings in several establishments.

ANDREW COYLE is Chair of ISTD. Between 1991 and 1997 he was Governor of HMP Brixton, having previously governed four major prisons. He has also worked in the headquarters of the Scottish Prison Service. Dr. Coyle has written extensively on criminal justice matters and has visited prisons in many countries as an expert consultant for bodies such as the United Nations and the Council of Europe. In 1997 he was the founding Director of the International Centre for Prison Studies, based at King's College London.

NASHATER DEU obtained her Psych. D in clinical forensic psychology from the University of Surrey. She is currently the Principal Clinical Psychologist at Broadmoor Special Hospital, specialising in the assessment and treatment of mentally disordered offenders in conditions of maximum security. Her research interests include: sex offending, the development and use of fantasy in criminal activity, deliberate self-harm and cultural aspects of mental illness and anti-social behaviour.

ANITA DOCKLEY has been the Policy Officer for the Howard League since 1991. Her areas of particular interest include: discipline and control in prisons, prison suicide, women in prison and issues relating to prisoners' families. She is currently studying part-time, for a Ph. D at the London School of Economics.

255

KATE DONEGAN is Governor of HMP and YOI Cornton Vale. She joined the Scottish Prison Service in 1977 and has held a number of governor's positions in various establishments, as well as being at Headquarters between 1991 and 1994. From 1995 to 1996 she was an Inspector, then Deputy Chief Inspector of Prisons for Scotland, before taking up her present post in 1996.

MOIRA McALPINE is Deputy Governor of HMP and YOI Cornton Vale. She joined the Scottish Prison Service in 1990 as Head of Personnel. She was a residential manager at HMP Edinburgh and HMP Shotts before being posted to HMP Peterhead in 1995. She was appointed to her present position in 1996.

MARTIN McHUGH joined the Prison Service in 1980 and worked in maximum security prisons as a psychologist until 1990. He then moved to Prison Service Headquarters to work in recruitment and the training of psychologists. In 1994 he became head of the Suicide Awareness Support Unit.

KAREN PAGE has been involved in the training of probation and prison staff for a number of years. The main focus of her work has been with sex offenders, risk assessment, sentence planning, stress management and child protection issues. She is a visiting lecturer at the University of Kent.

CHRISTINA POURGOURIDES is a psychiatrist who has recently completed a 12 month research project into detention, which was funded by the Barrow Cadbury Trust and the North Birmingham Mental Health Trust. She liaises with other organizations on issues surrounding detention, asylum and health.

PAUL RUBENSTEIN has been a Samaritan volunteer for 24 years. Having held various posts within that organization at local and national level, he was appointed as The Samaritan's National Co-ordinator for prisons for three years until January 1997. He has liaised with and visited prison services in several other countries, working with them in developing suicide awareness for staff and prisoners. He is currently a director and trustee of Befrienders International, which aims to expand and develop volunteer resources in supporting the suicidal throughout the world.

HELEN SHAW has been Co-director of INQUEST since 1994. She previously worked in the mental health field and as a therapist. She is co-author of *Racial Discrimination and Deaths in Custody* (with Deborah Coles).

TRUDIE STOTT has been a Samaritan volunteer for 17 years, having been Director of the South Devon Branch. She was instrumental in setting up the Listener scheme at HMP Channings Wood and has for some time been a member of the National Prison Support Team which oversees the organization's work in prisons in supporting Samaritan branches and prison establishments, keeping closely in touch with the Suicide Awareness Support Unit at Prison Service Headquarters.

GRAHAM TOWL is chair of the Prison Service Suicide Awareness Support Unit Research and Development Group. He holds visiting academic posts at the Universities of Cambridge and Kent and has clinical experience of working with the suicidal in both psychiatric hospitals and prisons. His main areas of research and practice interests lie in suicide, risk assessment, groupwork and ethics. He has also co-authored *The Handbook of Psychology for Forensic Practitioners*.

TREVOR WALT is the full-time Chaplain at Broadmoor Special Hospital. He has worked at Broadmoor for 25 years, initially as a psychiatric nurse and nurse tutor, before becoming Chaplain in 1988.

Delegates

Name	Role	Organisation
Kathy	Befriender	HMP Holloway
Ken	Samaritan	HMP Holloway
Colleen Befriender	HMP Holloway	
Penny Samaritan	HMP Wormwood Scrubs	
Vaughan	Listener	HMP Wormwood Scrubs
Ann	Samaritan	HMP Holloway
Uju Agomoh	Director,	PRAWA, Nigeria
Justine Ashton	Snr Practitioner, Remand Rescue	The Children's Society
Bill Baker		ISTD
Olga Berezhnaya		Serbsky Nat Research Centre
Valodia Bernardo	Criminology Student	ISTD
Kathy Biggar		ISTD
David Bishop	Senior Officer	HMYOI Portland
Eric Blaauw	Forensic Psychologist	Vrije University, Amsterdam
Dorothy Black	Mental Health Act Commissioner	
Ashley Blackett	Supt. Complaints and Discipline	Cleveland Constabulary
Christine Blackman	Prison Officer	HMP Holloway
Sir Louis Blom-Cooper	Chair	National Victim Support
Jack Bloomer	Training Adviser	N Ireland Prison Service
Janos Boros	Director of Research	Nat Prison Admin, Hungary
Julia Braggins	Director	ISTD
Merg Bray	Regional Prison Support Officer	The Samaritans
Bill Brazier	Suicide Awareness Trainer	HMP Featherstone
Michael Brightmore	Superintendent	Humberside Police
Robert Brown	Principal Officer	HM Prison Service
Shane Bryans	Head of Management Training	HM Prison Service, Newbold Revel
Michael Burdett	Solicitor	
Bob Burlinson	Senior Probation Officer	Suffolk Probation Service
Eileen Bye	Solicitor	Joint Council for the Welfare of Immigrants
Robin Carter	Head of Regime and Throughcare	HMP Woodhill
John Cartwright	Deputy Chair (Investigations)	Police Complaints Authority
Ivica Chorvatova		Police Academy, Slovakia
Elaine Christian	Magistrate	Isle of Man
Felicity Clarkson	Head of Programmes Group	Prison Service
Karen Coates	Clinical Manager	Premier Prison Services
Sheila Coggrave	National Prisons Support Co-ordnr.	The Samaritans
Deborah Coles	Co-Director	INQUEST
Sue Constantine	Prison Officer	HMP Grendon
George Cooper	Sergeant	Northamptonshire Police
Dean Corbishley	Senior Officer	HMP Preston
Chris Cormack	Prison Officer	HMP Featherstone
Mary Cotter	Research Associate	Open Society Institute
Marieva Coughlan	Clinical Psychologist	Department of Justice, Eire
Andrew Coyle	Director	International Centre for Prison Studies
Mike Culverhouse	Supt. Complaints and Discipline	Merseyside Police
Paul de Boer	Behaviour Advisor	Ministry of Justice, The Hague
Nashater Deu	Principal Clinical Psychologist	Broadmoor Special Hospital
Robert Dixon	Head of Prison Medical Services	DHSS, Northern Ireland
Anita Dockley	Policy Officer	Howard League for Penal Reform
Kate Donegan	Governor	HM Institution Cornton Vale
Enda Dooley	Medical Director	Department of Justice, Eire
Sandra Downes		Marion Downes Memorial Trust
Anne Dunn	Policy Manager	NACRO Race Unit
Audrey Edwards	Parent of Victim	
Paul Edwards	Parent of Victim	
Barry Edwards	Senior Officer	HMP Bristol
Paul Fenning	Probation Officer	Merseyside Probation Service
John Fitzgerald	Chaplain	HMP Nottingham
Aurelie Freeman	Social Work Team Manager	Wandsworth Social Services

Name	Role	Organisation
Lucy Gampell	Co-ordinator	Fed. of Prisoners' Families Support Groups
Steve Gannon	Principal Nurse	HMP Wormwood Scrubs
Jim Gore	Director	Social Developments Ltd
Halya Gowan	Researcher	Amnesty International
Elizabeth Grayson	Force Welfare Officer	Northamptonshire Police
Paul Grierson	Black Prisoner Sup. Scheme Co-odnr.	Nottingham Black Initiative
Julie Grogan	Administrator	ISTD
Nic Groombridge	Criminology Lecturer	St. Mary's University College
Irene Guild		Scottish Assoc. for Study of Delinquency
Ann Hair	Retired Prison Governor	
John Harrison	Discipline Sub-Committee	Police Federation
David Hastings	Prison Chaplain	HMP Exeter
James Havercroft	Investigations Officer	Premier Prison Services
Gordon Hay	Chief Superintendent	Northumbria Police
Lindsay Hayes	Assistant Director	Nat. Centre on Institutions and Alternatives
Stephanie Hayman	Conference Organiser	ISTD
Olga Heaven	Director	Female Prisoners Welfare Project and Hibiscus
Jan Heyes	Operations Manager	HMP Garth
Jim Heyes		Securicor Custodial Services
John Hickman	Treasurer	ISTD
Peter Hill		The Zito Trust
Michael Hill	Health Care Officer	HM Prison Service
David Hillier	Directorate of Health Care	Prison Service
Leonie Howe	Student	University of Warwick
Rachel Hughes	'A' Wing Manager	HMP Wormwood Scrubs
Helen Anger	Prison Liaison Officer	The Samaritans
Alan Ingram	Inspector	Lancashire Constabulary
Steve Jackson	Prison Officer	HMP Grendon
Lee Jasper	Director	1990 Trust
Graham Johnson	Research and Development	Lancashire Constabulary
Robert Jones	Chief Inspector	Thames Valley Police
Alun Jones	Principal Officer	HMP Bedford
Anthony Jones	Principal Officer	HMYOI Portland
Margaret Jordan	Nurse	HMP Holloway
Sarah Joseph	Board of Visitors	HMP Holloway
Mariana Katzarova	Researcher	Amnesty International
Kelley	Suicide Awness Liaison Officer	HMP Full Sutton
James Kelly	Prison Programmes Manager	Scottish Prison Service
Bill Kelly	Hospital Officer	Isle of Man Prison
Linda Kemp	Health Care Manager	HMP Gateside
Jan Kenny	Probation Officer	Merseyside Probation Service
John Kerr	Prison Officer	HMP Greenock
Samantha King		HMP Wormwood Scrubs
Alexandra Kirkpatrick		Scottish Association for Study of Delinquency
Arena Kriznik	Director General	National Prison Administration, Slovenia
Peter Lake	Governor Opns and Lifer Liaison	HMP Dartmoor
Ladi Lapite	Community Safety Officer	Manchester City Council
Carlo Laurenzi	Executive Director	Prisoners Abroad
Simon Lewis	Chief Inspector	Metropolitan Police
Alison Liebling	Lecturer	Institute of Criminology, Cambridge
Nicholas Long	Chair	Lambeth Com/Pol Consult Group
Sarah Mackereth	Probation Officer	Merseyside Probation Service
Michael Macklam	Principal Offr Suicide Awareness	HMP Full Sutton
Askala Mariam	Seven Star Productions	
Carol Martin	Research Development	ISTD
Liz Mayne	Director	WISH
Moira McAlpine	Deputy Governor	HM Institution Cornton Vale
John McCaig	Deputy Governor	HMP Greenock
Fergal McDonagh	Head Chaplain	Department of Justice, Eire

Name	Role	Organization
David McDonald	Social Scientist	The Australian National University
Brian McGivern	Prison Officer, Suicide Awareness	HMP Preston
Gail McGregor	General Secretary	Assn of Black Probation Officers
Martin McHugh	Head, Suicide Awns Sup Unit	HM Prison Service
Geraidine McKean	Probation Officer	Merseyside Probation Service
Jan McLean	Prison Officer	HMP Liverpool
Diana Medlicott	Lecturer	Buckinghamshire College
Sharon Moore	Co-ordinator, Remand Rescue	The Children's Society
Natalie Morel	Project Co-ordinator	The Inverness Council on Alcohol
Sebastian Naidoo	Journalist	
Keith Napthine	Inspector	Surrey Police Authority
Paul Neary	Head of Remand Population	Group 4 Prison Services Ltd
Michael Newell	Governor	HMP Hull
John Newell	Governor 5	Northern Ireland Prison Service
Sally Newton	Head of Nursing Services	Northern Ireland Prison Service
Debbie Nimblette		Marion Downes Memorial Trust
Evgeny Novikov	Chair	Belarus League for Human Rights
Jackie Owens	Senior Probation Officer	HMP Pentonville
Una Padel	Co-ordinator	London Prisons Community Links
Karen Page	Senior Probation Officer	Kent Probation Service
Lee Parker	Youth and Community Worker	Lambeth Education Services
Tony Pearson	Director of Security and Progs	Prison Service
Hubert Percival	Head of Healthcare	HMP Whitemoor
Mary Piper	Acting Head, Standards and Audit	Prison Service
Louise Pirouet	Co-ordinator	Charter ' 87 for Refugees
Christina Pourgourides	Psychiatrist	
Herschel Prins		Loughborough University
Beverly Provost	Director	Black Female Prisoners Scheme
Fiona Radford	Chair, Suicide Awareness Team	HMP Holloway
Cari Raybold	Regional Officer	Commission for Racial Equality
Carol Rigby	Project Worker	WISH
Colin Ring	Prison Officer	Isle of Man Prison
Cameron Ritchie	Procurator Fiscal	Stirling
Brigid Roberson	Probation Officer	Probation Board for Northern Ireland
Joe Rowan	President	Criminal and Juvenile Justice International, USA
Paul Rubenstein		The Samaritans
Peter Rudgard	Senior Psychologist	HMP Doncaster
Mick Ryan	Department of Humanities	University of Greenwich
Lynn Saunders	Head of Healthcare	HM Prison Service
Frans Schilder	Dept of Clinical Psychology	Vrije University of Amsterdam
Heinz Schurmann-Zeggel		Amnesty International
Valeri Sergueev		Moscow Centre for Prison Reform
Helen Shaw	Co-Director	INQUEST
Barry Siddaway	Health Care Officer	HMYOI Portland
Ursula Smartt	Researcher	Thames Valley University
Janice Smiley	Staff Officer	Northern Ireland Prison Service
Louisa Snow	Asst Information/Research Officer	HM Prison Service
Clare Sparks	Policy Officer	Prison Reform Trust
Catherine Stancer	Case Worker	Women in Prison
Christopher Stephens	Police Inspector	Devon and Cornwall Constabulary
Vivien Stern	Director	Penal Refor m International
Trudie Stott		The Samaritans
Norman Taylor	Chief Inspector	Northumbria Police
Paul Tidball	Governor 3	HMP Drake Hall
Richard Tilt	Director General	HM Prison Service
Heather Tomlinson	Assistant Psychologist	Broadmoor Hospital
Graham Towl	Area Forensic Psychologist	HM Prison Service
Michael Underhill	Security Officer	HM Prison Service
Vasiiy Vandysh-Boubko		Serbsky Nat Research Centre
Justina Vaughan	Probation Officer/Pre-Trial Services	Inner London Probation Service
Jana Viktoryova	Head of Faculty of Law	Police Academy, Slovakia
John Wadham	Director	Liberty
Andy Wainwright	EIF Unit Manager	Group 4 Prison Services Ltd

Trevor Walt	Chaplain	Broadmoor Special Hospital
Tony Ward	Senior Law Lecturer	De Montfort University
Orchid White	Legal Advocate	
Richard Whittington	President	Coroners' Society of England and Wales
Chris Williams	Governor	HM Prison Service
Albert Zaalberg	Senior Staff Member	National Agency of Correctional Institutions
Frank Zorge	Deputy Head of Policy Information	National Agency of Correctional Institutions

Expanded List of Contents

Introduction *vii*

PART ONE POLITICS, THEORY AND INQUIRY

1 Deaths in Custody: The Politics and Language of Culpability in Post-modern Britain *Mick Ryan 21;* Sudden and unexpected deaths in custody: growth of public concern 22; Police 22; Prisons 23; Families 24; Defending civil rights 25; Inquests 27; Denying culpability 28; Ways forward 29; Conclusion 30.

2 Changing Perspectives on Deaths of Prisoners *Richard Tilt 33;* Prison Service Statement of Purpose 33; Deaths during 1995 34; Suicide rates in the community 36; Self-inflicted deaths against average daily population 37; Deaths in Scottish and Northern Ireland prisons 38; What has the prison service done about self-inflicted deaths? 39; Key features of strategy 39; Work in progress 40; Homicides 41; Aftermath of death 42; Conclusion 43.

3 'Man Passeth Away Like a Shadow': Deaths Associated with the Australian Criminal Justice System, Six Years After the Royal Commission into Aboriginal Deaths in Custody *David MacDonald 44;* The Australian Royal Commission into Aboriginal Deaths in Custody 46; Civil court actions for compensation 48; Current position and trends with Australian custodial deaths 49; Trends and components of change 50; Deaths in police custody and police operations 52; Why has there been a fall in deaths in police lock ups? 54; Duty of care 55; Two special issues: 'Suicide by cop' and high speed police pursuits 57; How far does the duty of care extend? 58; Deaths in non-custodial correctional settings 60; Conclusion 61.

4 Prison Suicide and the Nature of Imprisonment *Alison Liebling 64;* Prison and the neglect of suicide 65; Understanding suicide 66; A cry of pain 68; Suicide and the pain of imprisonment 70; Responding to vulnerability in prison 73; To conclude 74.

5 Untoward Deaths in Special Hospital Care: Implications of These and Other Inquiries *Herschel Prins 75;* The avoidance of scandal 75; The Blackwood inquiry 76; The death of Orville Blackwood 78; Similarities between the deaths of three patients 79; Aftermath 79; Do inquiries serve their purposes? 80.

6   Deaths of Offenders: The Coroner's Inquiry *Richard Whittington 85;*
    Nature of an inquest *85;* The law and procedure at inquests *87;* Verdict
    88; Considerations for the coroner *89.*

PART TWO DEATHS OF OFFENDERS IN POLICE CUSTODY: SPECIAL
ISSUES

7   Investigating Deaths in Police Custody *John Cartwright 95;* Constitution
    and powers of the Police Complaints Authority *95;* Deaths in police
    care or custody *96;* Problems and concerns *99;* Suicides *99;* People who
    appear to be drunk *99;* Arrest *100;* Action to reduce deaths in custody
    101; Disclosure of statements *103;* Conclusion *104.*

8   Investigating Suspicious Deaths in Police Custody *Tony Ward and
    Deborah Coles 105;* The cases *106;* Richard O'Brien *106;* Shiji Lapite *107;*
    Wayne Douglas *107;* Racism and deaths in police custody *108;* The
    investigative process *109;* The coroner's inquest *113;* Conclusion *118.*

9   What Are the Lessons From Tragedies? *Nicholas Long 120;* Lessons
    from tragedies *120;* The 'Lambeth index' *121;* Deaths while in custody
    (1990-1996) *122;* Recommendations 1 to 22 with Metropolitan Police
    responses etc. and comment *124-137;* Appendix and tables *138-144.*

10 Self Harm and Suicide by Detained Persons: A Study *Alan Ingram,
    Graham Johnson and Ian Heyes 145.*

PART THREE VOICES OF PRISONERS, FAMILIES AND SUPPORT
GROUPS

11 The Right to Life and the European Convention On Human Rights *John
    Wadham (with the assistance of Richard Wald) 151;* The European
    Convention On Human Rights in context *151;* Incorporation of the
    Convention into UK domestic law *152;* Article 2: The Right to Life *152;*
    The Right to Life as a fundamental right *152;* Practical implications of
    article 2 jurisprudence in UK domestic law *153.*

12 Recognising Responsibilities to Families *Paul Edwards and Audrey
    Edwards 158;* Christopher's story *158;* The killer's story *160;* Christopher's
    death *161;* Our experience with the police *161;* Our experience with the
    Prison Service *163;* Relations with other criminal justice agencies *164;*
    Conclusions *168;* Advice to families *170;* Appendices *171-173.*

263

13 Black Deaths in Custody: A Human Rights Perspective Lee Jasper (Conference transcript) *174*.

14 Deaths In Custody; What Lessons?: An Overview of the Nigerian Situation *Uju Agomoh 182*; The trend *182*; Characteristics of the victims *185*; Causes of deaths in Nigerian prisons *188*; Lessons: Issues and intervention *192*; Responses from the voluntary sector *194*; Conclusion *195*; Appendix *197-9*.

PART FOUR PREVENTION OF DEATHS IN CUSTODY

15 Prevention of Suicides in the Dutch Criminal Justice System *Eric Blaauw, Frans Schilder and Stef van de Lande 201*; Explanations for different suicide rates *202*; Suicide prevention in police stations *205*; Screening for suicide risk *206*; Monitoring procedures *207*; Disarmament of suicidal instruments *208*; Provision of psychological support *209*; Transfer of suicidal detainees to other institutions *211*; Protocols and training *211*; Suicide prevention in houses of detention *212*; Screening for suicide risk *213*; Monitoring procedures *214*; Disarmament of suicidal instruments *215*; Provision of psychological support *216*; Transfer of suicidal detainees to other institutions *218*; Protocols and training *220*; In conclusion *221*.

16 Jail Suicide: Preventing Future Casualties *Lindsay M. Hayes 224*; Case 1: Suicide of Mathew Cullen *224*; Case 2: Suicide of Carol Grant *227*; Case 3: Suicide of John Keller *230*; Case 4: Suicide on the block *232*; Conclusion *232*.

17 Impact of the Custodial, Controlled Environment and Inmate/Patient Behaviour on Practices of Some Health Care Providers: Recommendations for Resolution of this International Problem *Joseph R. Rowan 234*; Falling victim to 'Manipulation Syndrome': the greatest peril *234*; Authoritarian environment *234*; Practice in privacy abridged *235*; Imbalance in staff gender in male institutions *235*; Insensitivity increases longevity *235*; Inadequate self-understanding by practitioners lessens treatment benefit *236*; Negative outcomes: deaths, permanent injuries/disabilities and/or pain/suffering *236*; Remedial/preventive measures *236*.

18 Deaths in the Care of the State: Issues and Lessons (closing address) *Vivien Stern 238*.

References, Cases cited, Speakers' biographical details etc *246 onwards*.

Some Other Waterside Press Titles

The Sentence of the Court Michael Watkins, Winston Gordon and Anthony Jeffries. Foreword by Lord Bingham, Lord Chief Justice. Excellent *The Law*. An extremely clear, well written book *The Magistrate*. (Second Edition, 1998). ISBN 1 872 870 64 3. £12.

Introduction to the Youth Court Winston Gordon, Michael Watkins and Philip Cuddy. Foreword by Lord Woolf, Master of the Rolls. A comprehensive, up-to-date and readable overview *Law Society Gazette*. A must for people interested in the work of the youth courts *The Magistrate*. An extremely useful and practical guide *The Law*. (1996) ISBN 1 872 870 36 8. £12.

Introduction to the Family Proceedings Court Elaine Laken, Chris Bazell and Winston Gordon. Foreword by Sir Stephen Brown, President of the Family Division of the High Court. (1997) ISBN 1 872 870 46 5. £12.

Introduction to the Criminal Justice Process Bryan Gibson and Paul Cavadino. Rarely, if ever, has this complex process been described with such comprehensiveness and clarity *Justice of the Peace* (First reprint, 1997) ISBN 1 872 870 09 0. £12.

Introduction to the Magistrates' Court Bryan Gibson (Second edition, 1995) A basic outline — plus a *Glossary of Words, Phrases and Abbreviations* (750 entries). An ideal introduction *Law Society Gazette*. (1995) ISBN 1 872 870 15 5. £10.

Introduction to the Probation Service Anthony Osler. An overview of probation work including the role of the Court Welfare Service in family matters. (1995) ISBN 1 872 870 19 8. £10.

Introduction to the Scottish Children's Panel Alistair Kelly. The first basic book in 20 years about the Scottish approach to juvenile offenders. (1996) ISBN 1 872 870 38 4. £12.

Children Who Kill Paul Cavadino (Ed). From the tragic Mary Bell and Jamie Bulger cases to comparable events world-wide. Contributors include Gitta Sereny. Published in conjunction with the British Juvenile and Family Courts Society. Highly recommended: *The Law*. (1996) ISBN 1 872 870 29 5. £16.

Interpreters and the Legal Process Joan Colin and Ruth Morris. For all people interested in spoken language or sign language in the legal context. (1996) ISBN 1 872 870 28 7. £12.

Justice for Victims and Offenders Martin Wright. A completely fresh treatment of this influential work — including sections on family group conferencing and restorative justice. (Second edition, 1996) ISBN 1 872 870 35 X . £16.

Transforming Criminal Policy Andrew Rutherford. (1996) 'Spheres of Influence' in the USA, The Netherlands and England and Wales in the 1980s. ISBN 1 872 870 31 7. £16.

Capital Punishment: Global Issues and Prospects Peter Hodgkinson and Andrew Rutherford (Eds). Deals with the topic world-wide. (1996) ISBN 1 872 870 32 5. £18.

Criminal Justice and the Pursuit of Decency Andrew Rutherford. By reminding us that, without 'good men and women' committed to humanising penal practice, criminal justice can so easily sink into apathy and pointless repression, Andrew Rutherford has sounded both a warning and a note of optimism *Sunday Telegraph*. (First reprint, 1994) ISBN 1 872 870 21 X. £12.

Growing Out of Crime: The New Era Andrew Rutherford. The classic and challenging work about young offenders. (Second reprint, 1995) ISBN 1 872 870 06 6. £12.50

Juvenile Delinquents and Young People in Trouble Willie McCarney (Ed). An *international* survey of youth justice. Published in conjunction with the International Association of Juvenile and Family Court Magistrates. (1996) ISBN 1 872 870 39 2. £18.

Criminal Classes: Offenders at School Angela Devlin. A wise and absorbing volume: if you are in any doubt about the links between poor education, crime and recidivism, read it: Marcel Berlins *The Guardian*. (First reprint, 1997) ISBN 1 872 870 30 9. £16.

Prison Patter Angela Devlin. A unique 'dictionary' of prison slang. (1996) ISBN 1 872 870 41 4. £12.

Relational Justice: Repairing the Breach Jonathan Burnside and Nicola Baker (Eds). Foreword by Lord Woolf. (1994) ISBN 1 872 870 22 8. £10.

Bail: The Law, Best Practice and the Debate Paul Cavadino and Bryan Gibson. (1993) Bail badly needed a basic general text, and now it has one *British Journal of Criminology*. ISBN 1 872 870 11 2. £14.

Paying Back: Twenty Years of Community Service Dick Whitfield and David Scott (Eds). Foreword by Lord Taylor, Lord Chief Justice. (1993) ISBN 1 872 870 13 9. £12.

Drinking and Driving: A Decade of Development Jonathan Black. Strongly recommended *Justice of the Peace*. (1993) ISBN 1 872 870 12 0. £14.

Punishments of Former Days Ernest Pettifer. (1992) A good read *The Magistrate*. ISBN 1 872 870 05 8. £9.50.

Tackling the Tag: The Electronic Monitoring of Offenders Dick Whitfield. A comprehensive and balanced guide *Prison Report*. (1997) ISBN 1 872 870 53 8. £16.

I'm Still Standing Bob Turney. A true story by a dyslexic ex-prisoner, now a probation officer. A truly remarkable book *Prison Writing*. (1997) ISBN 1 872 870 43 0. £12.

Black Women's Experiences of Criminal Justice Ruth Chigwada-Bailey. As featured in *The Guardian*. (1997) ISBN 1 872 870 54 6. £16.

Prisons of Promise Tessa West. Foreword by Sir David Ramsbotham, HM Chief Inspector of Prisons. Counteract images of prisons as negative places – and challenges people to identify and encourage the 'goodwill, energies and skills which might be maximised so as to make prisons *safe* and *purposeful* communities'. Extremely well-researched *Justice of the Peace*. (1997) ISBN 1 872 870 50 3. £16.

Hanging in the Balance Brian Block and John Hostettler. The history of the abolition of capital punishment in England and Wales. Foreword by former prime minister Lord Callaghan. A masterwork *Justice of the Peace*. (1997) ISBN 1 872 870 47 3. £18.

Bogus Law Reports Bryan Gibson. (1993) ISBN 1 872 870 0 82. £9.

A to Z of Criminal Justice Paul Cavadino. A unique 'mini-encyclopaedia' of criminal justice terms and terminology. (1998) ISBN 1 872 870 10 4. £18.

Domestic Violence and Occupation Orders Chris Bazell and Bryan Gibson. A key work for family law practitioners. The Family Law Act 1996, the associated regulations – and the important interface with the Protection from Harassment Act 1997. (1998) ISBN 1 872 870 60 0. £18.

Magistrates Bench Handbook: A Manual For Lay Magistrates. Loose-leaf. With the support of the Judicial Studies Board, Magistrates' Association and Justices' Clerks' Society. A must for people wanting to understand decision-making in magistrates' courts. Contains *The Sentence of the Court* (normally £12), the full *Magistrates' Association Sentencing Guidelines* (normally £15), new JSB Structured Decision-making Charts plus a range of Reference Sheets. Main revision every 18 months. (February 1998) ISBN 1 872 870 62 7. £28.50 (with binder).

All the above are available from Waterside Press, Domum Road, Winchester SO23 9NN Tel or fax 01962 855567. Cheques: 'Waterside Press'. Organizations invoiced for two or more books on request. Direct mail price given above. Please add £1.50 per book p&p (to a maximum of £6: UK only: postage abroad is charged at cost). Delivery of the *Magistrates Bench Handbook* is included in the price quoted.

ISTD Publications

The Directory of Criminology
A *new* edition of the indispensable guide to UK institutions in which criminology is taught and researched, and the courses available, together with the individuals involved and their research interests. Published in association with the British Society of Criminology. Edited by Carol Martin and Roger Tarling. June 1997. 186 pp. ISBN 0 901 541 44 3. £6.50 members, £11.50 non-members.

Sentencing in the 80s and 90s: The Struggle for Power
The eighth Eve Saville Memorial Lecture, given by Professor Andrew Ashworth, Edmund Davies Professor of Criminal Law and Criminal Justice at King's College London in May 1997. July 1997. ISBN 0 901 541 50 8. £1.50.

Repairing the Damage: Restorative Justice in Action
Stephanie Hayman (Ed.). Introduction by Martin Wright. Collected and edited papers from ISTD's conference held in Bristol in March 1997. *Contributors:* Mark Umbreit (University of Minnesota), Tony Marshall (Home Office), Caroline Nicholl (Thames Valley Police) and Lesley Moreland. September 1997. 30 pp. ISBN 0 901 541 46 X. £6.

Treating Sex Offenders in a Custodial Setting
Claire Holden and Stephanie Hayman (Eds.). Collected and edited papers from ISTD's conference held at HMP Brixton in March 1997. *Contributions from:* Dr A R Beech (STEP), Jo Clarke (HMP Brixton), Colin Turner (Rampton Hospital) and Eoin McLennan-Murray (HMP Blantyre House). Introduction by Dr Andrew Coyle. October 1997. 20 pages. ISBN 0 901 541 47 8. £5.

Tackling Drugs Together: One Year On
Julia Braggins (Ed.). Collected and edited papers from ISTD's international conference in June 1996. *Contributors include:* Jud Barker, Anna Bradley, Paddy Costall, Mark Gilman, Eilish Gilvarry, Paul Hayes, Keith Hellawell, Roger Howard, Libby Joyce, Howard Parker, Stephen Rimmer, Mike Trace. April 1997. 102 pp. ISBN 0 901 541 43 5. £10.

Absent from School: Truancy and Exclusion
Carol Martin and Stephanie Hayman (Eds.). A combined report from ISTD's two conferences on this theme held in February (London) and September (Manchester) 1996. *Contributions from:* Marva Buchanan, Avril Calder, Sue Chesterton, Angela Devlin, Lorna Farrington, Liz Jones, Edwin Lewis, Nicola Mackereth, Carl Parsons, John Simkins and Patrick Younge. February 1997. 66 pp. ISBN 0 901 541 41 9. £8.50.

Child Sexual Abuse: Myth and Reality
Stephanie Hayman (Ed.). A report on the conference held at King's College London on 25 November 1996. *Papers from:* Lady Justice Butler-Sloss, Donald

Campbell, Robert Hale, Barbara Kahan, Allan Levy QC, Kevin Smith, Sara Swann, Brian Waller, Norman Warner. February 1997. 36 pp. ISBN 0 901 541 42 7. £7.

Deaths in Custody: Caring for People at Risk
Alison Liebling (Ed.). *Contributions from:* Sir Louis Blom-Cooper, Ian Dunbar, Lindsey Hayes, Alison Liebling, David McDonald, Gethin Morgan, Rod Morgan, David Neal, Terry Waite and selected seminar papers from the ISTD conference organized in Cambridge in 1994. Published by Whiting and Birch. December 1996. 226 pp. ISBN 1 871 177 86 3. £12.

Does Punishment Work?
Proceedings of a conference organized by ISTD, the What Works Group and Positive Justice in November 1995 and edited by James McGuire and Beverley Rowson. *Contributors include:* Dr Andrew Coyle, David Garland, Bryan Gibson, James McGuire, Jerome Miller, Philip Priestley, Jenny Roberts, Michael Schluter, Joanna Shapland, Stephen Shaw, Rosemary Thompson, Martin Wasik, Dick Whitfield, Rt Hon Ann Widdecombe MP (1996). 88 pp. ISBN 0 901 541 39 7. £7.

What Works with Young Prisoners?
Stephanie Hayman (Ed.). Collected papers from a conference organized by ISTD with the Trust for the Study of Adolescence at HMYOI and RC Glen Parya in November 1995. *Contributors include:* Susan Bailey, Roger Bullock, Roger Graef, Alison Liebling. 52 pp. ISBN 0 901 541 38 9. £6.

Managing Risk: Achieving the Possible
Julia Braggins and Carol Martin (Eds.). Collected papers from a conference organized by ISTD in April 1995. *Contributors include:* Sir Louis Blom-Cooper, Graham Smith, Richard Tilt, John Wadham, Jayne Zito. 90 pp. ISBN 0 901 541 37 0. £7.

Contracts to Punish: Private or Public?
Carol Martin (Ed.). Collected papers from a conference organized by ISTD in Manchester in November 1994. Papers by Paul Cavadino, Robin Halward, Ken Pease, Mick Ryan and Stephen Shaw. 32 pp. ISBN 0 901 541 36 2. £5.

Juvenile Justice in England and Wales
Briefing Paper by Dr Julia Fionda, King's College London. 16 pp. December 1997. £2.50.

The Incorporation of the European Convention on Human Rights and Criminal Proceedings
Lord Williams of Mostyn QC. Address to ISTD's AGM on 4 November 1997. 8 pp. January 1998. ISBN 0 901 541 49 4. £1.50.

Imprisoning Women: Recognising Difference
Stephanie Hayman (Ed.). Collected and edited papers from a conference held at HMP and YOI Styal in October 1997. *Contributors include:* Dr Silvia Casale, Marie-Andree Dronin, Kate Donegan and Moira McAlpine, Olga Heaven, Rosemary King, Elaine Player, Carole Rigby, Chris Tchaikovsky. ISBN 0 901 541 51 6. £7.

Young People in Prison
Selected and edited papers from three conferences held in 1997 at HMYOI Stoke Heath, HMYOI Portland and King's College London and which looked at the needs of imprisoned juveniles and young offenders. *Contributors include:* Joyce Quin, MP, Minister of State, Home Office, Sir David Ramsbotham, HM Chief Inspector of Prisons, David Waplington, Governor, HMYOI Moorland, Juliet Lyon, Trust for the Study of Adolescence, Norman Tutt, Social Information Systems, Mary Graham, Atkinson Secure Unit, Mark Grindrod, The Howard League. ISBN 0 901 541 52 4. £10.

The ISTD Handbook of Community Programmes for Young and Juvenile Offenders
Compiled and edited by Carol Martin. Detailed information on almost 200 programmes in England and Wales working with young people aged 10-21. Foreword by Dame Barbara Mills QC. Published by Waterside Press. January 1997. 255 pp. ISBN 0 901 541 40 0. £12.

The Second Edition of the above handbook is available from April 1998 onwards. ISBN 0 901 541 53 2.

Criminal Justice Matters (CJM) is the Institute's quarterly magazine sent free to members. Designed to be accessible and readable, CJM provides information and informed opinion on all aspects of criminal justice. Each issue concentrates on a particular theme of relevance to practitioners and criminologists alike. Subscriptions for non-members costs £15 (UK), £21 (Rest of Europe) and £27 (Rest of World) Please contact the office for details of availability of back issues.

All of the above titles/papers can be obtained from: The Institute for the Study and Treatment of Delinquency (ISTD), King's College London, Strand, London, WC2R 2LS. Tel: 0171 873 2822 Fax: 0171 873 2823 Email: istd.enq@kd.ac.uk. UK p&p is included in the price quoted. Cheques with orders, except for non-UK bulk orders, for which ISTD will provide an invoice.